D1583237

THE NEW TESTAMENT
DOCTRINE OF THE CHRIST

Works by the same Author

RELIGIOUS REALITY. A Book for Men.

AUTHORITY AND FREEDOM. The Bishop Paddock Lectures for 1923.

CATHOLICISM WITH FREEDOM: An Appeal for a New Policy.

FREEDOM WITHIN THE CHURCH. A Sequel to ' Catholicism with Freedom '.

THE CHURCH AND THE CHALLENGE OF TO-DAY.

THE CHURCH OF ENGLAND AND THE CHURCH OF CHRIST.

NEW TESTAMENT DOCTRINE OF THE CHRIST.

THE WORLD'S QUESTION AND THE CHRISTIAN ANSWER. A Visitation Charge delivered in the Diocese of Derby, with Additions and Appendices. Together with the Charge delivered by the Chancellor of the Diocese.

STUDIES IN HISTORICAL CHRISTIANITY.

THE GOSPEL ACCORDING TO ST. MARK. (Westminster Commentaries.)

CHRISTIAN INITIATION.

CHRIST IN THE GOSPELS.

Edited by the same Author

ESSAYS ON THE TRINITY AND THE IN-CARNATION. By Members of the Anglican Communion.

THE NEW TESTAMENT DOCTRINE OF THE CHRIST

THE BAMPTON LECTURES FOR 1926

BY

A. E. J. RAWLINSON, D.D. (Oxon),
Hon. D.D. (Durham), Bishop of Derby

LONGMANS, GREEN AND CO.
LONDON · NEW YORK · TORONTO

LONGMANS, GREEN AND CO. LTD
6 & 7 CLIFFORD STREET, LONDON, W.I

LONGMANS, GREEN AND CO. INC.
55 FIFTH AVENUE, NEW YORK 3

LONGMANS, GREEN AND CO.
215 VICTORIA STREET, TORONTO I

ALSO AT MELBOURNE AND CAPE TOWN

ORIENT LONGMANS LTD
BOMBAY, CALCUTTA, MADRAS

First published . . 1926
Second Impression . 1929
Third Impression . . 1949

Made in Great Britain.

TO MY SON

ANTHONY KEITH

WHO WAS BORN

DURING THE PERIOD IN WHICH

THESE LECTURES

WERE BEING DELIVERED

EXTRACT

FROM THE LAST WILL AND TESTAMENT

OF THE LATE

REV. JOHN BAMPTON

CANON OF SALISBURY

' . . . I give and bequeath my Lands and Estates to the
Chancellor, Masters, and Scholars of the University of Oxford
for ever, to have and to hold all and singular the said Lands
or Estates upon trust, and to the intents and purposes
hereinafter mentioned ; that is to say, I will and appoint that
the Vice-Chancellor of the University of Oxford for the time
being shall take and receive all the rents, issues, and profits
thereof, and (after all taxes, reparations, and necessary
deductions made) that he pay all the remainder to the
endowment of eight Divinity Lecture Sermons, to be
established for ever in the said University, and to be per-
formed in the manner following :

' I direct and appoint, that, upon the first Tuesday in
Easter Term, a Lecturer be yearly chosen by the Heads of
Colleges only, and by no others, in the room adjoining to the
Printing-House, between the hours of ten in the morning
and two in the afternoon, to preach eight Divinity Lecture
Sermons, the year following, at St. Mary's in Oxford, between
the commencement of the last month in Lent Term, and the
end of the third week in Act Term.

' Also I direct and appoint, that the eight Divinity Lecture
Sermons shall be preached upon either of the following
Subjects—to confirm and establish the Christian Faith, and
to confute all heretics and schismatics—upon the divine
authority of the holy Scriptures—upon the authority of
the writings of the primitive Fathers, as to the faith and
practice of the primitive Church—upon the Divinity of our

Lord and Saviour Jesus Christ—upon the Divinity of the
Holy Ghost—upon the Articles of the Christian Faith, as
comprehended in the Apostles' and Nicene Creeds.

' Also I direct, that thirty copies of the eight Divinity
Lecture Sermons shall be always printed, within two months
after they are preached ; and one copy shall be given to the
Chancellor of the University, and one copy to the Head of
every College, and one copy to the Mayor of the city of
Oxford, and one copy to be put into the Bodleian Library ;
and the expense of printing them shall be paid out of the
revenue of the Land or Estates given for establishing the
Divinity Lecture Sermons ; and the Preacher shall not be
paid, nor be entitled to the revenue, before they are printed.

' Also I direct and appoint, that no person shall be qualified
to preach the Divinity Lecture Sermons, unless he hath
taken the degree of Master of Arts at least, in one of the two
Universities of Oxford or Cambridge ; and that the same
person shall never preach the Divinity Lecture Sermons
twice.'

PREFACE

A RECENT writer, commenting upon the ' tradition of learned conservatism ' which he regards as being characteristic of English theological scholarship, remarks that its effect has been that, while ' English theologians have made important contributions to the study of the history of the text of the New Testament, to the literary analysis of the first three Gospels, technically known as the Synoptic Problem, and to the exegesis of the various books of the New Testament, they have generally refrained from attempting any comprehensive reconstruction of the development of primitive Christianity on the basis of these exhaustive preliminary studies, and have been content mainly with a criticism of the critics.' [1]   To have so far departed from such a policy of caution as to have attempted, within the brief space of eight lectures, and under the conditions imposed by the Bampton bequest,[2] to reconstruct, even in broad outline, the ' development of primitive Christianity ' in respect of an issue so central as that of the interpretation of the Person of Christ may appear a rash undertaking.   It must be my excuse that I have had in mind the idea of writing a book upon these lines for a number of years, and that the time appeared to be ripe for some attempt to be made to grapple constructively in English with the work of Bousset and of other writers belonging to the so-called *religions-geschichtliche Schule* in Germany.   If I have not abstained in these lectures from ' criticism of the critics,' I can at least claim to have attempted to understand them ; and indeed I am conscious of having not infrequently learnt most from

[1] Sir Edwyn C. Hoskyns in *Essays Catholic and Critical*, p. 160.
[2] The lectures must all be composed and delivered within a period of a little more than a year from the date of the lecturer's appointment, and are directed to be published within two months of their delivery.   With the latter condition hardly any of the lecturers appointed in recent years have in practice found it possible to comply.   It is understood that under the provisions of the new Statutes made for the University by the Commissioners appointed in 1923 a longer period will in future intervene between the date of the lecturer's appointment and the dates of the actual delivery of the lectures.

the work of precisely those writers from whose conclusions I have in some respects differed most strongly.

The *religionsgeschichtliche Schule* approaches the study of the New Testament from the point of view, not primarily of the literary analysis of documents, but of the comparative study of the history of religion as such. It sees in the New Testament documents the reflection of a missionary movement, a new, creative, wholly distinctive and original movement of religious life, of which the essence was devotion to Jesus Christ, the exalted Lord, on the basis of the conviction that through Him God had visited and redeemed His people, and that through Him also (and that in the near future) the world would shortly be judged. The attempt is further made to study the successive forms in which the new Message came to be presented in relation to new contexts, new forms of thought, new peoples and environments, and to envisage the process of its development in relation to the rival and competing movements of contemporary pagan religious thought and life in the Graeco-Roman world. It has been the strength of the writers of this school that they have set the books of the New Testament in their proper historical context. The New Testament writings, in actual historical fact, are the literature of a missionary movement, which from one point of view may be said to have formed part of the general religious movement of the time ; and it is probable that the earliest readers of the New Testament were in almost all cases either hellenized Orientals or orientalized Greeks. It has been the weakness of the writers in question that in their enthusiasm for the new point of view they have tended to overlook or to underestimate the significance of the fact that, if the earliest readers of the New Testament were in almost all cases Gentiles, its writers were in almost all cases (S. Luke, who had probably been a ' God-fearer,' is an exception) originally Jews.

I have laid stress in these lectures upon the essentially Jewish character of the New Testament, because I believe it to be of vital importance. It is the Jewish character and presuppositions of the original Gospel—the inheritance of the monotheistic faith of the Old Testament—which, persisting continuously throughout, constitutes the indispensable

and vital link in the whole process of development. Wherever this element has been ignored, or has been inadequately
emphasised (as in the writings, for example, of Bousset,
or of his faithful disciple in English, Professor Kirsopp
Lake in his later publications), the resulting picture of the
development of New Testament Christianity has tended to
fall apart into a succession of virtually unrelated and disconnected phases, like the successive patterns of a kaleidoscope.
It is impossible in reading criticism of this type to avoid being
reminded of the words of Mephistopheles in *Faust* :

> ' *Wer will was Lebendig's erkennen und beschreiben,*
> *Sucht erst den Geist heraus zu treiben :*
> *Dann hat er die Theile in seiner Hand,*
> *Fehlt leider nur das geistige Band !* '

In the case of Christianity the ' spiritual bond ' is the
persistence, throughout all stages of development, of the
essential character of the original Gospel as being first and
foremost a message of ' good news about God.'   Christianity
as a religion does not consist either in the *cultus* of Christ
as a saint (a *cultus* sometimes combined, it is to be feared,
in modern times with theological agnosticism) or in the
attempt to follow, not very successfully, His human example.
It is an essentially monotheistic faith, which from the beginning of its career has consistently claimed to be the true heir
of the Jewish ' promises.'   It presupposes the faith of the Old
Testament.   It proclaims the one God, who is also the God of
the Jews ; the living God, who is the Creator of the ends
of the earth ; the God both of Nature and of History, who is
also and equally the God of Redemption and of grace.

The new religion, accordingly, was quite unable to make
terms with either pantheism or polytheism.   It refused to
be syncretistic, in the sense in which its rivals were syncretistic.   It retained and carried forward the old Jewish
jealousy on behalf of the one God, the Creator, whose solitary
majesty no creature might share.   It was this conviction,
deep-rooted in the inheritance of the Church from the Old
Testament faith, which rendered eventually inevitable the
explicit affirmation in set terms of the implications of that
attitude of Christians towards Christ as the ' Man appointed

by God ' to be the Mediator of Messianic Redemption which
had been characteristic of Christian discipleship from the
beginning. The Church affirmed in the end that the Christ
who was the Mediator of Redemption, and through whom
sinners were reconciled to God, was Himself, in the ultimate
roots of His Being, co-essentially and eternally one with the
Father ; and the Church was right in so doing. The doctrine
in question, as I have remarked in the course of my last
lecture, can only be repudiated at the cost of regarding
Christianity as having involved from the beginning the
idolatrous deification of a Jew

*   *   *   *   *   *

It was pointed out to me after the delivery of the first
lecture, by more than one friendly critic, that my use of the
term ' Modernism ' was liable to be misunderstood. I have
sought to use the word only in a strictly technical meaning,
which I have done my best to define. The word first came
into prominence in theological circles as a result of the
publication in 1907 of the Papal Encyclical *Pascendi dominici
gregis*,[1] issued in condemnation of the views of Loisy and
others. As defined by the Pope, the word denoted essentially
the separation of Jesus from Christianity in the interests
of the latter. It was applied, that is to say, to the theories
of those who were desirous of retaining Christianity in its
traditional form as a dogmatic and devotional system,
but who were prepared if necessary to discard, as being both
critically questionable and from the point of view of religion
no longer essential, the alleged basis of the Gospel in history.
In my lecture I have used the term ' Modernism ' to describe
also the converse position—the attempt, namely, to build
up a new version of the Christian religion upon the basis of
what is believed to have been the religion of Jesus, while at
the same time discarding Christianity in its historical forms,
and attempting to dispense with any explicitly formulated
doctrine of the relation of Jesus to God. The two forms of

[1] According to the writer of an article in the *Catholic Times* for April 4,
1924, the word ' *Moderniste* ' was employed by Rousseau as early as the
year 1769 to describe the views of a sceptical writer of the period. The
theories of Loisy and of his Italian sympathizers were denounced as
' *Modernismo* ' in the pastoral letters of certain of the Italian bishops in
1905, two years before the Papal Encyclical on the subject. It was the
publication, however, of the latter document which first made the term
known to the wider public.

'Modernism' thus recognized, while in one sense the precise
contraries of one another, have in common the unhistorical
assumption of a radical cleavage between 'Jesus' and
'Christianity.' It is to those theories, and to those theories
only, which involve such an assumption that I would suggest
that the application of the term 'Modernism,' in view of its
theological history, ought strictly to be confined.

I am of course well aware that in recent years the terms
'Modernism' and 'Modernist' have become current in a
much wider and more ambiguous sense. There are theological
circles in which 'Modernist' is a term of self-approbation,
and there are theological circles in which it is a term of abuse.
It can be used to convey the insinuation of heresy, and
conversely it can be used to convey the suggestion of a kind
of monopoly of intellectual enlightenment on the part of those
using it, and to make the flesh of the older generation of
theological conservatives creep. Neither of these uses of the
word is particularly edifying. There is a sense, no doubt, in
which to be 'modern' is the duty of all modern theologians.
The adoption of the term 'Modernist' in the Church of
England as the shibboleth of a party appears none the less
to be unfortunate, as being calculated both to darken theological counsel and to arouse undesirable passions.

*   *   *   *   *   *

Apart from the use of the term 'Modernism,' there are
one or two other points in relation to which I have been
invited by correspondents to reconsider my opinions before
publishing the lectures. I was asked, for example, whether
I did not really regard it as probable that the sense of spiritual
dissatisfaction with the religion of the Law and the experience so powerfully described in the seventh chapter of
the Epistle to the Romans were among the psychological
causes contributory to the conversion of S. Paul. I think that
the case for such a view can be powerfully and attractively
put ; but I have been impressed also with the fact that it is
essentially a modern speculation, and that S. Paul's own
words, though they do not of necessity exclude it, do not
directly imply it. Accordingly, after some hesitation, I have
decided to leave the passage on pp. 88 *sq.* as I originally wrote
it, and to submit the issue to the judgment of my readers.

The same also is true of the theory which I have adopted in Lecture VII. with regard to the original purpose and destination of the Epistle to the Hebrews. The view that the readers to whom the Epistle was in the first instance addressed were not Jewish but Gentile is one which attracts me ; and I have followed the guidance of some recent authorities in assuming its truth. But the point is not one with regard to which I should wish to be dogmatic. An alternative theory, very carefully worked out, is set forth in the *Expository Times* for November 1922, by Dr. J. V. Bartlet of Mansfield College, Oxford, who thinks of Italy as the place of origin, Ephesus as the place of destination, and a group of conservatively-minded Jewish Christians of Hellenistic culture, discouraged by the prospect of impending persecution, as the recipients. Dr. Bartlet is disposed further to think of Apollos as a probable author, and of the period immediately following S. Paul's martyrdom at Rome as the probable date. He would plead that his theory has the merit of ' " linking up " certain data of the Apostolic Age which hitherto have had to be read out of relation to their historic relations and setting.' It does not, however, really explain the description of the Epistle as being written to the ' Hebrews,' a term which, according to the analogy of its use in the New Testament, should mean properly ' Aramaic-speaking Jews ' ; and the difficulty that the ' apostasy ' which is dreaded in Heb. 3 [12] is an apostasy not from Christ but from theism—a ' falling away from the living God '—still remains to be met.

* * * * * *

I have brought my task to an end. It remains that I should express my gratitude to those who have helped me, and particularly to my father-in-law, the Rev. P. A. Ellis, who has again given most generous help in the verification of references and the correction of proofs, and to the staff of Messrs. T. and A. Constable Ltd., the printers, for the care and accuracy with which the book was set up in type.

A. E. J. RAWLINSON

Oxford,
September 1926.

CONTENTS

APPENDED NOTES

'If there be any true myth, if the Divine nature has at any time in any wise directly revealed itself to man, if any voice shall ever reach us out of the infinite circle of silence, where else shall we look but to the words of the Gospel?'—P. E. MORE, *The Christ of the New Testament*, p. 293.

'The Catholic faith is the reconciliation because it is the realization both of mythology and philosophy. . . . It met the mythological search for romance by being a story, and the philosophical search for truth by being a true story. That is why the ideal figure had to be a historical character. . . . But that is also why the historical character had to be the ideal figure.'—G. K. CHESTERTON, *The Everlasting Man*, pp. 283, 286.

LECTURE I
THE JEWISH RELIGIOUS HOPE

SYNOPSIS

THE modern world derives its knowledge of Jesus from Christian sources, which presuppose faith in Him as the Christ. The modern historical spirit attempts to go behind ' faith ' in order to arrive at ' facts.' Hence arises ' Modernism ' (= the separation of ' Jesus ' from ' Christianity ') in its two forms (Catholic and Protestant), of which the one seeks to build upon ' Christianity,' the other upon ' Jesus.'

Historical orthodoxy affirms the identification of Jesus with the Christ. It is the purpose of these lectures to study the forms assumed by this identification within the period of the New Testament itself. But already the simplest form of the doctrine—the assertion that Jesus is the Messiah—involves a doctrine of the Person of Jesus, the validity of which is bound up with the assertion of the validity of Israel's religious hope.

The Modernist assumption of a divorce between Jesus and Christianity has given rise to an astonishing variety of competing reconstructions of the alleged ' facts ' of the life of Jesus. The question therefore arises whether the fundamental hypothesis of Modernism is not mistaken. It was as a Claimant of Messiahship that Jesus was condemned. The faith that He was the Messiah must have arisen during His lifetime. The Gospels rightly represent Him as Himself believing that He was the Messiah.

What was, or what might be, the meaning of such a claim from the standpoint of Judaism ? Foakes-Jackson and Lake on the ambiguity of the term ' Messiah.' Analytical tendency of modern scholarship, which results in a disposition to treat the different and disparate conceptions of the ' Messiah ' in Judaism as logical alternatives. Nevertheless, it has been the claim of Christianity that the Old Testament as a whole is fulfilled in Christ. It is important not to separate Christianity from Judaism, inasmuch as the validity of Judaism as a religion of hope, and also as embodying a true revelation of God, is presupposed by the Christianity of history. The argument from Old Testament prophecy in the light of historical criticism. What is really at stake is the validity of the Jewish monotheistic faith in the living God. It is in this context that the hope of the Messiah must be understood. For the Jewish hope was set ultimately upon God, and there is a sense in which even the Messiah was not strictly indispensable. Nevertheless, Israel hoped for a Messiah.

The titles applied in Scripture to the hoped-for Messiah are all applicable also to the nation of Israel. The Messiah is the fulfilment of Israel's hope because He is the actualization of Israel's ideal. But Israel could not produce the Messiah. It remained therefore that God must send the Messiah for the redemption of Israel.

What is meant by ' redemption ' ? It is not an adequate answer to say merely ' redemption from foreign oppression.' The ideal of the Zealots was not co-extensive with the hope of the nation, which was ultimately religious, and included the fulfilment of everything that was, or that might be, involved in the Kingdom of God upon earth.

The coming of Jesus, and the tragedy of His rejection by Judaism.

LECTURE I

THE JEWISH RELIGIOUS HOPE

For because of the hope of Israel I am bound with this chain.

Acts 28 [20].

A SINGLE passage in Tacitus,[1] a possible confused allusion in Suetonius,[2] scattered references (for the most part polemical in tone) in Jewish Rabbinical literature,[3] and two passages (suspected of being Christian interpolations) in Josephus [4] constitute the sum total of the information with regard to the beginnings of Christianity which has come down to us from writers standing apart from the Christian tradition. The existence of Jesus of Nazareth as an historical character is otherwise known to the modern world exclusively through the medium of the witness borne to Him and the tradition handed down concerning Him by the community of those who believed in Him as the Christ. This means that the Gospels, for example, are written—as a modern writer has expressed it, borrowing a phrase used in a different connexion by S. Paul—'from faith to faith.' [5] They presuppose on the part of their readers, as on the part of their writers, an acceptance of the

[1] Tac. *Ann.* xv. 44.

[2] Sueton. *Claudius*, 25 ; cf. *Nero*, 16.

[3] For a discussion of the possible or probable allusions in Jewish litera-ture see J. Klausner, *Jesus of Nazareth : His Life, Times and Teaching* (translated from the Hebrew by H. Danby), pp. 18 *sqq.*

[4] Joseph. *Antiq.* xviii. 3 ; cf. also *Antiq.* xx. 9, as quoted by Euseb. *H.E.* ii. 23. I have not thought it necessary to take account of the further allusions to our Lord which occur only in the Slavonic version of Josephus. The arguments on the strength of which the attempt has recently been made to defend their genuineness are hardly such as to be likely to commend themselves to the considered judgement of scholars.

[5] J. Weiss, *Das älteste Evangelium*, p. 41 ; for the phrase cf. Rom. 1 [17].

faith of the Church. They set before us no merely neutral or undogmatic version of the story of Jesus. They are highly Christological documents, presupposing and taking for granted at every turn, both explicitly and implicitly, a doctrine of the person of Christ. This is as true of the earliest Gospel—that of S. Mark—as it is of the Fourth Gospel, or of the Gospels according to S. Matthew and S. Luke.

It has been the effort of historical criticism, steadily renewed by successive generations of scholars for a century or more, to get behind this state of affairs. Albert Schweitzer, in his study of the history of the critical investigation of the Gospels from Reimarus to Wrede, speaks of ' the long agony in which the historical view of the life of Jesus came to birth.' [1] The modern mind desires above all things to know what actually happened. It desires to discriminate history from legend, to eliminate what it is apt to regard as the distorting medium of idealizing dogma, and to establish with stark historical objectivity a version of the ' facts ' which shall be wholly independent of the point of view of ' faith.'

Hence arises the problem of what is called ' Modernism,' a term which (however ambiguously used) may be here taken to denote essentially the separation of Jesus from Christianity. I quote as typical a passage from the recently published work of Eduard Meyer. ' With the foundation,' he writes, ' of the Church and of the Mission, the teaching of Jesus was replaced by Christianity, that is to say, by the proclamation of the superhuman Son of God, who by His Resurrection had overcome death and had opened for men the way to deliverance from sin and to a new and eternal life of inner fellowship with God on the basis of faith in Himself, and who was shortly to come again as Judge of the quick and the dead to establish God's Kingdom.' This is described as ' a new religion, going far beyond the teaching of Jesus,'

---

[1] A. Schweitzer, *The Quest of the Historical Jesus*, p. 4.

a religion, however, which ' arose immediately after His death in the circle of His disciples, to whom it gave the requisite strength for their work.' [1]

We have here the fundamental assumption of ' Modernism,' alike in its Catholic and in its Protestant forms. The Catholic forms of Modernism assert Christianity, but deny, or are prepared to discard, its historical basis. For Catholic Modernists the Jesus of history may be all that the most sceptical criticism suggests ; it suffices for the purposes of practical religion that the Gospels are at least good mytho- logy, that the credal constructions of later theology conserve the religious values of the faith of the Apostles, and that the Catholic religion breeds saints. Conversely, the Protestant forms of Modernism, while claiming to recover and to reaffirm the religion of Jesus, discard Christianity. It is assumed that, behind the Gospels as they stand, there is discoverable by criticism the figure of a purely human and non-supernatural Jesus, who is nevertheless the world's supreme teacher in the sphere of religion. The assumption of a sharp, and indeed of a fundamental, antithesis between Jesus and Christianity is the common presupposition of both of these otherwise so radically contrasted reconstructions of theology and of religion.

It is clear that we are here touching the very nerve of the modern religious problem—that of the real relation of Jesus to Christianity. Historical orthodoxy has always affirmed the identification of Jesus with the Christ, and has claimed that the Church's later doctrine interprets truly the life of Jesus. It is the purpose of these lectures to attempt an historical study of the various forms which were successively assumed by the Christian doctrine of the person of Jesus within the period of the New Testament itself. We shall find that Christians of different types were led to express what they believed to be the significance of Jesus in a

[1] E. Meyer, *Ursprung und Anfänge des Christentums*, i. p. 52.

remarkable variety of different ways. We shall have occasion to trace what may from one point of view be described as a development of the doctrine from forms which were relatively rudimentary to forms which were relatively more mature ; there are early forms of Christology which, judged by the standards of later orthodoxy, are apt to appear, not indeed insignificant or untrue, but inadequate, elementary, jejune. Nevertheless, it is important to observe that implicit already in the earliest interpretation of all—in the simplest and most rudimentary acknowledgement of Jesus as the Messiah—there is involved the affirmation that not merely the teaching of Jesus, but Jesus Himself, is of vital significance for the people of God. To affirm the Messiahship of Jesus, in however rudimentary a sense, was to affirm already a doctrine of His person. It was to assert that this particular historical personage, Jesus of Nazareth, a first-century Jew, was of ultimate significance for mankind : that Jesus stood both towards God and towards Israel—and through Israel eventually towards mankind—in a relationship which was wholly unique. It was to affirm by implication the validity of Israel's religious hope : and it was to assert that through this particular Person the hope of Israel was destined to be fulfilled. The question of the essential validity of Christianity in this earliest form of it is bound up with that of the validity and real significance of the Jewish religious hope.

Meanwhile it is to be observed, on the one hand, that already in this earliest form of Christian affirmation about Jesus the gulf postulated by Modernism as yawning between Jesus and Christianity has been crossed, and on the other hand that historical criticism, as pursued on the basis of the tacit assumptions of Modernism, has not been unanimous in respect of its results. The popular Liberalism of such writers as Harnack and Wernle (which attempted, as it were, to domesticate Jesus) has found itself challenged not only by the 'eschatological' criticism of Johannes Weiss and of Schweitzer (for whom Jesus is essentially 'a stranger and an enigma to our time'), but also by the historical scepticism of Wrede and by the radically mythological theories of Jensen and Drews. The leading representatives of the school which adopts as its watchword the comparative study of the history of religion [1] have virtually abandoned as insoluble the problem of the Jesus of history, while proceeding to explain Christianity as the product of a mighty movement of the spirit, in which a highly syncretistic fusion of traditions and mythologies derived from many sources, Jewish, Greek and Oriental—with some contribution, no doubt, from the still living influence and memory of Jesus of Nazareth—gave rise (and that within a surprisingly short period) to the religion of which the New Testament writings are the expression   In the view of such writers the figure of Jesus as He is presented to us in the Gospels, so far from standing towards Christianity in any relation of contrast, is itself in large measure the product and the eventual outcome of the rapidly developing *cultus* of Jesus as the Christ   The original facts about Jesus, it is alleged, have been in such fashion developed and transformed (for the most part unconsciously) by the missionary, apologetic, and devotional needs of the Church, as to be no longer recoverable. A history of Christianity is possible, but no longer a history of Jesus   What the Gospels contain is not properly history, but a cross-section, or a succession of cross-sections, of the traditions and beliefs of Christianity at various stages of its first-century development.

Now, there is a sense, as I have indicated, in which these latter contentions, allowance being made for exaggeration, contain an element of truth.   It is through the medium of the Christian tradition, and not otherwise, that the story of

---

[1] I can find no less cumbrous way of expressing in English *die religionsgeschichtliche Schule.*

Jesus is made known to us, and the Jesus of the Gospel tradition is not *simply* the Jesus of history : He is equally the super-historical Lord of the Christian community, the present Object of the worship and faith of the Church, of whom a New Testament writer affirms that He is 'the same yesterday and to-day and for ever.'[1] The question, nevertheless, which inevitably suggests itself is the question whether the fundamental assumption of Modernism —the assumption of so sharp an antithesis between Christianity and Jesus—is true. If it was Christianity that created the figure of the Christ of the Gospels, what was it that created Christianity ? The only adequate answer is that behind Christianity is the Jesus of history, and that behind the Jesus of history is the redemptive activity of the living God. To drive in a wedge between Jesus and Christianity after the manner of the Modernists is simply to destroy in advance all hope of being able to arrive at a genuinely historical understanding of Christian origins.

And the wedge ought not to be driven in. It is no doubt the case that, from the point of view of orthodoxy itself, a contrast exists between the period before, and the period after, our Lord's Resurrection—a contrast (to use the old-fashioned traditional language) between the Christ in the days of His humiliation, and the Christ subsequently risen and exalted in glory. 'I have a baptism to be baptized with,' says the Jesus of the Synoptic tradition; 'and how am I straitened till it be accomplished ! '[2] But there is also continuity from the one to the other. The more extreme forms of scepticism and Modernism, opposing Jesus to Christianity, ignore the plain fact that Christianity is organically continuous with its own past, and that it has its roots not simply in the community of Jesus'

---

[1] Heb. 13 [8]. On the 'meta-historical' character of such religious narratives as those of the Gospels see A. Deissmann, *Paulus*, 2nd edn., p. 97.
[2] Lk. 12 [50] ; cf. Mk. 10 [38].

disciples, but in Jesus. It was as a Messianic Claimant that Jesus was condemned by the Jews and put to death by the Romans, a fact which involves that He must have Himself claimed to be the Messiah in His lifetime.

The belief in our Lord's Messiahship could not, in point of fact, have arisen simply as a conviction formed with regard to Him after His death by His disciples. Not even the Resurrection, regarded as an objective historical event, could have given rise by itself to such a remarkable belief. The disciples might have concluded, from the fact that their Master was believed to have been seen again after His Passion, that He was in some sense alive. They might have inferred from the fact that His tomb was believed to be empty that He had been raised from the dead. From the fact that He was believed to have been seen ascending into heaven they might have inferred that He had been caught up to God, and in virtue of such an ' assumption ' they might have been led to rank Him with Moses and Enoch and Elijah and Isaiah, about whom Hebrew tradition told similar stories. The conviction that He was the Messiah could not possibly have arisen in this way, but must have existed already. Regarded as the vindication of a Messiahship *already* ascribed to Jesus, the Resurrection falls into line. We can understand how it served to restore and to reconstitute the disciples' faith in Him, in spite of the Cross. But the Resurrection could not have given rise to the belief in His Messiahship *ab initio* ; [1] and if this be so, then the inevitable inference is that Jesus before His death must already have been regarded as the Messiah, and presumably that the Gospels are right in suggesting that He so regarded Himself. We have here, in fact, the decisive point at which the hypothesis of Modernism breaks down. The Messiahship of Jesus was vital, not merely to the community of Jesus' disciples, but to Jesus Himself. It is, indeed,

[1] J. Weiss, *Das Urchristentum*, p. 22.

antecedently probable that the Christology of the earliest Church did not stand in any very marked contrast with our Lord's own conception of His Messianic vocation and mission.

We are driven, then, to consider what was, or what might be, involved by the claim to be the Messiah, as it might be made by a Jew, and as it appears to have been made by our Lord ; and we are immediately confronted by the difficulty that the term ' Messiah,' in itself, is ambiguous.   It is pointed out (with entire justification) by Foakes-Jackson and Lake that the word ' Messiah ' is not a technical expression in Old Testament usage, though the Gospels are evidence that by the time of our Lord it was in common use to denote a divinely appointed head of the Jewish people who should one day appear, a Deliverer, who (it was expected) would be a descendant of the ancient royal house of Judah, and, as such, ' the Son of David.' [1]   As used in Jewish writings, ' " Messiah" is essentially an adjective meaning consecrated or appointed by God, and was not the prerogative title of any single person until later than the time of Christic.   It was applied in various forms of literature to the expected scion of the house of David, to the supernatural Son of Man, and to the High Priest ; but its use does not show that these figures were habitually identified with each other in Jewish thought.   It therefore follows that though the title was undoubtedly applied by his disciples to Jesus, their meaning must be sought from the context in which the word is used rather than from its established significance   In itself, it might merely mean

---

[1] Foakes-Jackson and Lake, *The Beginnings of Christianity*, i. p. 356. Cf. Mk. 12 [35], etc.   The earliest known example of the technical use of the word ' Christ ' as a title is apparently the passage in *Pss. Sol.* xvii. 36, where καὶ βασιλεὺς αὐτῶν χριστὸς κύριος should probably be emended to χριστὸς κυρίου (*sc.* ' and their King shall be the Lord's Anointed ').   The *Psalms of Solomon* allude to the death of Pompey, and presumably were written in the second half of the 1st century B.C.

that Jesus was divinely consecrated, without specifying the exact function to which he was appointed.' [1]

The two scholars whom I have quoted attack vigorously what they describe as the ' methodical error ' of grouping together the various and often widely divergent forms which at different periods and in different types of Jewish literature were assumed by the Jewish religious hope with regard to the future, and of labelling them all indiscriminately as ' Messianic.' [2] They would have us distinguish carefully, not only between the ' Age to Come ' and the ' Days of the Messiah,' [3] but also between the ' Messiah ' (in the sense of the ' Son of David,' foreshadowed in prophecy and portrayed in the *Psalms of Solomon*),[4] and the ' Elect One,' the super-natural ' Son of Man,' of the *Book of Enoch*.[5] They draw attention, as other writers have done before them, to the fact that for a brief period the Jewish religious hope had attached itself to the Maccabaean priest-kings, who were described, like Melchizedek, as ' priests of the Most High God.' [6] The expectation of a ' prophet like unto Moses,' to which reference

---

[1] Foakes-Jackson and Lake, *op. cit.* i. pp. 362 *sq.*

[2] *Op. cit.* i. p. 355.

[3] *Op. cit.* i. p. 277. Cf. Bousset, *Die Religion des Judentums*, 2nd edn., p. 332. There is no evidence that this particular distinction is anything more than a late rabbinical refinement.

[4] Is. 11 [1] *sqq.*; Jer. 23 [5], 33 [15]; Ezek. 34 [23] *sq.*; Zech. 3 [8], 6 [12]; *Pss. Sol.* 17, 18.

[5] *Eth. Enoch*, 37-71.

[6] Cf. Gen. 14 [18] *sqq.*, Ps. 110 [4], and for the glorification of the Maccabees *Test. Levi*, 8 [14], 18 [1] *sqq.*, *Jubilees*, 31 [15]; also *Test. Judah*, 21 [1] *sqq.*, where the priesthood is ranked higher than the kingship. In Bousset's words, ' the glory of the tribe of Levi, which had been made so illustrious by the priestly clan of the Maccabees, began despite all the Old Testament pro-phecies to outshine the glory of the tribe of Judah ' (Bousset, *Die Religion des Judentums*, 2nd edn., p. 256). So Josephus writes of John Hyrcanus that he ' was thought worthy by God of the three privileges— the rulership of the nation, the dignity of the high-priesthood, and pro-phecy ' (Josephus, *Antiq.* xiii. 10. 7). But the religious glory of the Macca-baean dynasty was short-lived. The Pharisees broke with Hyrcanus, and the *Assumption of Moses* (dated by Charles between A.D. 7 and A.D. 30) denounces those who ' call themselves priests of the Most High God ' as working ' iniquity in the holy of holies ' (*Ass. Mos.* 6 [1]).

is made in two passages in the Acts of the Apostles,[1] and
apparently also in a passage of the Fourth Gospel,[2] they are
disposed to connect with Samaria,[3] though admitting that
in Jewish midrashic teaching on the subject of the Messiah
' the parallel between Moses, the first deliverer, and the
great [future] Deliverer was fruitful of suggestions.' [4] The
figure of the Suffering Servant of the Lord in Isaiah,[5] or
again that of the Righteous Sufferer of the twenty-second
Psalm, they rightly point out was not regarded by Jewish
interpreters of Scripture as having reference to the Messiah.
Their general conclusion is that although there existed in
Judaism a widely accepted belief in the coming of the
Messiah, yet ' the more concrete traits with which homi-
letical *midrash* or popular imagination clothed this vague
expectation were varied and inconstant, drawn miscel-
laneously from prophecy and poetry, from the visions of
apocalyptic seers, from the circumstances of the times. . . .
It cannot be too strongly emphasized that there was no
generally accepted opinion, no organized and consistent
teaching, above all no orderly Messianic doctrine possessing
the faintest shadow of authority. The thing itself was of
faith, all the rest was free field for the imagination.' [6]

It is not altogether surprising that in view of this state
of affairs a large number of New Testament scholars should
have been of the opinion that in interpreting the doctrine
of the Messiahship of Jesus as affirmed in the earliest beginnings of the Christian Church it is necessary to choose as
between various possible alternative meanings of the term
' Messiah.' Either one thing or another, they would suggest
to us : either the King-Messiah of Old Testament prophecy
and the *Psalms of Solomon*, or the supernatural and future

---

[1] Acts 3 [22], 7 [37].   [2] Jn. 1 [11].
[3] Foakes-Jackson and Lake, *op. cit.* i. p. 406.
[4] *Op. cit.* i. p. 356.
[5] Is. 52 [13] *sqq.*
[6] Foakes-Jackson and Lake, *op. cit.* i. p. 356.

Son of Man of apocalyptic fantasy ; either David's Son or David's Lord, but not both. Or again, it is suggested virtually that the Lord Jesus came not to fulfil, but to destroy : that the Christian conception of Messiahship, as applied to our Lord, is something which is not only wholly new, but wholly out of relation to any or all of the Messianic beliefs and anticipations of pre-Christian Judaism.

Now, it is of course true enough that the various conceptions of the coming Messiah, and the various types of expectation with regard to the coming salvation of Israel, which at different periods were entertained by different schools of religious thought in Judaism, taken literally, are not mutually compatible. The pre-existent supernatural heavenly Man, the ' Elect One ' of the *Book of Enoch*, is not capable of logical identification with the descendant of David who is to be in a literal sense Israel's king. There is a sense in which, on the level simply of Jewish expectation, the lines run parallel : they do not meet.[1] It is nevertheless certain that it has been the claim of Christianity from the beginning that in Christ is the fulfilment and consummation, not simply of this, that, or the other particular line of

[1] That is to say, they do not *logically* meet : for it is worth noticing that, even within Judaism, conceptions which are logically incompatible are nevertheless not infrequently combined. Thus the ' Son of Man ' in the *Book of Enoch* is described, with an echo of one of the ' Servant ' passages of Isaiah, as ' the light of the Gentiles ' (*Eth. Enoch* 48 [4]; cf. Is. 42 [6], 49 [6]), and again is represented, in terms borrowed from the description of the King-Messiah in Is. 11 [1] *sqq.*, as being equipped with ' the spirit of wisdom, and the spirit which gives insight, and the spirit of understanding and of might ' (*Eth. Enoch* 49 [3]; cf. Is. 11 [2]). So again in the ' Son of Man ' vision of 2 Esdras 13, the figure ' as it were the likeness of a man ' who comes up ' from the midst of the sea ' is described by God as His ' Son '—that is to say, he is identified with the King-Messiah of the second Psalm (2 Esdras 13 [32]; cf. Ps. 2 [7]). In the previous chapter (2 Esdras 12) the Lion with a man's voice which arises to consume the Eagle (=Rome) is similarly identified (according to the Syriac text) with ' the anointed one, whom the Most High hath kept unto the end of the days, who shall spring up out of the seed of David ' (2 Esdras 12 [32]). It is clear that in the mind of the final editor of the book the Son of Man, the Son of God, the Lion and the Messiah are all somehow identified with one another.

prophetic anticipation, but of the religion of the Old Testament, taken spiritually as a whole, and interpreted as a religion of God-given hope. ' How many soever are the promises of God,' writes S. Paul, ' in him is the yea.'[1] It is perhaps permissible to doubt whether in point of fact the essentially modern and critical, literal-minded and analytical temper which persists in taking separately and in isolation each of the several types and forms of the Jewish hope, and in interpreting them remorselessly *au pied de la lettre*, is really quite the best mode of approach towards an adequate understanding of what is after all an essentially imaginative and Oriental religious literature ; but however this may be, it is clear that what the Church actually claimed with regard to the Lord Jesus was that, provided the Scriptures were interpreted not according to the letter, but according to the spirit, in Him the lines met. It was claimed that in Him was the fulfilment of the Old Covenant.

And the point is of some importance : for just as confusion arises when Jesus is set in fundamental antithesis to Christianity, so also confusion arises when Christianity is set in fundamental antithesis to Judaism. It is not merely an historical accident that Christianity arose in a Jewish environment, or that the Church has claimed as her own the Old Testament Scriptures and endorsed them as conveying ' by divers portions and in divers manners '[2] a preparatory revelation which the New Testament fulfils and completes. It is the teaching of the New Testament that salvation really *is* ' from the Jews.'[3] Its fundamental faith rests upon Judaism, presupposes the validity of Judaism, and takes it for granted that there really were such things as purposes and promises of God, which in Christ are fulfilled. The same assumption was certainly made by the Jesus of history Himself. In claiming to be the Messiah, in whatever precise sense He may have understood and interpreted

[1] 2 Cor. 1 [20].   [2] Heb. 1 [1].   [3] Jn. 4 [22].

the term, our Lord was emphatically claiming to be the Fulfiller of Israel's hope, and was thereby implying that the hope of Israel, rightly understood, was no empty illusion, but was validly grounded in the spiritual purposes and the eternal reality of God.   It is not altogether surprising that those who regard the Old Testament Scriptures, apart from a few passages of acknowledged beauty and spiritual distinction, as consisting mainly of a record of the tribal folklore and of the peculiar religious fantasies of a Semitic people who looked upon themselves as the special favourites of Heaven, should have difficulty in understanding the New Testament religion.   For the New Testament presupposes both the Old Testament monotheistic faith and also the reality of the promises of God.   What was new in Christianity, from this point of view, was simply the claim that *all* the promises of God were fulfilled in one Person.[1]

It is of course undoubtedly true that to modern minds, trained in the methods of strictly historical exegesis, the detailed arguments of New Testament writers from the Old Testament Scriptures appear quite artificial.   A generation which has ceased to regard prophecy in the light of an arsenal of predictive ' proof-texts ' no longer regards it as legitimate to argue from the wording of particular passages, taken wholly apart from their context and without regard to their primary meaning, that they were divinely intended beforehand to refer to our Lord.[2]   It is all the more important to

---

[1] ' It was a new thing that a single person should be regarded as fulfilling all the promises ' (J. H. A. Hart, *The Hope of Catholick Judaism*, p. 99 *n*.).

[2] Thus, for example, the experiences of Jonah are treated in the New Testament as predictive of the death and resurrection of Jesus (Mt. 12 [40]). It is probable that the emphasis upon the phrase ' the third day,' in 1 Cor. 15 [4], Mt. 16 [21], Lk. 9 [22], Mt. 17 [23], 20 [19], Lk. 18 [33] (contrast Mk. 8 [31], 9 [31], 10 [34]), is an echo of Hos. 6 [2].   The Resurrection was further held to be foreshadowed in Ps. 16 [10] *sq.*—whence ' the Holy One ' as a title of Jesus (Acts 2 [25] *sqq.*, 13 [35] : cf. also Mk. 1 [24], Jn. 6 [69], where however the word used is ἄγιος as against ὅσιος in the LXX of Ps. 16 [10]).   The phrase ' the kings of the earth ' in Ps. 2 [2] is treated in Acts 4 [25] *sqq.* as referring to Pontius Pilate and Herod.   For the Passion it is probable that appeal

recognize that the appeal of what may in a broad sense be described as the argument from prophecy is not bound up with the endorsement of such supposed triumphs of a frequently perverse exegetical skill, but depends rather upon the general relation of Christianity to Judaism as a religion of fulfilment to a religion of hope. The Church cannot consent to abandon the principle expressed in the saying *Novum testamentum in vetere latet, vetus testamentum in novo patet,*[1] or to capitulate to the new Marcionism which would divorce the religion of the Gospel from its historical roots.[2]

For in truth what is really at stake in these discussions is something which goes deeper than Christology. It is the fundamental faith of the Jew in the living God. It is the validity, as against what has been, upon the whole, the pantheistic tradition of much European philosophy, of that whole monotheistic apprehension and affirmation of God as

was made not only to Is. 52 [13]-53 [12] (cf. Acts 8 [32] *sqq.*), but also to Pss. 22 [6] *sqq.* and 69 [9, 21] (the influence of Pss. 69 [21], 22 [18, 7] *sqq.* is seen perhaps already in Mk. 15 [23, 36, 24, 29]; but cf. esp. Mt. 27 [34], Jn. 19 [24], and Mt. 27 [43] —a passage in which it is probable that the Evangelist has in mind not only Ps. 22 [8] but also Wisdom 2 [13-18]; so also the cry of our Lord in Mk. 15 [34] and parallels is derived from Ps. 22 [1]). The rejection of our Lord by the Jewish authorities was considered to have been predicted in Ps. 118 [22] *sq.* (cf. Mk. 12 [10] and parallels, Acts 4 [11], 1 Peter 2 [7]). J. Weiss suggests further that appeal might be made by Greek-speaking Christians, for whom ὁ κύριος was a standing title of Jesus (see Lecture III. pp. 76 *sqq.*), to the LXX of Is. 33 [10] as being predictive of the Resurrection and Exaltation of the 'Lord,' though the passage is not actually so quoted in the New Testament. It is curious that the only explicit appeal to Old Testament prophecy as predictive of the sufferings of the Messiah in the writings of S. Paul is Rom. 15 [3] (=Ps. 69 [9]), though it is probable that the language of Rom. 4 [25] is an echo of Is. 53 [12].

[1] Cf. Aug. *Quaestiones in Exod.* ii. 73 : *Ad vetus testamentum timor potius pertinet, sicut ad novum dilectio : quamquam in vetere novum lateat, et in novo vetus pateat.* Similarly Aug. *Serm.* clx. : *Novum testamentum in vetere velabatur : vetus testamentum in novo revelatur.* The passages are quoted by R. E. Bartlett in *The Letter and the Spirit* (Bampton Lectures for 1888), p. 39 *n.*

[2] It has been suggested by Harnack that the Books of the Old Testament should be regarded as being on a level with those of the Apocrypha (cf. Harnack, *Marcion : Das Evangelium vom fremden Gott,* pp. 248 *sqq.*).

the Living One, operative in history, concretely real and
personal, which mankind owes to the Jew.[1] Was the Jew
justified in his faith ? Is God truly the First and the Last
and the Living One, the Creator of the ends of the earth ?
Was it a true instinct, or was it only a false and delusive
hope, which led prophets and psalmists and seers to interpret
the record of history in the past as being in its deepest
essence a memorial of the ' marvellous works ' and ' mighty
acts ' of the Lord,[2] to affirm, in the face of present suffering,
persecution and oppression, that nevertheless ' the Most
High ruleth in the Kingdom of men,' [3] to look out into the
future, in spite of everything which upon the surface of
human affairs appeared manifestly to give the lie to their
conviction, in sure confidence and unwavering hope of the
coming, in God's good time, of the promised redemption ?
The Epistle to the Hebrews in magnificent phrases calls the
roll of the heroes of faith. It is the record of those who (if
a phrase from S. Paul may be linked with a phrase from the
writer of Hebrews) ' against hope believed in hope,' [4] inasmuch as they ' judged him faithful who had promised.' [5] It
is a record at once of the great names in the story of the
Old Testament and of those unnamed multitudes who left
no memorial, but who nevertheless ' through faith subdued
kingdoms, wrought righteousness, obtained promises . . .
were tempted, were slain with the sword,' and who ' all,
having had witness borne to them through their faith,
received not the promise, God having provided some better

---

[1] A writer to whose unpublished work I am permitted to have access
remarks that ' it is an element in the perfection of God that He is active
in the universe. . . . Any view which denies the real significance of
history for God either makes history and the moral struggle meaningless,
or else finds in them a meaning which is irrelevant to God, so that He is
not after all the supreme and all-inclusive Good. This is part of what is
meant by the Hebrew insistence that God is a living God.'

[2] Cf. especially Pss. 78, 105, 106.

[3] Dan. 4 [17], written in time of persecution under Antiochus Epiphanes.

[4] Rom. 4 [18].   [5] Heb. 11 [11].

thing concerning us, that apart from us they should not be made perfect.' [1]

The hope of the Messiah, as it was entertained by the Jewish people, is not rightly to be judged or interpreted apart from this wider context of Jewish religious faith in the Most High. For the Jewish hope was set ultimately upon God, and there was therefore a sense in which even the Messiah was not strictly indispensable. There are forms of the Jewish religious hope, as has often been pointed out, into which the figure of the Messiah does not enter at all.[2] God in a sense needs no instruments, and if need be, His own right arm would accomplish salvation : [3] the redemption of Israel is the work of the Lord. But it is equally the work of the Lord if—according to His promise—God raises up and bestows upon Israel the hoped-for Messiah.

Of the terms and titles which in the Biblical literature are bestowed upon the Messiah it is noticeable that all or most are as capable of being applied to the Church (whether Jewish or Christian) as they are of being applied to the Christ who is Lord of the Church. The term ' Christ ' or ' Anointed ' itself is applied, for example, to the Patriarchs—

> Touch not mine Anointed,
> And do my prophets no harm.[4]

In a true sense all God's people were His Anointed—all, in ideal and intention, were to be prophets and priests and kings.[5] So Moses is represented as saying, ' Would God that all the Lord's people were prophets,' [6] and in the Book

---

[1] Heb. 11 [33], [37], [39] sq.

[2] E.g., there is no Messianic figure in Joel, Is. 24-27, Daniel, *Eth. Enoch* 1-36, the ' Apocalypse of Weeks ' in Enoch (*Eth. Enoch* 93, 91 [12-17]), *Jubilees*, the *Assumption of Moses*, or the *Book of the Secrets of Enoch*.

[3] Is. 63 [5].   [4] Ps. 105 [15].

[5] For the anointing of prophets see 1 Kgs. 19 [16] ; for the anointing of priests Ex. 28 [41] ; for that of kings 1 Sam. 10 [1], 16 [13], 1 Kgs. 19 [15] sq.

[6] Num. 11 [29].

of Exodus Israel as a whole is a ' kingdom of priests '[1]—
whence the description of the Christian Church in the First
Epistle of S. Peter as a ' royal priesthood.'[2] If the Messiah,
in the sense of the King, is described in the second Psalm
as a ' son,' ' begotten ' of the Lord,[3] the prophet Hosea had
written of the nation, ' called . . . out of Egypt,' as God's
' son.'[4] The enigmatic title ' Son of Man,' as used of our
Lord in the New Testament, may have points of connexion
with the use of the same term in the *Book of Enoch*, but the
writer of *Enoch* derived it unquestionably from Daniel, and
in Daniel it denotes not any single individual but the Jewish
community, ' the people of the saints of the Most High.'[5]
A title peculiar, apparently, to Christianity in its Messianic
application is that of the ' Servant ' of God in certain passages
of Deutero-Isaiah ; it is the commonly accepted opinion
that in its Old Testament context the ' Servant ' is a personi-
fication of Israel.[6] The ' Messiah,' or the ' Christ,' according
to each of these several conceptions of Him, is the fulfiller
of the hope, or the realization of some aspect of the ideal, of
the elect nation, the people of God. We might be tempted
to say that the Messiah fulfils Israel's hope through the
actualization of Israel's ideal.

But the nation was incapable of fulfilling the ideal. It
was the teaching of the Rabbis that if Israel could perfectly
accomplish the keeping of the Law, the New Age would have
arrived ; that if Israel could keep but two Sabbaths—nay,
one Sabbath—perfectly, redemption would come ; that if
Israel could only completely and radically repent, the
Messiah would appear.[7] No such radical repentance,
no such perfect fulfilment of the Law on the part of the
nation, was ever forthcoming. Israel could not produce the

---

[1] Ex. 19 [6].   [2] 1 Pet. 2 [9].   [3] Ps. 2 [7].
[4] Hos. 11 [1]; cf. Ex. 4 [22].   [5] Dan. 7 [27].

[6] Or of the righteous element within Israel ; less probably an individual
in whom Israel's ideal vocation is regarded as being summed up.

[7] F. Weber, *Jüdische Theologie*, pp. 348 *sqq.*

Messiah.   It remained that God, without waiting for Israel, should send Him—for Israel's redemption.   ' We hoped that it was he which should redeem Israel.' [1]

Redeem Israel from what ?   It is a pertinent question. There are modern interpreters who would suggest (and there are no doubt a considerable number of passages from late Jewish literature which can be quoted in favour of the suggestion) that the redemption for which Israel was primarily looking was redemption from foreign oppression, political freedom from Rome—the ideal of the Zealots ! That surely is not an adequate interpretation of the scope and significance of Israel's hope.

> We do it wrong, being so majestical,

thus to limit its meaning.   The Zealots were a party within Israel ; they were not the nation.   According to Josephus, it was only in the days of the last Roman procurator, Gessius Florus, that ' the nation began to grow mad with this distemper.' [2]   No doubt the Jews did desire national freedom, and regarded it as no part of the ideal, but as essentially part of the evil of the present evil World-Age, which God in His own good time would bring to an end, that the Chosen Nation should be held down by a foreign oppressor   The Russian-American writer Simkhovitch has emphasized the necessity of taking account, if we are to understand the historical background of the story of our Lord's life, of the fiercely nationalist passion of political discontent with which it is manifest that some portions at least of the population of Palestine under Roman and Herodian administration were seething.[3]   There had been a serious revolt under Judas of Galilee ' in the days of the taxing.' [4]   There was destined to be trouble, involving the grave danger of a further fanatical outbreak, at a later

---

[1] Lk. 24 [21].   [2] Joseph. *Antiq.* xviii. 1. 6.
[3] V. G. Simkhovitch, *Towards the Understanding of Jesus.*
[4] Acts 5 [37].   Joseph. *Antiq.* xviii. 1. 1 ; xx. 5. 2 : *De Bell. Jud.* ii. 8. 1 ; ii. 17. 8.

date under Caligula, when that emperor gave orders that his statue should be erected in the Temple.[1] The war of A.D. 66-70, which saw ' Jerusalem compassed with armies ' and eventually sacked, was the outcome of a policy of patriotic despair which no doubt had exponents already in the time of our Lord, and against which certain of His sayings, and in particular the precepts about non-resistance to evil, on which stress has been laid in modern times by the Society of Friends and the followers of Tolstoi, may not impossibly have been originally directed. Jewish patriots were prepared at all times to die for their country, and the Zealots appear to have believed that when the moment came and the sword had been drawn, the Chosen People might count upon the miraculous intervention of God. In the case of the Zealots, the hope of a nationalist deliverance to be achieved by bloodshed and war was undoubtedly central. We may suppose the Zealot conception of the Messiah to have been modelled upon the history of Judas Maccabaeus. But the Zealots were balanced by those known as ' the quiet in the land,' who believed it to be their duty both to hope and also quietly to wait for the salvation of God. It is a crude caricature, as has been pointed out by the late J. H. A. Hart, to suggest that every pious Jew who cherished the hope of the coming of the Messiah, the Son of David, was secretly dreaming of an orgy of blood and fire.

The *rôle* of the Messiah in the *Psalms of Solomon*, for example, is at least as much religious as it is political or warlike. ' The Son of David, of whom the Psalmist dreams, does not appeal to the arm of flesh. He has not even sling and stones from the brook, with which to combat the latest representative of Goliath.

He shall destroy the ungodly nations *with the words of His mouth*,
He shall convict sinners *in the thoughts of their heart*.[2]

[1] Joseph. *Antiq.* xviii. 8. [2] *Pss. Sol.* 17 [27].

This is no ordinary conquering king, but a prophet whose message exercises an irresistible influence upon the consciences of his opponents. He deals with the oppressors of Israel as Nathan dealt with David in the matter of Uriah's wife, and his title identifies him as the antitype of Solomon,'[1] who (unlike David) was a king of peace.

The deliverance for which Israel was looking, with her hope set upon God, was in fact much more than a mere outward deliverance from the yoke of the Romans. It was at least equally deliverance from sin, and from all unrighteousness. It was the actualization of the ideal. It was religious salvation. It was bound up with the ideal of the coming theocracy, the manifested Sovereignty of God. It involved the fulfilment of everything that was, or that might be, implied in the new supernatural Age—in the Kingdom of God on the earth, or (as others might prefer to express it) in the new heavens and the new earth, wherein righteousness dwelt.

And at a particular date in the first century there came into this world—that is to say, in the first instance, into the Jewish world, which cherished such spiritual hopes—One who in some manifestly non-political sense was a Claimant of Sovereignty, and who to-day is the object of the passionate faith and of the adoring loyalty of multitudes whom no man can number, and who, in so far as they are upon earth, are 'dispersed' (to use the words of the Bidding Prayer) 'throughout the whole world.'

The coming of Jesus signalized the supreme tragedy of Judaism. The rulers condemned Him ; the common people, for the most part, preferred a Messiah of a different type— 'Not this man, but Barabbas ! '[2] Nevertheless, it was the conviction of a small sect, a little company of 'unlearned and ignorant '[3] persons from Galilee, that in Jesus the Messiah had arrived, that the appointed time was at hand,

---

[1] J. H. A. Hart, *The Hope of Catholick Judaism*, pp. 85 *sq.*
[2] Jn. 18 [40].   [3] Acts 4 [13].

and that God had in very truth 'raised up' for Israel 'a mighty salvation . . . in the house of his servant David.'[1] The verdict of Judaism upon Jesus was contained in the words of a verse from Deuteronomy—'He that is hanged is accursed of God.'[2] There came a stage in the life of a Jew subsequently known as S. Paul at which he found himself constrained to wrestle with this paradox.[3] He was enabled eventually to affirm it as his conviction, and to lay it down as a kind of test which might be found serviceable in the discernment of spirits, that 'no man speaking by the Spirit of God calleth Jesus accursed.'[4] For the verdict of Judaism was not according to God, but according to man.

[1] Lk. 1 69 (Prayer Book Version).   [2] Dt. 21 23.
[3] Gal. 3 13.   [4] 1 Cor. 12 3.

LECTURE II
THE CHRISTOLOGY OF
THE JEWISH-CHRISTIAN CHURCH

SYNOPSIS

THE reversal of the verdict of man by the verdict of God. The significance of the Resurrection and Ascension for the faith of the earliest Church. The crucified Christ is regarded as being from henceforth exalted in glory at God's right hand. The Messiahship transposed to a higher key. The Messiah, the Son of David, is already enthroned as David's Lord : but His Kingdom is not of this ' Age,' but of the ' Age to Come.''

And yet in a sense the New Age has already begun. The new supernatural order is already proleptically present. The Church as partaker of ' the powers of the Coming Age.' The assurance of fulfilment, as contrasted with the merely waiting attitude of Judaism; the Church still waits for the Kingdom, but with a new sense of its actuality. The eschatological setting of this earliest faith. The identification of Jesus with the coming ' Son of Man.'

But the expected Messiah is still Jesus. The old relationship of discipleship to Jesus is not broken off, but persists on a higher level. Jesus, the ' prophet like unto Moses,' who has become the exalted Messiah, is for Christians the very Lord of their lives. It is un-reasonable to doubt that they already spoke of him as *Maran* (i.e. ' our Lord '). The significance of the gift of the Spirit.

The advance from the relation of discipleship to that of religious dependence upon Jesus as Lord. Is it conceivable on Jewish soil and within the circle of the original disciples ? The new attitude less discontinuous with the old than is sometimes supposed.

Development of Christian thought, and of a Christian apologetic based upon arguments from Scripture. Jesus as ' Son of David ' and yet ' more than Solomon,' the ' Lord ' of David, the Messianic ' Son of God.' His life upon earth as a Messianic life. The Baptism as His ' anointing.' His ' authority ' and ' mighty works.' Jesus the Christ not merely of the future and of the present, but of the past. The ' Servant of the Lord ' of Deutero-Isaiah as a clue to the significance of the Passion.

The question of our Lord's own mind with regard to the Messiah-ship. The present tendency is towards scepticism, but the question is too vital to be simply ignored. The originality of the Christian Messianic conception implied a profoundly new and original inter-pretation of Scripture, which it is reasonable to hold may go back in essentials to Jesus Himself. In the mind of Jesus the *rôle* of the Messiah of prophecy was transformed by the interpretation both of the Davidic King and of the apocalyptic Son of Man in terms of the idea of the Servant of the Lord. Our Lord from the time of the Baptism onwards was inwardly sure that He was Messiah, and therefore clothed with supreme authority from God. The peculiar paradox of the Christian conception of the Messiahship is our Lord's own paradox.

Behind the Messiahship is the further mystery of our Lord's Person. Was He accustomed to speak of God as His ' Father,' and of Himself in distinctive fashion as ' the Son ' ? The ' filial consciousness ' as the psychological presupposition of the Messiahship. The Synoptic *Logion* about the mutual knowledge of the Father and the Son (Mt. xi. 27 ; Lk. x. 22) not absolutely impossible from the standpoint of Judaism, though the saying was later exploited in the interests of Gnosticism. The conception of Jesus as ' Son ' in relation to God was in any case an idea which was capable of fruitful development upon Gentile-Christian soil.

LECTURE II

THE CHRISTOLOGY OF
THE JEWISH-CHRISTIAN CHURCH

God hath made Him both Lord and Christ, this Jesus whom ye
crucified.—Acts 2 [36].

THUS the verdict of man was reversed by the verdict of God,
and the Galilaean Prophet whose Messianic claims had been
rejected by the rulers of the nation was by the supreme act
of Almighty God decisively vindicated as Lord and Christ.
To ask from the point of view of modern scientific history
what actually had happened is to ask a question to which
it is probable that there will never be in the strict sense any
finally adequate scientific reply. I must be allowed to state
my own personal conviction that apart from the recognition
of a supernatural factor as having been at work the beginnings
of Christianity are not really to be explained, and that in
the events which for us are represented by the New Testament accounts of the Resurrection and Ascension of Jesus
and of the pouring out of the Holy Spirit the Church
rightly discovered the laying bare of the arm of the Lord.
The earliest Christians, in and through the events in question,
became seized of the truth of a spiritual conviction about
Jesus which they expressed in the vivid language of Hebrew
religious poetry by saying that the crucified Christ was from
henceforth exalted in glory at God's right hand.[1]

The significance of this conviction, and of the language
(derived from the 110th Psalm) in which it was expressed,[2]

[1] Cf. the Lukan form of the words ascribed to our Lord at His trial,
viz. : ' From henceforth (ἀπὸ τοῦ νῦν) shall the Son of Man be seated
at the right hand of the power of God ' (Lk. 22 [69]).
[2] Acts 2 [34] sq. ; cf. Ps. 110 [1].

is drawn out in a famous argument with regard to the
Messiahship ascribed in the Gospel tradition to the Lord
Jesus Himself, viz. : ' How say the scribes that the Christ
is the Son of David ?   David himself said in the Holy Spirit,

> The Lord said unto my Lord,
> Sit thou on my right hand,
> Till I make thine enemies the footstool of thy feet.

David himself calleth him Lord ; and whence is he his son ? ' [1]
It is probable that the nationalist hope of a literally restored
Kingdom of David had been cherished during the lifetime of
Jesus by some at least of His disciples.   The author of Acts
represents the Apostles, even after the Resurrection, as
raising the question, ' Lord, dost thou at this time restore the
Kingdom to Israel ? ' [2]   But the question was from henceforward irrelevant.   A Messiah who had been called ' Lord '
by King David himself, and whose throne was at the right
hand of God, could be no successor of David in the literal
and political sense.   The Messiahship of Jesus—to use a
musical metaphor—had been transposed to a higher key
On the one hand His exaltation (and He was from henceforth
the *exalted* Messiah) betokened already His enthronement
as King.   He was reigning in majesty at the right hand of
God, in the unseen world of heavenly reality and glory, and
the ' Kingdom of the Messiah,' which for the Jews had been
an object of hope and expectation, was for the disciples of
Jesus already begun.   On the other hand, it was clear that
the Kingdom of the Messiah was not destined to be a
' kingdom ' of the political sort at all.   It was ' not of this
world.' [3]   It lay on the further side of the cleavage between
' this Age ' and ' the Age to Come.'

And yet it was nevertheless a kingdom which was actual
and real, and to which Christians already belonged.   The
new supernatural order was already, as it were, proleptically

---

[1] Mk. 12 [35] *sqq.* and parallels.   [2] Acts 1 [6].   [3] Jn. 18 [36].

present. S. Paul, when he spoke of the Father as having delivered Christians 'out of the power of darkness,' and translated them 'into the Kingdom of the Son of his love,'[1] was expressing a thought which there is no reason to suppose was distinctively Pauline. For Christians the New Age was already begun. Already those who had been 'made partakers of the Holy Ghost' had experienced 'the powers of the Coming Age.'[2] As for the Jews—to quote some words of Johannes Weiss—' in the midst of all the eloquence concerning the hope of Israel a profound hopelessness finds utterance. When is all this to happen? No one knows; there may still have to be endless waiting. "Blessed is he who shall be alive in those days, and shall see the salvation of Israel";[3] but no one dares to hope that he himself will be among those happy ones. And now there comes into the midst of these hopeless men of hope a band of people who with joyous and enthusiastic conviction declare : " We have found the Messiah, he is come ; the glorious time of consummation is dawning,the Kingdom of God is at the door." '[4]

It is true that ' the End ' was ' not yet.'[5] The disciples were still ' looking for the Kingdom of God.'[6] Their prayer was still ' Thy Kingdom come.' But they awaited the Kingdom, and prayed for its coming, with a new sense of its actuality, a new confidence, a new joy. It was not only that they were convinced that the New Age was at hand, and that they themselves, the ' little flock ' of Jesus' disciples, were elect according to ' the Father's good pleasure ';[7] they were, beyond this, convinced that the decisive step with a view to the bringing in of the Kingdom of God had already been taken. The end was not yet, but already the Lord Christ was enthroned ; and the investiture of the Christ with His heavenly sovereignty betokened

---

[1] Col. 1 [13].   [2] Heb. 6 [4] sq.   [3] Pss. Sol. 17 [44].
[4] J. Weiss, *Christ : the Beginnings of Dogma*, E.T., p. 17.
[5] Mk. 13 [7].   [6] Mk. 15 [43].   [7] Lk. 12 [32].

C

already the beginning of the end, the decisive hour in the great world-drama of redemption. It has been remarked truly enough that this earliest Christian Messianic conception is only adequately understood when it is interpreted in the context of the great apocalyptic world-view which anticipated in the ' last time ' the final issue of the eternal conflict between God and His Adversary, between the Kingdom of God and the Kingdom of Satan.[1] We may say, if we will, that in effect the Lord Jesus had become identified with the apocalyptic ' Son of Man,' who in the near future was destined to be manifested ' coming in clouds, with great power and glory,'[2] as the predestined ' Judge of quick and dead.'[3] It has been maintained by at least one modern scholar[4] that in this equation of Jesus with the future apocalyptic ' Son of Man ' was comprised the sum total of all that was distinctive in the religion of the original Jewish-Christian community of believers in Jesus—a typical example of the riding of a thesis to death.

For indeed even in the earliest Christianity there was involved, side by side with the apocalyptic confidence that the last decisive hour of the world's history was at hand, from which the earliest preaching derived its peculiar note of urgency and haste, a more personal element, which proved capable of persisting, and even of becoming intensified, at a later stage of the Christian religion, when the first vividly literal expectation of the immediate approach of the End

[1] J. Weiss, *Das Urchristentum*, p. 25. For the decisive importance attached to the idea of the enthronement of the risen and exalted Christ, cf. Rom. 1 [4] and Acts 13 [33], and note that in the latter passage the words of Ps. 2 [7] are quoted not (as in the Gospels) in connexion with our Lord's Baptism, but with reference to the action of God in raising Him from the dead.

[2] Mk. 13 [26] and parallels.

[3] Acts 10 [42]; cf. also Acts 17 [31], where it is probable that a ' Son of Man ' Christology underlies the description of our Lord as the ' *man* ' whom God has ' ordained ' with a view to the judgement of the world in righteousness.

[4] The late Wilhelm Bousset; see below, p. 39, *n.* 4, and Appended Note I. pp. 231 *sqq.*

was in process of fading, if not indeed of completely dying away.[1] The Messiah, or Christ, was, as we have seen, for strictly Jewish expectation an essentially abstract, in-determinate figure. He was ' he that should come,' [2] ' of whom Moses in the Law, and the prophets, did write,' [3] who had been variously conceived in different periods by prophets and psalmists and seers, but who was essentially an object of vague, indeterminate hope. For Christians, on the other hand, the expected Christ was identified with Jesus. They knew not only that the time was at hand : they knew who the Christ was. Their faith could be summarily stated in the form of the simple assertion ' that the Messiah was Jesus.' [4] And Jesus was One whom they knew. The supernatural Son of Man, whose approaching manifestation in glory they were awaiting, was for them no merely vague, mythological figure, but a concrete and definite personality, the Master and Lord whom they loved. If the salvation for which they were looking was primarily an eschatological salvation, bound up with the idea of the ' times of restoration of all things,' [5] it was still to Jesus that they looked. It was Jesus of whom they so confidently asserted that He had been ' designated beforehand ' [6] for the Messianic rank and

---

[1] What actually happened was that the religious tension between ' this Age ' and ' the Age to Come ' became gradually merged in, and virtually replaced by, the religious tension between the world of things seen and temporal and the world of things eternal and unseen. The first Christians lived in this Age as not belonging to it, because their true life was in the Age to Come ; later Christians, in so far as they were true to their Chris-tianity, lived in this world as not belonging to it, inasmuch as their true life was rooted in the sphere of the things unseen and eternal, ' hid with Christ in God.' ' Whatever this or that critic may think of the spiritual value of the process, it is a fact that for three centuries the development of Christianity is marked by a slow merging of the eschatological other-worldliness of Jesus with the philosophical other-worldliness of Plato ' (P. E. More, *The Christ of the New Testament*, p. 84).

[2] Mt. 11 [3], Lk. 7 [19].

[3] Jn. 1 [45].

[4] εἶναι τὸν χριστὸν Ἰησοῦν (Acts 18 [5, 28]).

[5] ἄχρι χρόνων ἀποκαταστάσεως πάντων (Acts 3 [21]).

[6] τὸν προκεχειρισμένον ὑμῖν Χριστὸν Ἰησοῦν (Acts 3 [20]).

dignity. He, and none other, was the ' man appointed by God,' [1] the hoped-for ' Prince and Deliverer,' [2] who was to bestow upon Israel the gifts of ' repentance and forgiveness of sins.' [3] Thus in their new faith the old relationship of discipleship to Jesus was not broken off, but was retained and continued upon a higher level They were the new community of Jesus the Messiah. They spoke of themselves as the followers of the Way.[4] Committing themselves absolutely to Jesus, they sought to regulate their lives in accordance with His remembered sayings—a fact to which

[1] ἄνδρα ἀποδεδειγμένον ἀπὸ τοῦ θεοῦ (Acts 2 [22]).

[2] The terms ἀρχηγός and σωτήρ suggest in a Jewish context the analogy of Moses the first great ' leader and deliverer ' : see J. Weiss, *Das Urchristentum*, p. 326 *n.*

[3] τοῦ δοῦναι μετανοίαν τῷ Ἰσράηλ καὶ ἄφεσιν ἁμαρτιῶν (Acts 5 [31]). Repentance was the constant demand of the great O.T. prophets from Isaiah onwards (cf. Is. 1 [6] *sq.*, etc.). The Divine requirement of a perfectly holy and righteous people (Lev. 20 [26]) could only be met upon the basis of a repentance so radical as to involve a complete and final breach with sin, an inward renewal, or change of heart, of so drastic a kind as to amount to a virtual re-creation of human nature. Already in Judaism it was perceived that it was not in the power of sinful man thus radically and completely to repent, that an inward renewal of human nature could be brought about only by the action of God (cf. Ezek. 36 [26] *sq.*, Jer. 31 [33]). Nevertheless it appears to have been taught in some circles that the coming of salvation was contingent upon the repentance of Israel (see Bousset, *Die Religion des Judentums*, 2nd edn., p. 285), and it was a widely-held doctrine, based on the Book of Malachi (cf. Mal. 4 [5, 6]), that it should be the work of Elijah to come back from heaven and by his preaching inaugurate the ' Great Repentance ' of Israel as the immediate prelude of the End. The Christian tradition identified the Baptist with the expected Elijah (Mt. 11 [14]), but regarded him as having been essentially the Herald of One greater than himself, *i.e.* of Jesus (Mk. 1 [7] and parallels). From the point of view of effective salvation he had been only one more great prophetic preacher of repentance, and his Baptism of water required to be completed by the more efficacious Baptism of the Holy Spirit (Mk. 1 [8] and parallels). As contrasted with merely Judaistic appeals for a ' repentance ' which, taken strictly, was beyond the reach of man's power, Acts 5 [31] stands already upon distinctively Christian ground in representing not merely the forgiveness of sins, but the actual capacity to repent, as itself forming part of God's gift to Israel through the Messiah. It was the conviction of Christianity that in Jesus the gift of repentance had been bestowed, and that correspondingly the great ἄφεσις ἁμαρτιῶν had taken place. Cf. H, Windisch, *Taufe und Sünde im ältesten Christentum*, pp. 34 *sqq.*

[4] Acts 9 [2], 19 [9, 23], 24 [14, 22] ; cf. 16 [17], 18 [25] *sq.*, 22 [4].

we are indebted for the record of such of His teaching as has come down to us in the Gospels. Jesus, they taught, was the 'Prophet like unto Moses,' foretold in the Scriptures by Moses himself, to whom Israel was commanded to ' hearken ' [1] —a manifestly early form of Christology which is quite incompatible with the theory that the whole of their religious attitude towards Jesus was summed up in the conviction that He was the predestined apocalyptic ' Son of Man.' The exalted Messiah, upon whom their devotion was focussed, was still to them Jesus, the Prophet and Teacher who had aroused men's astonishment by teaching ' as having authority, and not as the scribes.' [2] It was He, and none other, who, having been gloriously vindicated by God and exalted in supernatural majesty, was from henceforward the very Lord of their lives, a Lord whom they could utterly trust, and to whom absolute allegiance was due. It appears hardly reasonable to doubt—though the fact has been doubted—that already in the language of Christian devotion men spoke of the Lord Jesus as *Maran*, that is to say as ' our Lord.' [3] His very name had become to them a name of power : a saying preserved in S. Matthew's Gospel is confirmatory of the evidence of the Acts that in His name men prophesied, and in His name cast out demons, and in His name did many wonderful works.[4]

---

[1] Cf. Dt. 18 [15] *sqq*. The Messianic interpretation of this passage (for which cf. Acts 3 [22], 7 [37]; perhaps also Mk. 9 [7], on the assumption that ' hear ye Him ' is an echo of Dt. 18 [15] and means that the disciples are to ' hearken' to the new Prophet, who is also the ' Beloved Son,' and no longer to pay heed merely to ' Moses,' and to the other O.T. prophets, typified by ' Elijah ') seems to have been original in Christianity. There is no evidence that it was interpreted Messianically in Judaism, and the Samaritan doctrine of a future ' Restorer,' apparently based upon a combination of Dt. 18 [15] *sqq*. with Dt. 34 [10] (for which see Bousset, *Die Religion des Judentums* [2], pp. 258, 266), is extremely unlikely (despite Foakes-Jackson and Lake, *The Beginnings of Christianity*, I. pp. 404 *sqq*.) to have influenced the Christian tradition.

[2] Mk. 1 [22].   [3] See Appended Note I. pp. 231 *sqq*.

[4] Mt. 7 [22]. The saying is peculiar to Mt., and may not be a literal utterance of Jesus, more especially as it appears clearly to reflect the

Moreover, a strange new power had taken possession of the disciples themselves—a Power which they identified with the promised gift of the Divine Spirit, destined to be poured out in the last times.[1]   They spoke of the Spirit indifferently as the Spirit of Jesus [2] or as the Holy Spirit—that is, the Spirit of God.   The exalted Jesus, they said, had received the promised Holy Spirit from the Father, and had poured it out upon His disciples.   That He should have been able to do so was at once an evidence of His exaltation to the right hand of Power,[3] and to the disciples an assurance and pledge [4] of the certainty and imminence of the coming salvation.   In the power of the Spirit they were taken out of themselves, transformed, and endued with a strange boldness and confidence [5] to speak and to act in the name of the Lord Jesus.

The decisive step had in fact already been taken.   The advance had been made from the original relationship of discipleship towards Jesus as the Rabbi or Teacher [6] to the newer relationship of religious dependence upon Jesus as the

experience of a later time.   But it seems nevertheless probable that the experience in question goes back to Palestinian and Aramaic-speaking Christianity.   The investigation of Heitmüller (*Im Namen Jesu*, Göttingen, 1902) has made it probable that a literal invocation of the Name of Jesus is implied.   Cf. Acts 3 [6, 16], 19 [13].

[1] Acts 2 [15] *sqq*.   The experience described as that of ' receiving the Holy Spirit ' was beyond question the essential and distinctive thing in early Christianity, the secret of its transporting joy and power, the source of the confident faith which could be described as ' the victory that overcometh the world.'   See the admirable pages devoted to the subject in J. Weiss, *Das Urchristentum*, pp. 28 *sqq*.

[2] So Acts 16 [7].

[3] Cf. Eph. 4 [8].

[4] Cf. Rom. 8 [23] (ἀπαρχή), 2 Cor. 1 [22] (ἀρραβών).   The ' first-fruits ' is an assurance of the reality of the coming harvest : the ' earnest ' (i.e. a first instalment paid in advance as a guarantee of the *bona fides* of a bargain) is a pledge that the full and completed payment is to come.

[5] παρρησία (Acts 4 [13, 31]).

[6] Cf. for the use of ' Rabbi' by the disciples in addressing our Lord, Mk. 9 [5], 11 [21], 14 [45], and for ' Rabboni ' Mk. 10 [51], Jn. 20 [16].   The Greek equivalent form Διδάσκαλε occurs in Mk. 4 [38], 9 [38], 10 [35], 13 [1].   The later Evangelists avoid this usage, Mt. tending to replace Διδάσκαλε by Κύριε, Lk. by Ἐπιστάτα.

exalted Messiah and Lord of the Church. It would appear probable—though the evidence, at the stage which we have thus far reached, is naturally scanty [1]—that already they were becoming accustomed to address Jesus directly in prayer. They depended utterly upon Him, in the sure confidence that He was ' with them always, even unto the End of the Age.' [2] In this faith they were prepared to endure persecution—they were ready, if need be, to suffer martyrdom—' rejoicing that they were counted worthy to suffer dishonour for the Name.' [3]

The question has not unnaturally been raised whether such an advance from the relationship of discipleship to that of an essentially religious dependence, amounting to virtual or actual worship, is really conceivable as having taken place upon strictly Jewish soil, or within the circle of the original disciples who had known Jesus in the days of His flesh.[4] But the facts of history appear to be indisputable. No

[1] See, however, Acts 7 [59, 60], on which Lebreton remarks, ' si d'instinct, à l'heure suprême du martyr, le chrétien invoque Jésus, c'est que cette innocation était devenue pour lui une profonde habitude religieuse ' (Les Origines du Dogme de la Trinité, p. 329) ; and cf. the early Christian formula Marana tha (i.e. ' Our Lord, come ! ' cf. Rev. 22 [20]), quoted by S. Paul in 1 Cor. 16 [22], on which see E. Meyer, Ursprung und Anfänge, III. 232 n.

[2] Mt. 28 [20].   [3] Acts 5 [41].

[4] More especially by W. Bousset in Kyrios Christos, Chapter I. According to Bousset the religion of the earliest Christians was purely and simply a Menschensohndogmatik ; that is to say, it was a faith which identified Jesus with the expected ' Son of Man,' but which involved the belief that, having ascended into the heavens, He was from henceforth absent from His Church until the Parousia (cf. Acts 3 [20] ; the Gospel sayings about the taking away of the Bridegroom—Mk. 2 [20]—and the vain desire to see one of the days of the Son of Man—Lk. 17 [22] ; and such phrases as those of Mt. 24 [48], Lk. 12 [45] —' My lord delayeth his coming '—and Mt. 25 [5], ' While the bridegroom tarried '). For Bousset the idea of any present possibility of direct com munion and fellowship with the exalted Lord on the part of the Christian proceeds from a false mysticism which is the illegitimate product of Hellenistic, rather than of Jewish or properly Christian, religious devotion. He roundly denied, therefore, the existence of any cultus of Jesus within the circle of the original disciples, or of any sense, on the part of the original Jewish-Christian community, of present communion with Christ. Bousset's position was sharply challenged in an article on Jesus und Paulus in the Zeitschrift für Theologie und Kirche by P. Wernle, to whom Bousset replies

doctrine of the deity of Christ had as yet been thought out. The essential relation of Christ to the Father had not been defined. The Christological thought of the disciples moved wholly within the range of the half-mythological, pictorial and imaginative categories of Jewish Messianism. Nevertheless, already they were looking upon Jesus as enthroned at the right hand of the Father, already they were yielding to Him an allegiance of such a kind as is legitimately due only to God, already they were depending upon their relationship to Him for such spiritual gifts as only God can bestow.

Nor was the new attitude in reality so wholly discontinuous with their pre-Resurrection faith as might at first sight appear. The effect of the Resurrection, as we have seen,[1] had been not to create for the first time the conviction that Jesus was the Messiah, but to restore a faith temporarily shaken. Already in the lifetime of Jesus the faith had arisen that He was, or might be, the Christ ; and that meant already that He was more than the Master of a band of disciples, that already He was the Chosen One, the Elect of the Father, through whom the Hope of Israel was destined to be fulfilled. To recognize Jesus as the Messiah was already to depend wholly upon Him as the predestined Mediator of the religious salvation of Israel. The relation of religious dependence had already in that moment begun. It was re-established and raised to a new power by the conviction

in *Jesus der Herr* (see esp. pp. 23 *sqq.*). Apart from the question of the use of the title ' Lord ' (on which see Appended Note I. pp. 231 *sqq.*), the discussion is largely concerned with the implications of the early Christian practice of exorcism in the name of Jesus—a practice which is admitted by Bousset to go back to Palestinian Christianity, and to be suggestive at least of the beginnings of something approximating to a *cultus* of Jesus on the part of the Christian community. There is the question, further, of the original meaning of the Sacraments. So far as the Eucharist is concerned, it would be denied by Bousset that it carried with it in Palestinian Christianity the implication of present communion with the exalted Christ which it undoubtedly involved for S. Paul. Baptism in the name of Jesus is a difficulty for his theory : and he would like to think that it was a later and distinctively Hellenistic development. So also *Kyrios Christos*, 2nd edn., pp. 90 *sqq.*   [1] Lecture I. p. 11.

that Jesus was risen and exalted to the right hand of God, but its beginnings were earlier. In the last resort it was essentially the culmination and crystallization in terms of a living faith of the entire impression made by the personality and character, the life and teaching, the death and resurrection of Jesus upon the souls of those who had been His most intimate companions in the days of His flesh.[1]

That there should have ensued, even within the circle of the earliest believers, a fairly rapid development both of doctrine and of practice was really inevitable. Deep, new and transforming religious experiences oblige men to think, and it was impossible for the disciples of Jesus simply to rest in their dramatically re-established conviction of their Master's Messiahship. They were constrained, no doubt partly for the satisfaction of their own proper minds, but still more with a view to the necessities of missionary apologetic in a Jewish environment, to think out their new faith and to relate it to the presuppositions and inherited beliefs of the Judaism in which they had been brought up. If Jesus were indeed the Messiah, if ' the things which were come to pass '[2] were in very truth no accident but an essential part of the eternal purposes of God, then it must surely be possible to find them foreshadowed in those Old Testament Scriptures in which it was the faith of every Jew that God's promises and purposes for Israel were set forth. The apologists of the new faith must be able to show that the things which had been fulfilled in Jesus were such as had been ' written in the law of Moses, and the prophets, and the psalms,' concerning Him.[3] They must be able to argue that it was ' according to the Scriptures ' that Christ had died, that He was ' raised on the third day according to the Scriptures,'[4] and that according to the same Scriptures it

---

[1] Cf. J. Weiss, *Das Urchristentum*, p. 28 ; A. Deissmann, *Paulus*, 2nd edn., pp. 98 *sqq.*

[2] Lk. 24 [18].   [3] Lk. 24 [44].   [4] 1 Cor. 15 [3] *sq.*

had ' behoved the Christ to suffer these things, and to enter into His glory.' [1]

For these earliest Christians the Old Testament was a Book which spoke everywhere of Jesus. Brought up in the inheritance of Judaism, and convinced of the Messiahship of Jesus, they proceeded confidently to put together the Scriptures in the conviction that they were spiritually fulfilled in Him. As Messiah He was clearly the Son of David—' born of the seed of David according to the flesh ' [2] —the heir of one who could be described as being ' of the house and lineage of David ' ; [3] and yet ' more than Solomon ' : [4] in a true sense not only David's Son, but his ' Lord.' [5] He might even be described, on the ground of His enthronement at God's right hand, as the ' Son of God,' since a Psalmist had written, with reference to the enthronement of a Davidic king,

> I will tell of the decree :
> The LORD said unto me, Thou art my Son :
> This day have I begotten thee.[6]

---

[1] Lk. 24 [26].   [2] Rom. 1 [3].

[3] Lk. 2 [4] : cf. Acts 13 [23] ; Mk. 10 [47] and parallels ; and the genealogies in Mt. and Lk. (Mt. 1 [1] sqq., Lk. 3 [23] sqq.). No doubt both these genealogies, which diverge at points from one another, are in a sense artificial compilations. On the possibility, nevertheless, that there may have been an actual tradition of Davidic lineage in the family into which our Lord was born see Dalman, The Words of Jesus, E.T., pp. 319 sqq. ; F. H. Chase, Belief and Creed, pp. 60 sqq. ; J. Weiss, Das Urchristentum, p. 89. Familiarity with such a family tradition may even have played a part in suggesting to our Lord's human mind in boyhood at Nazareth the possibility that it might one day be His vocation to fulfil the rôle of the promised Messiah.

[4] πλεῖον Σολομῶντος (Mt. 12 [42], Lk. 11 [31]).

[5] Ps. 110 [1], Acts 2 [34] sqq., Mk. 12 [35] and parallels. It does not appear to me to be necessary to read into the last of these passages a polemical denial, on the part of some early Christian interpreters of Scripture, of the Davidic sonship asserted on behalf of our Lord by others. The suggestion is rather, I think, simply that the ' Son of David ' conception, taken by itself, is inadequate. See the discussion of the passage in my Commentary on the Gospel according to S. Mark (Methuen, 1925).

[6] Ps. 2 [7] ; cf. Acts 13 [33], Mk. 1 [11] ; 2 Sam. 7 [14], Ps. 89 [26]. In view of these passages it is difficult to think with Bousset (Kyrios Christos, pp. 52 sqq. ; but see also Jesus der Herr, pp. 4 sqq.) that the title ' Son of God '

The life, too, of Jesus had been in a true sense a Messianic life. His enthronement as King had not been the beginning of His Messiahship. Like David himself, who according to the Old Testament had been anointed by Samuel beforehand (so that ' the Spirit of the LORD came mightily upon David from that day forward '),[1] with a view to a sovereignty upon which he was only actually to enter in the future, so also the great Messianic ' Son of David ' had been anointed beforehand—in the hour of His Baptism ! God, it was held, had ' anointed Him with the Holy Spirit and with power,' so that He ' went about doing good, and healing all that were oppressed of the devil : for God was with Him.' [2] Looking back upon the past, men remembered the impression which Jesus had made—the impression as of One clothed with supreme spiritual authority from God,[3] the impression as of a Person divinely equipped and enabled by the power of the Spirit of God to work miracles.[4] It was believed that the Lord Jesus had opened blind eyes,[5] that He had unstopped the ears of the deaf ; [6] it was believed that the lame had been enabled to walk, that the lepers had been cleansed, that the dead had been raised up, and that good tidings had been preached to the poor.[7] Of a truth many prophets and kings had desired to see the things which the disciples of Jesus saw, and had not seen them, and to hear the things which the disciples of Jesus heard, and had not heard them.[8] The contemporaries of our Lord

---

was first applied to Jesus in Hellenistic Christian circles ; it appears clearly to go back to the Old Testament, and presumably, therefore, to Jewish Christianity. On the other hand, in a strictly Jewish context the title would not in itself signify more than enthronement as the divinely-upheld Monarch and Ruler of the People of God. For the combination of the idea of Davidic Sonship with that of enthronement as ' Son of God,' cf. Rom. 1 [3, 4].

[1] 1 Sam. 16 [13] ; cf. too the case of Saul (1 Sam. 10 [1] sqq.).
[2] Acts 10 [38].   [3] Cf. Mk. 1 [27].   [4] Cf. Mt. 12 [28], Lk. 11 [20].
[5] Mk. 8 [22-26].   [6] Mk. 7 [31-37].
[7] Mt. 11 [4] sq., Lk. 7 [22] sq. ; cf. Is. 35 [5] sq., 61 [1].
[8] Lk. 10 [23] sq., Mt. 13 [16] sq.

had no modern hesitations of mind as to miracles. They reported the story of the ' mighty works ' of Jesus with simple-minded enthusiasm, as clear evidence that the ' Days of the Messiah ' had begun. Especially did the *exorcisms* of Jesus appear to them to be significant. They meant that the power of the great Adversary of mankind and of God had been broken, that the ' strong man ' had been ' bound,' that the kingdom and tyranny of Satan were at an end.[1]   The Church saw in Jesus not merely the Christ of the present, victoriously seated at the right hand of the Majesty on high, or the Christ of the future, hereafter destined to be manifested coming in the clouds, but the Christ also of the past, who already in the days of His flesh had been the Anointed of the Spirit, the Fulfiller of Prophecy, the Herald of the Acceptable Year of the Lord.[2]

And because the Church thus saw in Jesus the Fulfiller of Prophecy, it seems that a Messianic significance was dis-covered in Old Testament passages which Judaism had not hitherto been accustomed to refer to the Messiah, but which to Christians spoke clearly of Jesus   There was the passage about the Anointed of the Spirit, to which allusion has already been made—the passage which S. Luke represents Jesus Himself as having read and expounded as being ful-filled in Himself in the Synagogue at Nazareth.[3]   There were the psalms of the Righteous Sufferer, repeatedly echoed in the Gospel accounts of the Passion.[4]   Above all, there was the great series of passages in Deutero-Isaiah, descriptive of the mysterious vocation and suffering destiny of the Servant of the Lord.[5]   What if the same prophet to whose writings the Church was indebted for the solitary passage of Scripture which contained the idea of One who,

---

[1] Mk. 3 [23] and parallels ; Lk. 10 [17] *sqq.*
[2] Lk. 4 [19].
[3] Lk. 4 [16] *sqq.*
[4] Pss. 22 and 69 : see note on pp. 17 *sq.*, *supra.*
[5] Is. 42 [1] *sqq.*, 49 [1] *sqq.*, 50 [4-9], 52 [13]-53 [12].

' anointed ' (and so made a ' Christ ') with an unction not of
the oil of earthly sovereignty, but of the Spirit of the Lord
God, was commissioned straightway as God's Anointed to
proclaim good tidings to the poor,[1] had in reality been speaking not of himself, nor of some other contemporary figure,
but of Jesus, in these passages also ? ' Himself took our
infirmities, and bare our sicknesses '—the passage is quoted
in the Gospel according to S. Matthew with reference to the
healing miracles of Christ.[2] Or again,

> He was led as a sheep to the slaughter,
> And as a lamb before her shearer is dumb,
> So he openeth not his mouth :
> In his humiliation his judgement was taken away:
> His generation who shall declare ?
> For his life is taken from the earth.

The words sounded indeed startlingly apt in their application to Jesus ; and the passage was so explained, according
to the account in the Acts, by S. Philip to the Ethiopian
Eunuch, who had ' come to Jerusalem for to worship.'[3]
Embodying as it did the idea that the sufferings of the Lord's
Servant were not for his own sake, but for the sake of others,
on account of whose transgressions he was wounded, and by
reason of whose iniquities he was bruised, the prophecy
appeared to illuminate what must otherwise have appeared
to be the well-nigh inexplicable mystery of the Crucifixion,
and formed the basis of what I must needs regard as the
earliest Christian theology of the Atonement. It would
seem that for a relatively brief period, and in those circles
of primitive Christianity in which the Old Testament was
read with some reference to the Hebrew original, the phrase
' ebed Jahweh ' (i.e. ' Servant of the Lord '), or whatever may
have been its equivalent in Aramaic, became a recognized
title of Jesus—a title which still shimmers ambiguously

---

[1] Is. 61 [1], Lk. 4 [17] sqq.   [2] Mt. 8 [17] ; cf. Is. 53 [4].
[3] Acts 8 [27] sqq. ; cf. Is. 53 [7] sq.

through the Greek of a few passages in the Acts,[1] though it is probable that in Greek-speaking circles the Septuagint rendering—παῖς Κυρίου—was from the first hardly distinguished in meaning from υἱὸς τοῦ θεοῦ, ' Son of God.'

A few words may be added with regard to the question of the historical mind of our Lord Himself in relation to the Messiahship, though the subject is notoriously one of extreme difficulty, and one, too, in respect of which the opinions of scholars have varied between the extremes of complete scepticism and the confident psychological dogmatism which, in the words of the late Dr. Sanday, was prepared to canvass our Lord's mind and motives with the same freedom as if He were ' a living statesman or one's neighbour in the next house.' [2]   Just at present the pendulum has swung violently in the direction of scepticism. It is perceived that the Jesus, not merely of the Johannine, but of the Synoptic, tradition is already the Christ who is the object of the worship and faith of the Church ; it is assumed that the Jesus of history has been somehow transformed by the faith of the Church ; but the attempt by some process of critical research to undo the transformation has been largely abandoned.

Nevertheless, the problem of the relation of Jesus to Christianity is too vital an issue to be thus simply set on one side ; a mere reaction in the direction of scepticism can hardly be permanent. It is antecedently probable that there were links of connexion between the disciples' faith

---

[1] Cf. Acts 3 [13], [26], 4 [27], [30], where the word παῖς is (probably rightly) rendered ' Servant ' in the R.V. as against the A.V. rendering ' Child.' For the ambiguity of παῖς in such a connexion in Hellenistic Greek, cf. Wisdom 2 [13-18] (παῖδα Κυρίου ἑαυτὸν ὀνομάζει . . . ἀλαζονεύεται πατέρα θεὸν . . . εἰ γάρ ἐστι δίκαιος υἱὸς θεοῦ), and see Bousset, Kyrios Christos [2], pp. 56 sq., Wetter, Der Sohn Gottes, p. 146, and Lebreton, Les Origines du Dogme de la Trinité, p. 327.   For a consideration and rejection of the theory that the ' Servant ' passages were first referred to our Lord in Hellenistic rather than in Aramaic-speaking circles, see Appended Note II. pp. 239 sqq.

[2] Sanday, The Life of Christ in Recent Research, p. 95.

in our Lord and our Lord's own belief with regard to Himself ; and in view of the fact that, as we have seen, it is historically certain that our Lord allowed Himself to be crucified in the capacity of a Jewish Messiah, the question of the sense in which He interpreted to His own human mind the Messiahship which He undoubtedly claimed cannot well be evaded. That our Lord was not the Messiah in any merely conventional sense is self-evident. A Messiah who did nothing to bring about the political freedom of Israel, who established no Kingdom of David, who appeared outwardly in the guise, not of a claimant of sovereignty, but of a Prophet, and who ended His days on a cross, could be to orthodox Judaism merely an unacceptable and blasphemous paradox, ' a stone of stumbling and a rock of offence.' [1] What is clearly demanded is such an interpretation of what is meant by Messiahship as shall render intelligible the behaviour of Jesus, on the assumption that He did actually believe Himself to be the Messiah whom the Scriptures foretold. The solution, as I venture to think, is perhaps to be found partly in a profoundly original reading of the Old Testament.

That the Hope of Israel should be fulfilled in the person of One who set Himself to establish no kingdom, but who proclaimed only the Kingdom of God ; that the primary work of the Messiah should be the work of proclaiming glad tidings to the poor ; that the Master and Lord should be in the midst of the disciples as One who came not to be ministered unto, but to minister, and that the Son of Man, predestined, according to the vision in Daniel, to receive in the clouds of heaven everlasting dominion, should be on the earth as One homeless, not having where to lay His head, appointed to suffer many things and to be rejected, betrayed into the hands of sinners, and put to death ; that the victory of the Elect Champion of the people of God should be gained

---

[1] Rom. 9 [33] ; cf. Is. 8 [14].

only through suffering and apparent defeat, at the price of a cup of anguish and of a baptism of blood ; that the life of the Messiah Himself should be poured out on behalf of others in sacrifice, and His blood be described as ' the blood of the Covenant, shed for many '—all these are ideas, profoundly new and original in Christianity, and yet in a true sense rooted in the soil of the Old Testament, and essentially Hebraic ; ideas which, I submit, were no afterthought on the part of the disciples, but may be reasonably held to go back to the historical mind of the Lord Jesus Himself.

The Lord Jesus claimed to be the Christ, and yet not to be the Christ of the popular theology—the true Christ, not the Christ of the scribes.[1] According to the account in S. Mark, He was not the Christ as the term ' Christ ' was understood by S. Peter at Caesarea Philippi,[2] but in a sense which involved sufferings and death. ' The Son of Man must suffer many things and be rejected. . . . And He spake the saying openly.'[3] It is exceedingly difficult not to believe that the Lord Jesus in some sense foresaw and anticipated His Passion, and that the vocation on behalf of the People of God to suffer martyrdom and to ' give His life a ransom for many' was for Him bound up in some mysterious fashion with the Messianic vocation in accordance with the inscrutable will and purposes of God. Is it too daring to suggest that the broad outlines of the distinctively Christian interpretation of the Old Testament were already implicit in the outlook of Jesus, that already in the mind of the Jesus of history the *rôle* of the Messiah of prophecy—the Davidic Messiah—had become inwardly transformed, and at the same time linked with that of the apocalyptic Son of Man, in virtue of the interpretation of both these originally distinct and independent conceptions in terms of the martyr vocation

---

[1] Cf. Mk. 12 [35] *sqq.* and parallels ; it is perhaps significant that the warning ' Beware of the scribes ! ' (Mk. 12 [38] *sqq.* and parallels) immediately follows this paragraph in the Gospel tradition.

[2] Mk. 8 [27] *sqq.* ; contrast Mt. 16 [13] *sqq.*   [3] Mk. 8 [31] *sq.*

and suffering destiny of the Servant of the Lord ? [1] On the broad issue as between the ' eschatological school of New Testament critics and their opponents I venture to think that the eschatological school is in the right in maintaining that the mind of our Lord was predominantly orientated in the direction of the future, that He envisaged the future in terms of the eschatological symbolism of the coming of the Son of Man and the End of the Age, and that like the prophets [2] He proclaimed that the time was at hand. But I do not believe that the eschatology was the whole of His Messianic doctrine. I believe that the Son of Man was identified in His mind with the Servant of the Lord, and that the peculiar paradox of the Christian conception of the Messiahship, according to which the Son of Man, who is the Representative of God and the Ultimate Judge, who has authority on earth to forgive sins [3] and is Lord of the Sabbath,[4] is at the same time the ' servant of all,' who ' came not to be ministered unto, but to minister, and to give his life a ransom for many,' [5] goes back to the historical mind of the crucified Prophet who ' dreamed that God would redeem the world through Him, and died to make the dream come true.' [6] I venture to think also that at least from the time of His Baptism onwards, and in virtue of the experience which then came to Him, our Lord knew Himself to be the Messiah, the Anointed of the Spirit, who as such was clothed with supreme authority from God.

Behind the question of the Messiahship there lurks the further question of the ultimate mystery of our Lord's Person. Who was this Jesus for whom such claims were made, and who, there is reason to think, made such claims

---

[1] I have attempted to work this out in a note on ' The Significance of our Lord's Baptism ' appended to my edition of *The Gospel according to S. Mark* in the Westminster Commentaries (*op. cit.* pp. 251 *sqq.*).

[2] Cf. Ezek. 12 [22] *sqq.*

[3] Mk. 2 [10].   [4] Mk. 2 [28].   [5] Mk. 10 [44] *sq.*

[6] B. H. Streeter in *Foundations*, p. 144.

on behalf of Himself ?   It was not the method of the Lord
Jesus—if we exclude from consideration the Fourth Gospel,
as for my own part I think that we ought for this purpose
to do—to indulge publicly in theological reflection with
regard to His own Person.   The whole mind of the Christian
Church was inevitably occupied with the subject for generations, and it was a matter of centuries before the problem
was even effectively stated in what has come to be regarded
as its classical form.[1]   Yet if the Gospels may be trusted
it would seem that our Lord was accustomed in a distinctive
and peculiar fashion to speak of God as His ' Father,' [2] and
from time to time also to speak of Himself in the third
person, as if by a kind of title, as ' the Son.' [3]   It is not
improbable that those scholars are right who have spoken
of the so-called ' filial consciousness ' of Jesus—the awareness as it were of an unique and peculiar inner spiritual
relationship towards God, expressed to our Lord's own
human mind in terms of the metaphor of sonship—as
having constituted the indispensable psychological pre-

---

[1] In the Definition of Chalcedon, A.D. 451.

[2] It is pointed out by Foakes-Jackson and Lake, following Bousset
(cf. *Kyrios Christos*, 2nd edn., p. 52 : ' *mit ersichtlicher Reflexion durch-
geführt ist jener Sprachgebrauch doch nur im Matthäus-Evangelium, und
dann später im Johannes-Evangelium* '), that this usage is primarily characteristic of the Gospel according to S. Matthew, the editor of which, as
they suggest, was in the habit of emphasizing our Lord's Divine Sonship
by the introduction of the phrase ' My Father ' into His sayings (see *The
Beginnings of Christianity*, vol. i. p. 402, and the statistics there given).
Nevertheless, although it is true, as the same writers have urged (*op. cit.*
p. 401), that ' the Fatherhood of God is a characteristically Jewish doctrine,
found in equal abundance in the Old Testament and in Rabbinic literature,'
it would seem probable that there was really something unusual in what
appears to have been our Lord's virtually exclusive use of the term
' Father ' as a title of God, a usage in which the Church so immediately
followed Him that the Aramaic form *Abba* (='Father') was carried
over into the prayers even of the Gentile and Greek-speaking Church
(cf. Rom. 8 [15], Gal. 4 [6], Mk. 14 [36]).

[3] Cf. Mk. 13 [32], 12 [1-12].   The authenticity of the Parable of the
Wicked Husbandmen has been strongly defended by Burkitt in the
Transactions of the Third International Congress for the History of Religion,
ii. pp. 321 *sqq.*

supposition of His acceptance of the mysterious vocation to be the Messiah. It is not likely that Professor B. W. Bacon of Yale University is right in believing that our Lord's Divine Sonship is to be explained by the theory that He regarded Himself as the Son of God merely in the sense of being the ' first-born of many brethren,' the champion of the Divine sonship of the spiritually disinherited masses, the ' lost sheep of the house of Israel.'[1] Jewish scholars like Montefiore have some pertinent remarks to make on the subject of these supposed ' spiritually disinherited masses.'[2]   On the other hand, there may be truth in the suggestion of McNeile that in the mind of our Lord His Sonship to God ' was Israel's moral sonship represented and consummated in His own human person.'[3]   And yet not the whole truth ; in my judgement an ultimate mystery remains.

The Synoptic tradition includes one passage—the famous words about the mutual knowledge of the Father and the Son[4]—which has been described as an erratic block in an alien environment, a thunderbolt from the Johannine sky. Grave critical doubt has been widely expressed with regard to the genuineness of the saying as an utterance of Jesus. It is certainly a difficult saying, and one which in later days was widely exploited in the interests of Gnosticism.[5]   On the other hand, it is not absolutely true to say that the central idea contained in the saying—the idea of an unique knowledge of God as being the privilege, partly communicable by teaching and revelation to others, of One who Himself was uniquely known by God—is foreign to Judaism.   We have

[1] B. W. Bacon, *Jesus the Son of God* (Yale University Press, 1911).

[2] C. G. Montefiore, *The Synoptic Gospels*, i. pp. lxxv. *sqq.*

[3] A. H. McNeile, *New Testament Teaching in the Light of S. Paul*, p. 31. The statement is quoted and criticized by Gore in *The Holy Spirit and the Church*, pp. 278 *sq.*

[4] Mt. 11 [27], Lk. 10 [22]. For a discussion of the passage, see Appended Note IV. pp. 251 *sqq.*

[5] Cf. E. Norden, *Agnostos Theos*, pp. 73 *sqq.*, 285 *sqq.*

only to think of the passage about Moses in the closing chapter of Deuteronomy, in which it is said that 'there hath not arisen a prophet since in Israel like unto Moses, *whom the Lord knew face to face.* [1] It was the conviction of Christianity that in Jesus such a 'Prophet' at length had arisen, a Prophet who, like Moses, was truly a 'servant of the Lord,' [2] but who, unlike Moses, was more than a 'servant,' inasmuch as He was also a 'Son.' [3]   And this conception of Jesus as more than a 'servant,' as in unique fashion entitled to be described as 'the Son' in relation to God, was an idea which was destined to prove capable of fruitful development upon Gentile-Christian soil.

[1] Deut. 34 [10].   [2] Deut. 34 [5].   [3] Hebrews 3 [5] *sq.*

LECTURE III
THE GENTILE-CHRISTIAN MISSION

SYNOPSIS

THE beginnings of Gentile Christianity due not to S. Paul but to the Christians of Antioch. The new Hellenistic environment. Its characteristics. An age of religious syncretism, of popular superstition, of intense realization of spiritual needs. The 'failure of nerve,' or the dawn of humility. Its historical causes. The longing for super-earthly salvation. The horror of death.

(1) The revival in this period of the religion of the mysteries, and the vogue also of 'mystery cults' of barbarian origin. Without accepting the exaggerated statements of those who ignore dates, it is certain that the Hellenistic-Egyptian religion of Serapis and Isis, and perhaps also the Phrygian religion of Cybele and Attis, were already widespread as 'mystery' religions in pre-Christian times. Initiation into the mysteries was *one* method of seeking salvation. And the 'salvation' which was sought was more particularly deliverance from death.

(2) But it was also deliverance from Fate. The vogue of astrology, or the belief in the determination of human destiny by the stars, interpreted optimistically by the philosophers, gave rise to the 'astral mysticism' of such thinkers as Posidonius; interpreted pessimistically by the Gnostics, it became a nightmare, from which deliverance was sought by means of *gnosis*. The Gnostic documents known to us are mostly of post-Christian date and often partially Christian. (Contention of Bevan that the figure of the Redeemer in Gnosticism is post-Christian and borrowed from Christianity.) But it is possible that both the essentials of the Gnostic world-view and the idea of salvation by *gnosis* were current in pre-Christian times.

(3) The wider sense of the term *gnosis*. Norden's *Agnostos Theos*: the idea that the supreme God was 'unknowable,' except by revelation. The resulting demand for revealers creates a supply.

The Hellenistic idea of a 'son of God' as a supernatural Being, a 'divine man,' at once benefactor, thaumaturge and prophet. Fluidity of the term 'god.' The deification of the Emperors finds its parallel in the deification, in certain instances, of the religious teacher and sage. On a background of paganism and polytheism deifications were easy.

In what way would the ' Greeks ' (*i.e.* Hellenized Orientals) understand Christianity ? The first converts were not pagans, but ' God-fearers ' who had been in contact with Judaism. But the Gospel spread outside this circle, and reached a class to whom the Jewish term ' Christ ' was unintelligible. So also the term ' Son of Man ' to non-Jews was obscure. It was otherwise with the terms ' Lord ' and ' Son of God.' The presentation of Jesus in the Synoptic tradition is in line with the popular Hellenistic significance of the term ' Son of God,' and the term ' Lord ' would suggest to a pagan the idea of the Church as a *thiasos* or community of devotees who were associated for the worship of a deity called ' Jesus.' (The significance of the term *Kyrios* : its associations on the one hand with the Old Testament and on the other hand with pagan religion.) The possible dangers of the Gentile-Christian situation apart from S. Paul.

LECTURE III

THE GENTILE-CHRISTIAN MISSION

They therefore that were scattered abroad upon the tribulation that arose about Stephen travelled as far as Phoenicia, and Cyprus, and Antioch, speaking the word to none save only to Jews. But there were some of them, men of Cyprus and Cyrene, who, when they were come to Antioch, spake unto the Greeks[1] also, preaching the Lord Jesus.—Acts 11 [19, 20].

THE beginnings of Gentile Christianity were due not to S. Paul but to the originators of the Christianity of Antioch. Had S. Paul never existed, there would still have come into being a mission of Christianity to the Gentiles, and that, too, upon lines which would almost certainly have involved ultimately the repudiation of the permanent obligation of the Law. The missionary impulse, already inherent in Judaism (we are told that even the Pharisees of Jerusalem were prepared to compass sea and land to make a proselyte),[2] was especially active in the Hellenistic or Greek-speaking synagogues of the Dispersion. It was quickened, in the case of the Christian disciples of S. Stephen, by the conviction, bound up with their faith in the Messiahship of Jesus, that the decisive hour of the world's history was at hand. It is not surprising that there were some of their number—men of Cyprus and Cyrene—who, when they were come to Antioch, could not refrain from preaching the

---

[1] R.V. here rightly follows the Bezan text in reading Ἕλληνας. The translation 'Grecian Jews' of R.V. mg. represents the reading of Codex Vaticanus, viz. Ἑλληνιστάς, which makes nonsense of the passage. The followers of Stephen were already themselves 'Hellenists' (*i.e.* Greek-speaking Jews), and so were the Jews to whom at first they addressed their message. The new departure consisted in preaching to 'Greeks,' in the sense of Greek-speaking pagans.

[2] Mt. 23 [15].

message of the Lord Jesus not to Jews only, but also to Greeks.

The atmosphere of the strange many-coloured cosmopolitan world of Greek-speaking but in many respects un-Greek civilization upon which Christianity thus entered was radically different from that of Palestine. It was a world of great cities, superficially hellenized, but rich with the smells of the Orient, cities typified by Antioch itself, the former capital of the Seleucid Kings, now the administrative centre of the Roman province of Syria, a city in whose streets and colonnades and bazaars a bewildering variety of human types—Greek, Syrian, Anatolian, Chaldaean, Arabian, Jew— met and jostled and talked and gesticulated and bargained and exchanged ideas in the vulgar colloquial Greek which, as a result of the conquests of Alexander and by the policy of his successors, had become the common medium of intercourse in the Levant.

It was a world in which religious syncretism flourished— a modern scholar describes Syria as ' the true homeland of syncretism ' [1]—as was natural in a country and period in which three originally diverse religious and cultural traditions, Greek, Jewish and Oriental, were in intimate contact. The Jewish element is known to have been strong in Antioch : we are told by Josephus that the Jews of the Syrian capital enjoyed equal rights of citizenship with their non-Jewish neighbours, and that they had made many converts to their religion.[2]   But the Judaism of Antioch was of the Hellenistic and liberalizing type : the Christianity of Antioch became quickly more liberalizing still. The Church found itself confronted at Antioch, exactly as on the mission field to-day (for example, in the great cities of modern India), with the problem of how best to present its essential message in terms

---

[1] ' *Diesem eigentlichen Mutterboden des Synkretismus* ' (J. Weiss, *Das Urchristentum*, p. 577).

[2] Josephus, *De Bell. Jud.* VII. iii. 3.

intelligible to the minds of its hearers without itself incurring the danger of becoming partially paganized in the process.

The age was one of intense spiritual yearning, of widespread consciousness of religious need, and at the same time of widespread popular superstition. We are told in the Acts that the populace of Athens derived from the preaching of S. Paul the impression that he was ' a setter forth of foreign demons '—two ' foreign demons,' to wit, whose names were respectively ' Jesus' and ' Anastasis.' [1] So too the formula of exorcism employed by the seven sons of Sceva at Ephesus, ' I adjure you by Jesus whom Paul preacheth,' [2] finds its parallel in the formula of a magical papyrus discovered in Egypt, ' I adjure you by Jesus the god of the Hebrews.' [3] Quacks, prophets and charlatans, magicians, astrologers and hierophants of strange cults, were everywhere. So too were the popular street preachers of philosophy, picturesque figures in rough philosopher's cloak, equipped with staff and wallet, travelling barefoot and penniless to proclaim the gospel according to Stoicism, or the more deliberately ascetic, but in other respects hardly distinguishable precepts of the Cynics.[4] We may suspect, no doubt, that the adjurations addressed to the multitudes by these philosophic friars of antiquity to bethink themselves of their true good, to abandon idolatry, and to live according to reason, were on the whole as ineffective as are the adjurations of philosophy in relation to the multitudes in every age of the world's history. The apostles of new cults and religions were

---

[1] Ξένων δαιμονίων δοκεῖ καταγγαλεὺς εἶναι · ὅτι τὸν Ἰησοῦν καὶ τὴν ἀνάστασιν εὐηγγελίζετο (Acts 17 [18]).

[2] Acts 19 [13].

[3] Ὁρκίζω σε κατὰ τοῦ θεοῦ τῶν Εβραίων Ἰησοῦ (Reitzenstein, *Poimandres*, p. 14 *n.* ; Dieterich, *Eine Mithrasliturgie*, 2nd edn., pp. 44 *sq.* The words occur in the Paris magical papyrus from which Dieterich has unearthed the so-called ' Mithras Liturgy.' According to Dieterich the MS. dates in its present form from about 300 A.D., but most of the material is much older).

[4] Cf. Wendland, *Die hellenistisch-römische Kultur*, p. 44 ; Dill, *Roman Society from Nero to Marcus Aurelius*, Bk. III. Chap. ii. ; and J. Weiss, *Das Urchristentum*, pp. 172 *sqq.*

more efficacious. The average man finds it a good deal easier to accept a new form of religious worship than to turn over a new leaf, and it would seem that the faith of Christ was only one out of a number of foreign religions which were in process of becoming disseminated at this period in the Graeco-Roman world

In the interval which separates the campaigns of Alexander from the age of the New Testament a new spirit and temper had come over the Greek-speaking world. The old self-confident humanism of classical Hellas, the rationalism which had believed it possible to ' see life steadily and see it whole,' which had looked out on the world with a certain directness,[1] and had believed in the capacity of philosophical thought to attain speculative truth, had given place to a mood of pessimism, a doubt as to the ultimate competence of human reason, a despair of enquiry, a longing for some sure word of revelation. We may call it, according to our taste and predilection, ' a failure of nerve,'[2] or the dawn of humility. Certain it is that men no longer felt ' at home in the universe ' ;[3] there was a sense of insecurity, of strange terrifying possibilities, of the enigma of the Unknown. It was partly due, no doubt, to the break-up of the City State, to the experience of foreign conquests, of war, pestilence and famine, of great disasters and sudden reversals of fortune which made men feel as though the old gods had abdicated, as though the affairs of mortals were controlled by Chance or Destiny ; it was partly due to the rise of an individualism which was no longer satisfied to immerse the individual in the concerns of a civic life which, with the loss of civic

---

[1] On the ' note of directness ' as being characteristic of the Greek view of life, see R. W. Livingstone, *The Greek Genius and its Meaning to us,* Chapter iii.

[2] Gilbert Murray, *Five Stages of Greek Religion,* Lecture iv.   Professor Murray informs us in his Introduction, pp. 8 *sq.,* that he was indebted for the phrase to a conversation with Professor J. B. Bury.

[3] Edwyn Bevan, *Stoics and Sceptics,* p. 96 *sqq.*

independence, had largely lost its significance ; and partly, too, to a resurgence of the mystical temper which looks away from the affairs of this world altogether to seek a more abiding home of the spirit in the world beyond change and death

It was a period in which the old gods of the City were discredited, while at the same time the new worship of Rome and Augustus, though it gave genuine expression to the sense of gratitude for the new era of prosperity and stable government which had been inaugurated by the victory of Actium and the subsequent pacification of the world, did little to satisfy the heart. Men were looking for a super-earthly salvation, for some assurance of life to come. Dr. Bevan has rightly drawn attention to the fear of death, as having been in the Hellenistic period ' much more powerful and more widely diffused than it is among ourselves,' so that ' a New Testament writing speaks of men as being "through the fear of death all their lifetime subject to bondage." ' [1] It is not altogether surprising that the ancient Greek mysteries, the solemn rites of Eleusis, the teaching of Orphic and Pythagorean brotherhoods with regard to the life after death, experienced in this period a kind of renaissance, or that, outside Greece proper—or, indeed, in Greece itself in such seaport cities as the Athenian Peiraeus and Corinth—the vogue of mystery cults of barbarian origin was beginning to be fashionable. Exaggerated statements have been made on this subject by scholars who believe themselves to be entitled to disregard dates, and the blunt statement of Schweitzer, that S. Paul, for example, ' cannot have known the mystery religions in the form in which they are known to us, because in this fully-developed form they did not yet exist,' [2] is worth

[1] E. Bevan, *Hellenism and Christianity*, p. 82 ; Heb. 2 [15].
[2] Schweitzer, *Paul and his Interpreters*, p. 192. On the Mystery Religions, see further Appended Note VI. pp. 270 *sqq.*

bearing in mind. Schweitzer's point is that the greater part of our evidence with regard to these cults is of later than first-century date, that their origins were savage and primitive, and that it is in most cases quite uncertain at what period they began to be made the vehicle of higher aspirations. It would seem, however, that already in pre-Christian times at least the Hellenistic-Egyptian religion of Serapis and Isis, and probably also the Phrygian worship of Cybele and Attis, had become associated with ' mysteries ' in which a mythology and ceremonial originally connected with the decay and revival of vegetable life was so interpreted as to suggest the hope of immortality. Initiation into the mysteries was at least *one* of the methods by which in the Hellenistic period men sought for salvation. And the ' salvation ' for which they were looking was primarily deliverance from death.

But it was also, at least in some cases, deliverance from Εἱμαρμένη, or Fate. The word εἱμαρμένη recurs continually in the religious literature of the period, and appears commonly to have been connected in the popular mind with the belief in the control of human destiny by the stars. ' Astrology '—to quote a sentence from Professor Gilbert Murray—' fell upon the Hellenistic mind as a new disease falls upon some remote island people.' [1] It came in from the remoter East—from Babylonia : so much so that the term 'Chaldaean,' originally denoting an inhabitant of that country, came to bear commonly in Greek and Roman literature the sense of ' astrologer.' The Babylonians from very early times had been diligent observers of the heavens. The notion arose that the configuration of the sky corresponds with the phenomena of earth. ' Everything in sky and earth alike,' writes Cumont, ' was incessantly changing, and it was thought that there existed a correspondence between the movements of the gods above and the alterations which

---

[1] Gilbert Murray, *Five Stages of Greek Religion*, p. 177.

occurred here below. This is the fundamental idea of astrology.'[1] It was capable of being interpreted either in an optimistic or in a pessimistic sense.

The optimistic interpretation was that of the Stoics,[2] whose teaching, especially in the eclectic and somewhat modified form in which it had been popularized by the Syrian Greek thinker Posidonius, tended to dominate the intellectual outlook of educated minds.[3] The Stoics were pantheists with a turn for morality and a disposition to make some sort of terms with the popular religion. They believed in a doctrine of εἱμαρμένη or Destiny, and in the universal sympathy of the elements in the Cosmos.[4] They were already committed to the belief that the stars were animate beings, and in some sense divine—a tenet which had formed part of the tradition of Greek philosophy from the time of Plato and Aristotle.[5] The stars were the ' visible gods,' and as such the proper objects of human veneration. A strong vein of what Cumont describes as ' astral mysticism ' is characteristic alike of Neo-Platonism and of the later representatives of Stoic thought.[6] ' It was precisely in the religion of the educated classes,' writes Bousset, ' that the stars from the time of Plato onwards were accounted the real gods. The figures of the popular gods begin to fade, and the inner truth of religion begins to be discovered in veneration for the stellar powers and ruling potencies of heaven, and together with these for the

[1] F. Cumont, *Astrology and Religion among the Greeks and Romans*, p. 18.

[2] Panaetius was an exception : see Schmekel, *Die Philosophie der mittleren Stoa*, pp. 191 *sqq.*

[3] On Posidonius, who became an adopted citizen of Rhodes, and who was the philosophical master of Cicero, see Edwyn Bevan, *Stoics and Sceptics*, Lecture iii., and Schmekel, *op. cit.*

[4] Συμπάθεια τῶν ὅλων : see Gilbert Murray, *op. cit.* p. 178, and the references there given.

[5] Cf. C. C. J. Webb, *Studies in the History of Natural Theology*, pp. 66 *sq.*, 92 *sqq.*, 153 *sq.*

[6] F. Cumont, *Astrology and Religion among the Greeks and Romans*, Lecture v.

spirits of the Elements [1] and the deified forces of Nature. The stars are the visible gods, and yonder world above, in which these shining beings move, is the world that is truly divine. Here on the earth, with its dim, gross atmosphere, in this sublunar world, with its incalculable chances and fleeting phenomena, misfortune and evil may have their seat.[2] Above, where in unvarying order move the blessed, shining gods, where all happens according to unvarying law, in calculable and unbroken sequence, there is the world of Beauty, of Goodness and of Harmony : the Cosmos in the proper meaning of the word. Dependent upon that world is the whole of human life and destiny, for it is those heavenly Powers who determine the lives of men. Nay, they are no mere dead, cold Powers : they are gods, to whom men may legitimately (however illogically) lift up their hands in prayer. Man himself—that is to say, the highest part of man's being —belongs to that heavenly world : his higher Ego is a particle of the ethereal Light, his spirit is begotten of the

---

[1] The 'beggarly elements' of Gal. 4 [9]; cf. Col. 2 [8, 20]. The word στοιχεῖον, originally meaning a member of a row or line, came to be used of the letters of the alphabet, arranged in series, and eventually of the elemental forces of Nature. The ' elements ' of Earth, Air, Fire and Water were all deified, and so also were the Planets (Sun, Moon, Mars, Mercury, Jupiter, Venus and Saturn), represented in Greek magical writings by the seven vowels α ε η ι ο υ ω. In late Greek usage the word στοιχεῖον comes to mean a Daemon. The belief in demonic spirits of the various elements and planetary powers passed into Judaism in the form of the belief that the various departments of Nature (stars, fire, wind, clouds, rain, snow, etc.) were all administered, under God, by their appropriate ' angels ' (see R. H. Charles, *Apocrypha and Pseudepigrapha of the Old Testament*, vol. ii., Index, s.v. ' Angels '). Cf. also Lecture VI. pp. 142 *sqq.*

[2] Cf. Plutarch, *De Iside et Osiride*, 45, where, arguing against the Stoics in favour of dualism, Plutarch remarks that life is a mixed affair, and that *at least in the world beneath the moon* there is an evil principle at work (ὅ τε βίος μικτός, ὅ τε κόσμος, εἰ καὶ μὴ πᾶς, ἀλλ' ὁ περίγειος οὗτος καὶ μετὰ σελήνην, ἀνώμαλος καὶ ποικίλος γέγονε, καὶ μεταβολὰς πάσας δεχόμενος). The same idea is found in the *Somnium Scipionis* of Cicero, where after the description of the seven planetary spheres, of which the lowest is that of the Moon, we read that beneath the moon ' *nihil est nisi mortale et caducum praeter animos munere deorum hominum generi datos, supra Lunam sunt aeterna omnia* ' (Cicero, *De Republica*, vi. 17).

Sun and kindred with the stars. To that world return after their deaths the souls of the wise and religious among men, themselves to move henceforward in the rhythmic courses of the stars, and to be satisfied by the unutterable beauty of the gleaming universe of Light. And, lastly, the astronomer, who by his researches and calculations seeks to comprehend the secret eternal ordinances of heaven—the astrologer, who by means of his " science " attempts to penetrate the hidden counsels of the gods—filled with a secret rapture is conscious of exaltation above this darkling and troubled earth into the great free world of deity on high, and in the awareness of his soul's kinship with the divine experiences in blissful ecstasy a species of *unio mystica* with the starry firmament above.' [1]

Thus far the optimistic version of the philosophers ; the pessimistic interpretation was that of the Gnostics, for whom the entire visible universe was evil, and the stars consequently, so far from being deities, were demonic and sinister powers, the ' world-rulers of this darkness,' hostile to man. The stars and the seven circling planets were for the Gnostic the lords of this lower world, in unnatural subjection to whose harsh dominion the divine element in man was held a prisoner, the captive of an alien tyranny, the victim of unpitying Fate. To such minds the rule of the stars could be no rational system of wisely ordered Providence. It was a nightmare, an intolerable horror ; and salvation consisted not in the mystic ecstasy of union with the stars, but in deliverance from the unyielding grip

---

[1] W. Bousset, *Kyrios Christos*, 2nd edn., pp. 185 *sq.* Cf. the epigram of Ptolemy the Astronomer (end of the 2nd century A.D.) :

Οἶδ᾽ ὅτι θνατὸς ἐγὼ καὶ ἐφάμερος · ἀλλ᾽ ὅταν ἄστρων
μαστεύω πυκινὰς ἀμφιδρόμους ἕλικας,
οὐκέτ᾽ ἐπιψαύω γαίης ποσίν, ἀλλὰ παρ᾽ αὐτῷ
Ζανὶ θεοτροφίης πίμπλαμαι ἀμβροσίης.

(*Anthol. Palat.* ix. 577.)

A free rendering in English is printed by Robert Bridges in *The Spirit of Man* (Book ii., No. 160).

of Fate. Presupposed by the majority of Gnostic systems is the same astronomical or astrological view of the universe as is to be found in what is thought to have been the teaching of Posidonius. There is the same scheme of the seven concentric heavens, the same belief in the Κοσμοκράτορες or World-Rulers. Only now the goal of salvation is utter escape—escape beyond the seven spheres of the circling planets, beyond the region of the fixed stars, the *flammantia moenia mundi*, and that ' music of the spheres ' of which the philosophers spoke (but which to the Gnostic could only be harshest discord), escape altogether, beyond the confines of this visible universe, into the Silence, the great Abyss, the Ogdoad or Eighth Region, where dwells in unapproachable light the unnameable, Unknown God.

Here, again, as in the case of the mystery cults, the majority of our documents for the study of Gnosticism are of post-Christian date, and the systems described and perhaps travestied in the polemical pages of early Church Fathers are of course partially Christian. Dr. Bevan in an interesting essay has attempted to show in particular that the figure of the Redeemer in Gnosticism came in from Christianity, his argument being that in the definitely non-Christian systems, so far as they are known to us, the figure of the Redeemer is missing : that in the partially Christianized systems in which a Σωτήρ actually appears, the idea of salvation by *gnosis* and the idea of salvation by Christ ' present the appearance of two alternative schemes which have been imperfectly joined together ' ; and that in these systems the Gnostic account of the descent and re-ascension of the Redeemer is in its essence little more than a reduplication of the Hellenistic account of the soul.[1]

---

[1] Edwyn Bevan, *Hellenism and Christianity*, Essay v. (' The Gnostic Redeemer '). Cf. also W. Scott, *Hermetica*, vol. ii. p. 9, where the absence of the conception of a ' Saviour ' from the *Poimandres* document is regarded as an argument for the absence of Christian influence, and the conception of ' a " Saviour," i.e. a divine Person who has descended from a higher

Nevertheless, when all necessary cautions have been observed, it seems probable, or indeed almost certain, that the essentials of Gnosticism—the pessimistic cosmological dualism, the fantastic mythology, the magical formulae and rites, the disposition to seek salvation by *gnosis*, that is to say, by dabbling in the occult, with the very practical object of escape from the evils and miseries of material existence—are pre-Christian in origin (as they are certainly independent of Christianity), and that they represent a general system or body of ideas, a way of looking at the world, which there is reason to think may have been fairly widely disseminated in various forms in the first century of our era. It would seem that we ought to recognize as having been, so to speak, in the air, side by side with the idea of salvation by ' mysteries ' (in the sense of secret rites and initiations), the alternative idea of salvation by *gnosis*, that is to say, by revelation.[1]

For indeed the term *gnosis*, as has been made clear by the

world to rescue human souls from their fallen condition,' is described as ' the most distinctive characteristic of Christian doctrine, as compared with that of other religions of the time.'

[1] I venture to think that Reitzenstein in *Die hellenistischen Mysterien-religionen* goes seriously astray as the result of a failure to draw this distinction. In consequence he ascribes on the one hand to the mystery cults a theology which, in the earlier stages of their development, there is little reason to suppose that they involved, and tends on the other hand to regard the type of religion reflected, for example, in the various writings which make up the *Corpus Hermeticum* as having arisen by way of a spiritualization or ' interiorization ' (*Verinnerlichung*) of religious ideas derived originally from mystical experiences gained through initiation into a cult (cf. Reitzenstein, *op. cit.*, 2nd edn., pp. 106 *sqq.*) : this despite the fact that in the Hermetic religion the element of *cultus* does not enter at all, salvation being the result simply of instruction by means of a λόγος τέλειος, a phrase for which Prof. H. A. A. Kennedy suggests the translation ' a revelation which initiates ' (Kennedy, *St. Paul and the Mystery Religions*, p. 132). No doubt the Gnostic religions *commonly* involved an element of *cultus* ; and no doubt also as time went on the mystery religions may have come to involve increasingly an element of *gnosis*. But even so there was a difference of emphasis, which in turn was the result of a difference of origin and character. The mystery cults were essentially ancient and secret rituals, into which individual initiates were at liberty to read what

work of Norden [1] among others, bears a much wider significance in the religious thought and language of the period
than that which connects it specifically with Gnosticism.
It was used most characteristically in Gnosticism to denote
the occult 'knowledge' which enabled a man to escape from
the tyranny of an alien universe into a world which was
wholly other, and which yet was the true home and place
of origin of the divine element within his soul. But the
word was used also in a wider sense, independently of any
dualistic cosmology or other tenets distinctive of Gnosticism,
to denote the idea of such a ' knowledge ' of God as was
attainable not by speculative thought but by revelation.
Plato already in the *Timaeus* had said that to discover the
Maker and Father of the universe was difficult, and that
when one had discovered Him it was impossible to speak
of Him to all men.[2]   Later Greek thought became even less
confident than Plato had been of the capacity of man by
searching to find out God, and in the Hellenistic period—
perhaps partly as the result of influences which came in
from the East, and which represent something of the spiritual
heritage of hellenized Semitic populations—the element of
ultimate agnosticism which is inherent in the specifically

significance they chose.   The Gnostic sects were all founded by individual
Gnostic teachers, who claimed to be able to impart the true *gnosis* of things
divine.   The use in a purely metaphorical sense, long established in the
language of religion, and indeed of common speech, of such terms
(originally technical in the language of the ' mysteries ') as τελετή (τέλειος),
and μυστήριον itself, ought not here to mislead us : compare S. Paul's
use of the verb μυεῖσθαι in Philipp. 4 [12], in which he speaks of having been
' initiated into the secret ' of how to be hungry and how to abound !

[1] The value of Norden's brilliant book *Agnostos Theos* is not destroyed
by the fact that his ingenious attempt to establish a dependence of the
speech ascribed to S. Paul at Athens in Acts xvii. upon a lost writing
of Apollonius of Tyana is essentially wrong-headed.   For a convincing
demolition of this particular theory see C. C. Torrey, *The Composition and
Date of Acts*, pp. 46 *sqq*.   According to E. Meyer (*Ursprung und Anfänge
des Christentums*, iii. p. 92 *n*.), the theory in question has now been abandoned by Norden himself.

[2] Τὸν μὲν οὖν ποιητὴν καὶ πατέρα τοῦδε τοῦ παντὸς εὑρεῖν τε ἔργον καὶ εὑρόντα
εἰς πάντας ἀδύνατον λέγειν (Plato, *Tim.* 28 c).

religious view of the universe [1] asserted itself as against the intellectualism of the philosophers. The feeling arose that God—or, at least, the ultimate God—was unknowable except by revelation, and that men—that is to say, the majority of men—in default of a Prophet who should guide them, were wandering in ignorance of God, and of the true meaning and end of human life.

The resulting demand for religious teachers and guides appears to have been met by a supply. We have to think not only of Stoic sages and itinerating philosophers and teachers of wisdom, but of such figures as those of Simon Magus and Apollonius of Tyana, as well as of the founders of various Gnostic sects, who appear in some cases (as in that of Simon Magus himself) to have claimed worship for themselves, as being in some sense divine.[2] There is a famous passage in Origen's work against Celsus in which the latter is reported as having affirmed that it was no uncommon thing for itinerant prophets in Syria and Palestine to put forward such claims. ' It is both easy and usual,' he writes, ' for such persons to say, "I am God, or a son of God, or a Divine spirit. I have come. Already the world is at the point of destruction, and you, O men, are lost through your unrighteousness ; but I am willing to save you ; and ye shall see me again coming upon you with heavenly power ;

[1] A God who was wholly unknown could not be worshipped ; but on the other hand a God who was completely understood would have ceased to be a possible object of worship. In this sense there is an element of agnosticism in all religion.

[2] The Samaritan Dositheus according to Celsus claimed to be the Christ predicted by Moses (Origen, Contra Celsum, i. 57) : Menander, also of Samaria, claimed according to Irenaeus to have been sent into the world by the invisible powers to be the Saviour of mankind—se autem eum esse qui missus sit ab invisibilibus Salvatorem pro salute hominum (Iren. Adv. Haeres. i. 17). For Simon Magus, cf. Hippolytus, Refut. vi. 7 (τὰ δὲ καὶ διὰ δαιμόνων κακουργήσας, θεοποιῆσαι ἑαυτὸν ἐπεχείρησεν, ἄνθρωπος γόης) and the statement in Acts 8 [10] that he was regarded in Samaria as being ἡ δύναμις τοῦ θεοῦ ἡ καλουμένη Μεγάλη : on the religion of Simon Magus, see further E. Meyer, Ursprung und Anfänge des Christentums, iii. pp. 277 sqq.

blessed is he who now worships me ; upon all others I will cast fire eternal, upon both cities and country estates ; and men, except they acknowledge their deserts, shall groan for it and repent in vain ; but those who obey me I will preserve for ever." ' [1] Celsus of course had read the Gospels, and the claims which he thus puts into the mouth of the typical Syrian prophet are to a large extent a deliberate parody of the claims made by the Church on behalf of our Lord. But the passage is an interesting one ; a Swedish scholar has taken it as the starting-point of a learned investigation as to the ideas popularly conveyed in the Hellenistic religious world by such titles as ' prophet,' ' son of God,' θεῖος ἄνθρωπος, and the like.[2] What appears to emerge from the enquiry as probable is that the phrase υἱὸς θεοῦ, which in Greek should mean properly ' son of a god,' came to mean, in accordance with Semitic idiom, in the Greek spoken by hellenized Semitic populations, ' a divine being,' ' a god,' ' a supernatural person,' the virtual equivalent of θεῖος ἄνθρωπος, or even of θεὸς ἐπιφανής. On a background of pantheism and polytheism deification was easy. The fundamental idea is that of τὸ θεῖον, supernatural quality or power,[3] which was the common characteristic both of gods and of other supernatural persons, such as deified men. The supernatural power might be manifested in a variety of ways—to use a modern classification, either physically, in miracles and wonders, or spiritually, in wisdom and gnosis, or psychically, in ecstasies and visions. In any

---

[1] Πρόχειρον δ' ἐκάστῳ καὶ σύνηθες εἰπεῖν· ἐγὼ ὁ θεός εἰμι ἢ θεοῦ παῖς ἢ πνεῦμα θεῖον· ἥκω δέ· ἤδη γὰρ ὁ κόσμος ἀπόλλυται, καὶ ὑμεῖς, ὦ ἄνθρωποι, διὰ τὰς ἀδικίας οἴχεσθε· ἐγὼ δὲ σῶσαι θέλω· καὶ ὄψεσθέ με αὖθις μετ'οὐρανίου δυνάμεως ἐπανίοντα· μακάριος ὁ νῦν με θρησκεύσας, τοῖς δ' ἄλλοις ἅπασι πῦρ αἰώνιον ἐπιβαλῶ καὶ πόλεσι καὶ χώραις· καὶ ἄνθρωποι, οἱ μὴ τὰς ἑαυτῶν ποινὰς ἴσασι, μεταγνώσονται μάτην καὶ στενάξουσι· τοὺς δέ μοι πεισθέντας αἰωνίους φυλάξω (Origen, Contra Celsum, vii. 9).

[2] G. P. Wetter, ' Der Sohn Gottes ' (Göttingen, 1916).

[3] On ' divine power ' see A. D. Nock's paper, ' Studies in the Graeco-Roman Beliefs of the Empire ' (Journal of Hellenic Studies, vol. xlv. pp. 84 sqq.).

or all of these ways a man might establish a claim to be a
θεῖος ἄιθρωπος, an inspired, wonder-working prophet, or
' son of God.' [1] Attention has been drawn by Bishop Gore
to a passage quoted by Origen in the preface to his
Commentary on the Psalms with regard to the use of the
term θεός, in which a number of definitions are given.
According to one view it is said that ' every comely soul
is already a god, even though it be encompassed by a human
body.' [2] So, too, in the third-century work of Philostratus
in honour of Apollonius of Tyana, Apollonius, when asked
why men call him a god, is represented as replying that
' every one who is regarded as a good man is honoured with
the appellation of a god.' [3] Presumably the theory of
Euhemerus,[4] who, arguing by analogy from the current
practice of deification, had contended that all the recognized
gods, with the exception of the heavenly bodies, were
originally deified benefactors of mankind, had done something towards promoting in educated circles this weakened
sense of the term ' god.' But the populace took deifications
seriously, especially in the hellenized East. It was in the
Eastern provinces that the worship of the Emperors was
first introduced. The reigning Augustus (Σεβαστός) was
not only θεοῦ υἱός in Greek, as he was divi filius in Latin ; [5]
he was a ' present deity' (praesens deus, θεὸς ἐπιφανής,

---

[1] Wetter, op. cit. p. 48.   On ἄνθρωποι θεῖοι see also Reitzenstein's
note (Die hellenistischen Mysterienreligionen, 2nd edn., pp. 99 sqq.).

[2] ὥστε πᾶσαν ἀστείαν ψυχὴν θεὸν ὑπάρχειν, κἂν ἐν ἀνθρώπῳ περιέχηται (Origen,
In Psalmos, Prolog. § B ; cf. Gore, Belief in Christ, pp. 9 sq.).

[3] ὅτι πᾶς ἄνθρωπος ἀγαθὸς νομιζόμενος θεοῦ ἐπωνυμίᾳ τιμᾶται (Philostratus, Vita
Apoll. viii. 5).

[4] Euhemerus appears to have been anticipated by an earlier writer,
Hecataeus, a contemporary of Ptolemy I. of Egypt (see Wendland, Die
hellenistisch-römische Kultur, pp. 68 sqq.).

[5] Deissmann refers to an inscription in honour of Augustus at Tarsus:
Αὐτοκράτορα Καί]σαρα θεοῦ υἱὸν Σεβαστὸν
ὁ δῆμ]ος ὁ Ταρσέων,
remarking that ' perhaps the young Paul may have seen here the expression
Son of God for the first time—long before it came to him with another
meaning ' (Deissmann, Bible Studies, E.T., p. 167).

ἐναργὴς ἐπιφανεία) ; he was εὐεργέτης, σωτήρ and κύριος, like the Ptolemies and Seleucids before him.[1] The fact that it was politically worth while, from the point of view of the government, to promote and foster the *cultus* of the Emperors is clear evidence that in the popular mind it corresponded to something which was real. If the Emperor was called σωτήρ, it was because he had been the ' rescuer ' of the world from confusion and havoc, and because he had bestowed on his subjects the blessings of order and settled peace.[2] If the Emperor was θεοῦ υἱός, it was not merely for the formal reason that as the representative of the deified Julian house he was styled officially *divi filius*, but on the ground of his achievements, or, as a Greek inscription expresses it, ' because of his virtue and benevolence.'[3] On both grounds it was held that he was rightly to be regarded as being something more than merely a man amongst men : he was worshipped not simply for political reasons, but because by the popular mind he was seriously regarded as a divine being, a god upon earth.

So also was it, apparently, at least in some cases, with the religious teacher and sage, who on the ground either of teaching or miracles or both made the right kind of impression upon the popular mind ; he, too, might very easily come to be regarded by those who accepted his claims as a kind of

---

[1] Ptolemy Epiphanes (205-181 B.C.), in the great Rosetta inscription of B.C. 196, bears also, along with a large number of other divine titles, the descriptions θεὸς ἐκ θεοῦ and εἰκὼν ζῶσα τοῦ Διός.

[2] For the idea that the work of Augustus coincided with the beginning of a new religious era, cf. Vergil's fourth Eclogue, especially the passage beginning at lines 4 and 5 :

Ultima Cumaei venit iam carminis aetas :

magnus ab integro saeclorum nascitur ordo, etc. ;

and for the conception of Augustus as ' Saviour,' see H. Lietzmann, *Der Weltheiland* (Bonn, 1909). On the distinction between Christian and pagan conceptions of the ' Saviour,' see E. Meyer, *Ursprung und Anfänge*, iii. pp. 390 *sqq.* Cf. also Lecture VII. *infra*, pp. 172 *sq.*

[3] ἀρετῆς ἕνεκεν καὶ εὐνοίας, κ.τ.λ. (Dittenberger, *Syll. Inscr. Gr.* ², i. No. 351). Such phraseology is, however, a common form in Greek honorific inscriptions.

divinity, as a person supernatural in origin, and therefore supernatural also in wisdom and power. The terms 'son of God' and the like, in the popular usage of orientalized Hellenism, would appear to have conveyed just that meaning : they suggested the idea of a supernatural being who was in some sense divine, whose appearance among men was an epiphany of deity upon earth. According to the Acts of the Apostles, S. Paul and Barnabas at Lystra were regarded by the populace, on the ground of a miracle of healing wrought on an impotent man, as gods, divine beings come down to earth in the likeness of men. It was indeed hastily concluded by the Lystrans that they had to do with an epiphany of no less exalted divine personages than Hermes and Zeus.[1] So, too, the barbarians of Malta when S. Paul is uninjured by the viper imagine at once that he is a god.[2]

We have come round again to the Acts of the Apostles, the book which describes the first preaching of Christianity to the Greeks. The question must be asked : In what sense would the Greeks understand it ? In particular, what would be likely to be the interpretation put upon the Christian message about Jesus by such Gentile converts to Christianity as had had no previous contacts with Judaism, but whose religious background and presuppositions were pagan ? It is probable, no doubt, that the first Gentile converts of all were not pagans in the sense which has been indicated, but were drawn rather from the ranks of the so-called 'God-fearers,' or Gentile adherents of the Synagogue, to whose existence is due the double form of address in a speech ascribed in the Acts to S. Paul—'Men of Israel' (*i.e.* Jews), 'and ye that fear God' (*i.e.* Gentile adherents).[3] The intense monotheistic faith, the high ethical standards, and the imageless worship of the Synagogue were attractive in many cases to Gentiles who had learnt from

---

[1] Acts 14 [5] *sqq.*   [2] Acts 28 [6].
[3] Acts 13 [16] ; cf. 13 [26], 10 [2, 22].

contemporary philosophy to despise as irrational the polytheistic superstitions of the vulgar, but who at the same
time not unnaturally shrank from the acceptance of circumcision and the attendant burdens of the Law. Such men
remained on the fringe of the Synagogue and took part in
its worship, without actually joining it. Their existence
provided the first Christian missionaries in the Greek-
speaking world with a ready-made congregation of Gentiles.

Nevertheless, the result of the Christian propaganda in
city after city, as is clear from the record in Acts, was a
breach with the Synagogue, precisely as a consequence of the
conversion of such Gentile adherents. The Church broke
off, and a new Christian *ecclesia* was formed, the propaganda
of which was accessible to Gentiles as such ; and it is clear
that to Gentiles who had had no previous training in Judaism
the term Χριστός or ' Christ ' was unintelligible. By the
heathen it appears to have been early corrupted into Χρηστός,
a word which means 'kindly,' or in an ironical sense 'simple'
or ' silly.' [1] It is not impossible that the word may already
have been so pronounced and understood by the populace of
Antioch, who appear to have first coined the term Χριστιανοί
or Χρηστιανοί and applied it as a nickname to the followers
of our Lord.[2] Already in S. Paul's Epistles Χριστός is
most naturally read in the majority of contexts no longer
as a title, with conscious reference to the Old Testament

---

[1] Cf. Sueton. *Claud.* 25 : *Judaeos impulsore Chresto assidue tumultuantes,*
etc. ; Tertull. *Apol.* 3 : *Christianus vero, quantum interpretatio est, de
unctione deducitur. sed et cum perperam Chrestianus pronunciatur a vobis
. . . de suavitate vel benignitate compositum est.* E. Meyer notes that *Chres-
tianos* is the reading of the first hand in the MS. of Tac. *Ann.* xv. 44 ; so
also the Codex Sinaiticus has the corrupted form in Acts 11 [26], 26 [28], 1 Pet.
4 [16]. Is there a conscious reference, by way of *double entente*, to the
heathen pronunciation in the quotation from Ps. 34 [8] in 1 Pet. 2 [2] (εἰ
ἐγεύσασθε ὅτι χρηστὸς ὁ κύριος) ? There is perhaps a similar play upon
words in the ἄχρηστος and εὔχρηστος of Phmn. [11] (cf. F. C. Baur, *St. Paul,*
E.T., ii. p. 82). On the significance of the name ' Christians,' see further
J. Weiss, *Das Urchristentum,* p. 128.

[2] Acts 11 [26].

doctrine of the Messiah, but as a proper name, or, in the exceedingly frequent form ' Christ Jesus ' and the rather less frequent ' Jesus Christ,' as an integral part of a proper name. We may suppose him to have been following the established and customary usage of Gentile Christians, to whom (unless they were sophisticated by Biblical knowledge) the term ' Christ '' no more immediately suggested the idea of what Judaism meant by the Messiah than it does to ourselves.

As with the term ' Christ,' so also with the term ' Son of Man ' ; translated literally into Greek as ὁ υἱὸς τοῦ ἀν- θρώπου, it was a barbarism which, apart from a single passage in the Acts,[1] is found in the New Testament only in the Gospels, where it appears as the mysterious self-desig- nation of Jesus ; translated idiomatically into Greek as ὁ ἄνθρωπος, it is probably used once by S. Paul,[2] who in any case was certainly familiar with its usage and meaning.[3] Neither the idiomatic nor the literal translation of barnāshā, however, could convey very much to a Greek who was unfamiliar with the Jewish antecedents of the expression Except as surviving in the Gospel tradition of the sayings of Jesus, ' the Son of Man ' as a title of our Lord virtually passed out of use.

If, however, the terms ' Christ ' and ' Son of Man ' were thus devoid of associations, and in practice hardly intel- ligible to Gentiles, the case was otherwise with the alter- native, though perhaps in Aramaic-speaking Christianity less prominent, designations of Jesus as ' Lord ' and as ' Son of God.' The latter phrase was calculated, as we have seen,

---

[1] Acts 7 [56] ; cf. Rev. 1 [13], 14 [14], where, however, the wording is influenced by the LXX of Dan. 7 [13].

[2] ὁ δεύτερος ἄνθρωπος ἐξ οὐράνου—so the true reading in 1 Cor. 15 [47].

[3] S. Paul's familiarity with ' the Son of Man ' as a title of our Lord follows from his use of Ps. 8 [6] in 1 Cor. 15 [27] ; cf. also Eph. 1 [22]. The Psalm was regarded as prophetic of the humiliation and exaltation of Jesus on the ground of the use of the phrase ' son of man ' as a paraphrase for ' man ' in the second half of verse 4. Cf. Lecture V. pp. 124 sq.

to suggest the idea of a supernatural Being—supernatural in origin, and therefore also in wisdom and power—a divine Wonder-worker and Prophet, at once the Healer of men's diseases, and a Teacher come from God. It is interesting to observe that it is precisely this Hellenistic interpretation of the term ' Son of God ' which on the whole underlies the presentation of our Lord as the Son of God in the Gospels. The Gospel according to S. Mark, which may be said to constitute roughly the narrative basis of the Synoptic tradition, sets forth our Lord as the Son of God to whom witness is borne by miraculous voices from heaven,[1] who is recognized by demons as their supernatural foe and predestined destroyer,[2] and who is manifested in works of miraculous power.[3]   The conception of our Lord as a supreme Teacher and Prophet may be said to underlie the second fundamental source of the Synoptic tradition, viz. : the document ' Q ' and its allies, representing perhaps the tradition of various Greek-speaking centres of Christianity with regard to our Lord's teaching.[4]   A similar presentation of our Lord, as the Son of God who on the one hand spake as never man spake,[5] and on the other hand wrought miracles and ' signs,' so that at least ' for the very works' sake '[6] men ought to believe, is to be found in the Fourth Gospel.[7]   The tradition is carried on by the Greek Apologist Justin Martyr, who argues that our Lord is worthy to be called the Son of God ' on account of His wisdom.'[8]

The case as regards the title ' Lord ' was not dissimilar. It conveyed an intelligible meaning in Greek, and the Christian phrase ὁ κύριος ἡμῶν, ' our Lord,' a translation of the Aramaic Maran, was likely to suggest to Greek minds the conception of the Christian Church as a kind of θίασος

---

[1] Mk. 1 [11], 9 [7].   [2] Mk. 1 [24, 34], 3 [11], 5 [7].   [3] Mk. 2 [12], 4 [41], 7 [37].

[4] B. H. Streeter, *The Four Gospels*, pp. 227 *sqq.*

[5] Jn. 7 [46].   [6] Jn. 14 [11].   [7] See Lecture VIII. pp. 221 *sq.*

[8] υἱὸς δὲ θεοῦ ὁ Ἰησοῦς λεγόμενος, εἰ καὶ κοινῶς μόνον ἄνθρωπος, διὰ σοφίαν ἄξιος υἱὸς Θεοῦ λέγεσθαι (Justin Martyr, *Apol.* i. 22).

or community of devotees, associated together for the worship of a Divine ' Lord ' whose name was ' Jesus.'

Materials illustrative of the use of the word κύριος, 'lord,' as a Divine title in the Hellenistic world have been collected by Bousset in his extraordinarily interesting and important, though in some respects mistaken, book *Kyrios Christos*.[1] The application of the title in current usage to the deified Emperors, on which stress has been laid more particularly by Deissmann,[2] is essentially part of a much wider religious and historical context. Oriental in origin—in which connexion a passage in Robertson Smith's *Religion of the Semites*[3] is still well worth reading—the title was characteristic of a number of hellenized cults, more particularly in Syria, Asia Minor, and Egypt.[4] It seems probable, indeed, that the choice by the translators of the LXX of the word Κύριος to serve as a paraphrastic rendering of the Divine Name Yahweh in the Old Testament belongs to the same general context of ideas : it expressed the conception of Yahweh as the solitary and unique Divine ' Lord ' to whom Israel might lawfully render allegiance. In its religious usage the term seems to have been more particularly a *cultus* title : that is to say, it was used by the worshippers themselves of the deity who was the object of their worship, and whom they invoked as the ' lord ' whom they adored, and whose servants or ' slaves ' (δοῦλοι) they acknowledged themselves to be. To speak in this connexion of ' Oriental servility ' is the result of a failure in understanding. The fact that a man in addressing a superior calls him ' my lord,' and speaks of himself and others as

---

[1] Bousset, *Kyrios Christos*, 2nd edn., pp. 91 *sqq.*

[2] Deissmann, *Light from the Ancient East*, E.T., pp. 355 *sqq.*

[3] Robertson Smith, *Religion of the Semites*, pp. 68 *sqq.*

[4] The invitations to ' sup at the table of the lord Serapis ' (δειπνῆσαι εἰς κλείνην τοῦ κυρίου Σαράπιδος) in *Oxyrhynchus Papyri*, Nos. 110 and 523, are illuminating parallels to 1 Cor. 10 [21, 27], though the papyri in which they occur are considerably later in date (2nd cent. A.D.).

'thy servants,' is (in Robertson Smith's phrase) 'a refinement of Semitic politeness'; and 'when a man is named the servant of a god, the implication appears to be, not merely that he belongs to the community of which the god is king, but that he is specially devoted to his service and worship.'[1]   As applied to our Lord, the original form ὁ κύριος ἡμῶν, 'our Lord,' translating the Aramaic Maran, quickly became 'the Lord Jesus,' or simply 'the Lord.'   On the one hand, the phrase gave expression to the Christian conviction of the absolute lordship of Jesus, His exaltation in majesty, and His unqualified claim to allegiance: on the other hand, the use of the title, in view of the usage of Κύριος as a paraphrase for Yahweh in the Septuagint (already the 'Bible' of the Greek-speaking Church), tended to promote more and more an unthought-out but very definite belief in the divinity of Jesus, based on the fact that to Him was applied the same divine title which in Greek was the Name of the Old Testament God.   We find in the New Testament a number of examples of the quotation with reference to the Lord Jesus of Old Testament passages in which the term Κύριος occurs, in spite of the fact that the original reference was of course, in the Old Testament context, to 'the Lord' in the sense of 'the Lord God';[2] clear evidence, if evidence were needed, that the Lord Jesus was more and more coming to be set on a level with God in the mind of the Church.

And the situation in the Gentile Christian Church was perhaps not without its dangers.   In the pagan world there were 'gods many and lords many,' and it was easy for pagans to believe in a divine 'lord,' or in a supernatural 'son of God.'   The Lord Jesus, in a context of hellenized paganism, might very quickly have been accepted as the centre of a cult, as the divine 'lord' of a θίασος of

---

[1] Robertson Smith, op. cit. pp. 68 sq.

[2] Cf. the use of Joel 2 [32] in Rom. 10 [13], Acts 2 [21]; of Is. 45 [23] in Philipp. 2 [9-11]; and of Ps. 102 [25-27] in Hebr. 1 [10] sqq.

worshippers, or as 'son of God' in the sense of a thaumaturge
and prophet, on a background of pantheism and polytheism.
No doubt the Church made for Him exclusive and uncom-
promising claims : He was *the* 'Son of God,' and beside
Him there was none other ; [1] so again, though there might
be 'gods many and lords many ' in paganism, for Christians
there was but ' one God, the Father,' and ' one Lord, Jesus
Christ.' [2] The inheritance of the Septuagint was of priceless
value as a safeguard of monotheism, and the presence
within each of the Gentile Christian Churches of an original
nucleus of converted ' God-fearers ' who had had previous
training in Judaism no doubt counted for something. But
there was need, if Christianity was not to be in danger of
becoming very rapidly hellenized in a fashion which would
have meant rather the paganization of the Gospel than
the christianization of the Hellenistic religious mind, of the
contribution of a great original thinker who was at once
fundamentally rooted in the Hebraic tradition and at the
same time capable of entering into and understanding the
mind of the Greeks. In other words, there was need of the
contribution of such a man as S. Paul, whose great work was
not that of promoting the hellenization of Christianity, but
rather that of proclaiming the Gospel in terms of so
tremendous an emphasis upon the love, the redemptive
activity and the ethical righteousness of the one, true,
living, and personal God, as to safeguard for ever the Hebraic
inheritance of the Christian religion.

[1] This was probably the sense conveyed to Greek readers by the phrase
ὁ υἱός μου ὁ ἀγαπητός in the Gospel accounts of our Lord's Baptism (Mk. I [11]
and parallels) : the word ἀγαπητός in Greek usage can mean in some
contexts—as in Gen. 22 [2] (LXX), Demosth. *Midias*, 567, Aristotle, *Rhet.*
i. 7—' only,' especially in the phrase ' an only son,' so that ἀγαπητὸς υἱός
in the Synoptists is in effect equivalent to μονογενὴς υἱός, for which cf.
Jn. I [18].

[2] I Cor. 8 [6].

LECTURE IV

THE CONTRIBUTION OF S. PAUL—I

SYNOPSIS

S. PAUL born and brought up in the Dispersion, but claims emphatically to be an Aramaic-speaking Jew. He was given a thorough command of Greek in his boyhood, but was sent to be trained under Gamaliel in Jerusalem. The character of his Pharisaism. Montefiore's contention that he was no typical Rabbinical Jew.

His conversion to Christianity. The question of its psychological antecedents. The theory that he had been previously tormented by scruples of conscience has little foundation. S. Paul should not be read in the light of the psychology of Luther. His baptism, and preaching of Christ in the Synagogues.

The strange theories of scholars with regard to S. Paul's Christianity, e.g. that he was deliberately ignorant of Jesus of Nazareth, that he was independent of tradition, that he evolved his Christology out of his own inner consciousness, that he brought it with him from Pharisaism. The theory that his thought contained non-Jewish elements, and that in his teaching the Jewish message about Jesus has been transformed into a ' mystery of redemption ' after the Hellenistic model.

The special theory of Bousset, according to whom the alleged transformation is pre-Pauline, and the Christianity of S. Paul is to be understood as having been developed from that of the Gentile-Christian Church. The essentials of Gentile-Christianity according to Bousset are (a) the *cultus* of Jesus as ' Lord,' and (b) the doctrine of the sacramental mediation of grace. S. Paul as developing out of ' cult and community mysticism ' a personal and individual mysticism in some sense peculiar to himself. The valuable elements in the theory of Bousset. The real question, however, is that of the extent to which S. Paul remained fundamentally a Jew. The weakness of Bousset's position. The insistence of Schweitzer that Christianity is for S. Paul simply Judaism with its centre of gravity shifted.

S. Paul as a Jewish Christian, for whom the gods of the heathen are akin to the ' demons.' The relatively superficial character of his Hellenism. His failure at Athens. His attitude towards ' the wisdom of this age.' His presentation of Christ to the Greeks as ' Son of God,' ' Lord ' and Redeemer. But he would have presented Christ also in equivalent terms to the Jews, and believes that the Gospel is the power of God ' to the Jews first.'

S. Paul's relation to Judaism has in fact been misunderstood. The controversial character of much of his writing about the Law. He is the champion of Gentile freedom, but believes nevertheless that the Law is ' holy.' He did not regard himself as having ceased to be a Jew. He incurred beatings in Jewish Synagogues, and the Acts is probably right in suggesting that he normally himself lived as a Jew in so far as was compatible with the claims of his work amongst Gentiles. At how early a stage in his career did the vocation to become the missionary of Christ to the Gentiles develop ? If the Acts is correct in suggesting that it was in the course of the mission organized from Antioch, then the first half of S. Paul's life as a Christian was spent probably in mission work amongst Greek-speaking Jews.

The Christendom, therefore, in the environment of which the Christianity of S. Paul was matured was still predominantly Jewish, and the development of a predominantly Gentile Christianity has been ante-dated by Bousset. If Bousset is right in discerning that both the *cultus* of Jesus as Lord and also the doctrine of the sacraments as media of grace are pre-Pauline, it follows that both the sacraments and the cult of the Lord Jesus go back in essentials to the earliest Church. It is in harmony with this supposition that no controversy appears to have arisen about either between S. Paul and his Judaistic opponents ; a strong argument in favour of the view which sees continuity, rather than discontinuity, between Greek-speaking Christianity and the Christianity of the original Church.

LECTURE IV

THE CONTRIBUTION OF S. PAUL—I

One called Saul, of Tarsus.—Acts 9 [11].

S. PAUL was a bilingual Jew from the Greek-speaking city of Tarsus, in Cilicia—a Jew who, despite the fact that he had been born and brought up in the Diaspora, was able to speak not only Greek, but Aramaic.[1] There is a passage in one of his letters in which, after having already emphasized his Israelite stock and his Benjamite descent, he proceeds to describe himself further as a ' Hebrew of Hebrews '[2]—a phrase which, in view of the use of the term ' Hebrew ' elsewhere in the New Testament to denote an Aramaic-speaking as distinct from a Greek-speaking Jew,[3] means probably that S. Paul's parents on both sides spoke Aramaic, and that Aramaic rather than Greek had been the language of his home ;[4] his family must necessarily, of course, have spoken Greek in their intercourse with the Greek-speaking citizens of Tarsus, but they appear still to have used the Aramaic of Palestine amongst themselves. It is

[1] Cf. Acts 21 [40], 22 [2], where the populace of Jerusalem, who expect S. Paul to address them in Greek, are in all probability surprised, as well as gratified, when he speaks to them in the ' Hebrew dialect,' *i.e.* in Aramaic.

[2] Ἑβραῖος ἐξ Ἑβραίων (Philipp. 3 [5]). Inscriptions with the words συναγωγὴ Αἱβρέων or Ἑβρέων, evidently from the doors of Jewish synagogues, have been found both in Rome and in Corinth, and denote presumably that in these particular synagogues the services were carried on in Hebrew and Aramaic, for the benefit of Aramaic-speaking Jews from the East (Meyer, *Ursprung und Anfänge*, iii. p. 271 *n.*).

[3] Cf. Acts 6 [1].

[4] So (e.g.) J. Weiss, *Das Urchristentum*, p. 131 ; Deissmann, *Paulus*, 2nd edn., p. 72 *n.* S. Paul's emphatic claim in Philipp. 3 [5], 2 Cor. 11 [22] to be a ' Hebrew ' suggests that his opponents had attempted to deny his affinities with Aramaic-speaking Judaism, and to rank him exclusively as a ' Hellenist.'

probable, therefore, that they had only recently migrated to Cilicia ; according to a tradition preserved by S. Jerome, their original home had been Gischala in Galilee.[1] That they still retained intimate links of connexion with the Judaism of Palestine is suggested further by the fact that S. Paul's married sister appears to have been settled in Jerusalem.[2] The convictions of the family were in any case strongly Pharisaic, and the youthful Saul, after having received in boyhood, perhaps from a Jewish *rhetor* of Hellenistic education,[3] a sufficient training in grammar and rhetoric to give him a thorough command of the Greek language as spoken and written by educated men of the period, was sent to complete his studies at Jerusalem, where he became the pupil of the famous Gamaliel, the most distinguished Pharisaic teacher of the day.[4]

S. Paul's youthful Pharisaism was clearly of an extreme and fanatical type. As S. Paul himself afterwards expressed it, he was, as compared with many of his contemporaries, ' more exceedingly zealous ' for the traditions of his fathers.[5] He is not likely, indeed, to have been in the political sense a ' Zealot,' an extravagance from which he was probably saved by the fact that he had inherited from his father not only the traditions of Pharisaism, but also the citizenship of Rome.[6] But he was plainly a zealot for the Law. Mr.

---

[1] Hieron. *Comm. in Philem.* 23. The suggestion in the *De Viris Illustribus* that S. Paul came himself from Gischala (Hieron. *De Vir. Ill.* 5) is clearly due to a blunder on the part of S. Jerome, but the statement as regards the Galilaean origin of the family is regarded by many modern scholars as being likely to have some basis in authentic tradition.

[2] Acts 23 [16] *sqq.*

[3] So J. Weiss, *Das Urchristentum*, p. 134.

[4] Acts 22 [3]. The statement is probably historical.

[5] Gal. 1 [14].

[6] Acts 16 [37] *sqq.*, 22 [25] *sqq.*, 25 [10] *sqq.* S. Paul appeals confidently to Roman justice, and consistently regards ' the powers that be ' as ' ordained of God ' (Rom. 13 [1] *sqq.*). In writing to his Greek-speaking converts he uses invariably the Roman name ' Paulus,' which presumably as a Roman citizen he had borne from his childhood, side by side with his Jewish name ' Saul ' (so Ramsay, *S. Paul the Traveller and the Roman Citizen*, pp. 81 *sqq.* ;

Montefiore, who thinks that S. Paul's religious views *after* his conversion are an inexplicable psychological enigma unless we assume that *before* his conversion his religion was ' less intimate and joyous ' as well as ' more theoretic and questioning ' than that of the typical Rabbinical Jew, is disposed to suggest that the strict observance of the Law on the part of Jews who belonged to the Dispersion may have tended in some cases to become self-conscious, fanatical, gloomy, and perhaps clouded by anxiety and scruple, in a way which was quite uncharacteristic of the Judaism of Palestine   The Jew of the Dispersion was on the defensive. If he clung to the Law, it was with the knowledge that to the majority of his non-Jewish neighbours his religion appeared foolish and irrational, a farrago of prohibitions and taboos. Of necessity the Hellenistic Jewish legalist was constrained to become an apologist for usages which to the Palestinian Jewish legalist required no apology. The Law to the typical Rabbinical Jew was not a burden ; it was ' the most adorable of God's gifts,' the highest of all religious privileges, the source of that purest of spiritual joys which the Rabbis described as ' the joy of the commandments.' If S. Paul had not learnt to regard the Law in this light, he was assuredly no typical Rabbinical Jew.[1]

It is perhaps hardly necessary to decide how far Mr Montefiore is right in his estimate of the pre-Christian religion of S. Paul. It is permissible to suspect that the attractive picture of first-century Judaism which is now set before us in the writings of modern Jewish apologists is in some respects an idealization, even though it must be

---

Deissmann, *S. Paul* (E.T.), p. 93, and *Bible Studies* (E.T.), pp. 313 *sqq.* ; J. Weiss, *Das Urchristentum*, p. 133.   E. Meyer in *Ursprung und Anfänge*, iii. p. 197, reverts to the older but less probable theory that the name ' Paulus ' was adopted by way of compliment to the ' Sergius Paulus ' of Acts 13 [7] *sqq.*).

[1] C. G. Montefiore, *Judaism and St. Paul*, pp. 96 *sqq.*

conceded that the picture traditionally painted by Christian apologists is to a large extent a polemical caricature. The fanaticism of Saul the disciple of Gamaliel may have been not wholly typical of the school to which his teachers belonged ; and it is certainly not improbable that he was in some respects unfair to the Pharisaic interpretation of Judaism in retrospect. A convert is rarely impartial in his estimate of the religious system which he has abandoned, and S. Paul is a man whose spiritual history is cut sharply in two by a dramatic conversion.

The abrupt metamorphosis of Saul the apostle of Pharisaism into Paul the apostle of Jesus Christ has been made the theme in modern times of much speculative psychological conjecture. S. Paul's own account of it is simply that it pleased God to reveal His Son in him, that he might preach Him among the Gentiles.[1] It is reasonable to suppose that the witness of Stephen had made more impression on the mind of S. Paul than S. Paul himself realized, perhaps also that certain of the arguments to which he had listened in the Synagogue of the Cilicians at Jerusalem[2] had suggested, albeit only subconsciously, a lurking doubt as to whether the followers of the new Way might not after all be in the right. The further suggestion that S. Paul was dissatisfied with Pharisaism, that devotion to the Law had resulted in scrupulosity and anguish of mind, and that the zeal of the persecutor was the mask of a soul inwardly tormented by the conviction of sin, is more doubtful. It is not certain that the description of the divided soul in the seventh chapter of Romans[3] is autobiographical ; the use of the first person singular may be little more than

---

[1] Gal. 1 [15] sq.

[2] Acts 6 [9]. J. Weiss thinks that two synagogues are here meant, the one consisting of *libertini* (*i.e.* Jewish freedmen) and Jews from Cyrene and Alexandria, the other of Jews from Cilicia and Asia. S. Paul as a Cilician Jew presumably frequented the latter synagogue (J. Weiss, *Das Urchristentum*, p. 120 *n.*).   [3] Rom. 7 [7-25].

a stylistic device, and it is at least possible that the picture which S. Paul so powerfully sets before his readers may be intended to represent rather a typical than a strictly individual case.[1] It is noteworthy that the specific sin of which S. Paul definitely accuses himself in his Epistles— that of having been formerly a persecutor of the Church [2]—is a sin which from the standpoint of Judaism would be regarded rather as a manifestation of zeal ; and that what he says of himself when he makes a direct and unmistakable statement about his former life as a Jew is that he was ' as touching the righteousness which is in the law, found blameless.' [3]   There is some force in the brusque comment of Wrede that the spiritual wrestlings of Luther have been taken as a model for the portrait of S. Paul ; [4] and it is not unlikely that S. Paul's eventual conviction of the utter wrongness of his former life as a Pharisee was the result, not of any pangs of conscience experienced at the time, but of the shattering discovery, made subsequently in the light of his conversion, that he had been involved by his very devotion to Pharisaism in the fearful sin of having rejected the Messiah, misread utterly the purposes of God, and cruelly persecuted the followers of Christ.

What is in any case beyond question is that the effect of the experience which befell Saul on the road to Damascus was to convince him that the Christians whom he had

---

[1] So (e.g.) W. Wrede, *Paulus*, p. 83 ; cf. J. G. Machen (*The Origin of Paul's Religion*, p. 65), who remarks with reference to Rom. 7 [7-25] that ' it is doubtful whether the description is taken from the Apostle's own experience,' and that ' with regard to the sense of sin as the goad which forced Paul to accept the Saviour, there is no evidence that before his conversion Paul was under real conviction of sin.'   On the rhetorical affinities of the passage from Romans, see R. Bultmann, *Der Stil der paulinischen Predigt und die kynisch-stoische Diatribe*, pp. 84 *sq.* ; and on S. Paul generally as a stylist, J. Weiss, *Das Urchristentum*, pp. 303 *sqq.*
[2] 1 Cor. 15 [9], Philipp. 3 [6] ; cf. 1 Tim. 1 [13] *sqq.*
[3] Philipp. 3 [6].
[4] *Die Wahrheit ist : die Seelenkämpfe Luthers haben für dies Bild des Paulus Modell gestanden* (W. Wrede, *op. cit.* p. 83).

persecuted were right, and that he himself had been utterly wrong. The Christ had appeared to him ; henceforth he believes himself called to be a witness of the resurrection of Jesus.[1] He is baptized,[2] and becomes a preacher of the faith of which he had formerly made havoc.[3] The Acts is most probably correct in suggesting that the newly-con- verted Saul at once proceeded to proclaim Jesus in the synagogues, and to enter into controversial arguments with the Jews.[4]

The most extraordinary views have been held and maintained by scholars with regard to the Christianity of S. Paul. It has been supposed that he was careful to know nothing about Jesus of Nazareth beyond the bare facts of His crucifixion and heavenly glory,[5] that he was utterly independent of all human teaching and tradition,[6] and that his religion henceforward consisted wholly in devotion to a heavenly Being whom he believed to have appeared to him, and whom he identified, for reasons which are not always made clear, with the glorified Christ. It has been supposed that his Christology, and indeed his whole system of doctrinal belief as a Christian, was either evolved from his own inner consciousness as the result of reflection

---

[1] I Cor. 9 [1], 15 [8] *sqq.* ; Gal. 1 [15] *sq.*

[2] Acts 9 [18].

[3] Gal. 1 [23].

[4] Acts 9 [20, 22].

[5] Those who adopt this view commonly misinterpret 2 Cor. 5 [16], as though S. Paul were distinguishing a ' Christ after the flesh ' from a ' Christ after the Spirit.' For S. Paul there is only one Christ—Jesus of Nazareth. What he is repudiating is not a fleshly kind of Christ, but a fleshly kind of knowledge. In virtue of the new life which he now lives in Christ Jesus, he no longer forms his judgements, whether about Christ or about any one else, κατὰ σάρκα, but in accordance with what he elsewhere describes as ' the mind of the Spirit ' (Rom. 8 [4] *sqq.*).

[6] A misunderstanding of Gal. 1 [12], the meaning of which is simply that he was converted to Christianity and commissioned to preach the Gospel directly by the Christ who had appeared to him, that he had not been ' taught ' by the original Apostles, and that therefore he did not owe them allegiance and was not in any sense their disciple.

upon his conversion experience,[1] or else was the result simply
of the attachment to the person of Jesus of a ready-made set
of predicates derived from a cut-and-dried conception of
the heavenly Messiah which he is supposed to have brought
with him from Pharisaism.[2]   Or again, it has been suggested
that S. Paul's thought contains non-Jewish elements, that
his doctrine of man, and more particularly his antithetical
use of the terms ' spirit ' and ' flesh,' is without parallel in
Judaism and must be set down to the credit of his Hellenistic
environment ; [3] that his interpretation of the sacraments
was derived from, or influenced by, the sacramentalism

---

[1] According to Karl Holsten (*Zum Evangelium des Paulus und des Petrus*,
1868), the Pauline Gospel of the Cross had already been thought out
hypothetically by S. Paul *before* his conversion.   He had reflected upon
what *would* be the consequences for religion if the assertions of his opponents
were true, and such was his theological acumen and insight that in him ' the
principle of the Messianic faith ' was ' alive in greater definiteness than
even in the consciousness of the followers of the Messiah whom he persecuted'
(see Schweitzer, *Paul and his Interpreters*, E.T., pp. 38 *sq*., and J. G. Machen,
The Origin of Paul's Religion, pp. 63 *sq*.).   Other scholars lay the main
stress on S. Paul's supposed pre-Christian agony of soul ; on the improbability of this, see above.   Those who imagine S. Paul to have excogitated
his Gospel in complete independence of the beliefs of his fellow-Christians
commonly interpret the reference in Gal. 1 [17] to his visit to Arabia as
meaning that he went into the solitudes of the desert to think out his
position ; it is sometimes suggested that the whole of the ' three years ' of
Gal. 1 [18] was spent in this way!   Kirsopp Lake (*The Earlier Epistles of
S. Paul*, pp. 320 *sqq*.) propounds the alternative hypothesis that S. Paul was
engaged in missionary work in the territory of the Nabataean Arabs who
were ruled by King Aretas IV. (cf. 2 Cor. 11 [32]), pointing out that S. Paul's
argument in Galatians is strengthened considerably if we understand him
to mean that he had been a preacher of the Gospel for the best part of three
years before making the acquaintance of S. Peter.   J. Weiss (*Das Urchristentum*, p. 144) thinks that ' Arabia ' means certainly not the desert but
the Nabataean Kingdom; that S. Paul's stay there was probably brief;
and that, although it is uncertain for what purpose he was led to visit
Aretas' dominions, he is not to be understood as having lived there as a
hermit.

[2] So M. Brückner, *Die Entstehung der paulinischen Christologie*, and
W. Wrede, *Paulus*.

[3] H. J. Holtzmann, *Lehrbuch der neutestamentlichen Theologie*, ii. pp.
13 *sqq*. ; R. Reitzenstein, *Die hellenistischen Mysterienreligionen*, 2nd edn.,
pp. 48 *sqq*., 159 *sqq*. ; W. Bousset, *Kyrios Christos*, 2nd edn., pp. 120 *sqq*. ;
W. Morgan, *The Religion and Theology of Paul*, pp. 16 *sqq*.

(real or alleged) of contemporary pagan mystery cults,[1] and his interpretation of the Passion by the notion, supposed to have been borrowed from the same mysteries, of a suffering and dying god ;[2] in a word, that Christianity, as taught and proclaimed by S. Paul, has become, by comparison and contrast with its Jewish beginnings, a religion of a new and different kind altogether—a religion in which for the hope of the coming Kingdom there has been virtually substituted the present *cultus* of the glorified Lord, and in which for the Gospel of the Messiahship of Jesus there has been substituted a strange semi-Gnostic mythological system according to which the divine grace of the Redeemer, conveyed by the sacraments, is believed to effect in the faithful, in the most literal and realistic of fashions, a metaphysical change, a supernatural transformation of their mortal and perishable nature, in virtue of which the ' old man ' in them is regarded as having been abolished and replaced by a new supernatural manhood, derived from the supernatural Christ, who as ' life-giving spirit ' imparts a new principle of life to believers.[3] In all these respects, it is maintained, the theology of S. Paul is essentially non-Jewish. The line separating the Jew from the Greek has been crossed. Jewish elements of course remain in S. Paul's teaching, but already the transformation is virtually complete which converted an originally Jewish message about Jesus into a predominantly Hellenistic mystery of redemption, in which individuals were offered a salvation involving not merely a change of will but a change of nature, a salvation which was regarded as being supernaturally mediated by *gnosis* and sacraments.

The most recent, as it is certainly the most challenging,

---

[1] W. Heitmüller, *Taufe und Abendmahl in Urchristentum* ; A. Loisy, *Les Mystères païens et le Mystère chrétien*, pp. 269 *sqq.* ; C. Toussaint, *L'Hellénisme et l'Apôtre Paul*, pp. 310 *sqq.* ; A. Dieterich, *Eine Mithrasliturgie*, pp. 106 *sqq.*, 176 *sqq.*

[2] Loisy, *op. cit.* pp. 248 *sqq.*, Bousset, *op. cit.* pp. 134 *sqq.*

[3] Reitzenstein, *op. cit.* pp. 50 *sqq.*; Bousset, *op. cit.* pp. 120 *sqq.*, 125 *sqq.*

presentation of Paulinism from this point of view is that of the late Professor Bousset, who believed that in essentials the transformation in question had already been effected before S. Paul came into the Christian movement at all.   S. Paul must no doubt have become acquainted, if only in the capacity of a persecutor, with the Messianic beliefs of the Church at Jerusalem ; his conversion on the road to Damascus would not otherwise have been psychologically intelligible.[1]   Nevertheless, S. Paul's affinities from the moment of his conversion onwards are, according to Bousset, wholly with Greek-speaking Christendom ; he must be regarded as having ripened and grown to maturity as a Christian in the spiritual environment of a Church which was already, it is suggested, syncretistic and predominantly Gentile.   Bousset believes further that it is possible by means of a discriminating study of the Pauline Epistles to distinguish with fair probability between those elements in S. Paul's teaching which were the fruit of his own original genius and insight, and those elements which belong rather to the general tradition of Hellenistic Christianity as such.   He attempts, therefore, in a chapter devoted to the original Gentile-Christian Church,[2] to describe the Christianity with which he conceives S. Paul to have been brought into contact.

It was a Christianity of which the essential and distinguishing characteristic was the *cultus* of Jesus as ' Lord.'   Believers in Christ are described by S. Paul as those who ' call upon the Name of our Lord Jesus Christ ' ;[3] that is to say,

---

[1] In the first edition of *Kyrios Christos*, Bousset was disposed to deny altogether that S. Paul had been brought up at the feet of Gamaliel or had persecuted the Christians of Jerusalem, and to suggest that he was already domiciled at Damascus and began his career as an opponent of Christianity there.   In *Jesus der Herr* (p. 31) he retracts these judgments, and in the second edition of *Kyrios Christos* contents himself with remarking that ' the relations of the Apostle Paul with Jerusalem were of the scantiest kind ' (*op. cit.* p. 75).

[2] *Kyrios Christos*, Chap. iii.   [3] 1 Cor. 1 [2].

they are those who *invoke* Jesus Christ under the title of
' Lord ' in their worship.   So again, it is ' in the Name of
the Lord Jesus '—that is to say, in connexion with a solemn
liturgical invocation of Jesus as ' Lord,' and on the basis
of the confession of Him as ' Lord ' by the candidate—that
converts are admitted to baptism,[1] a rite in respect of which
there is complete spiritual equality as between Gentile and
Jew, on the ground that ' the same Lord is Lord of all, rich
unto all that call upon him,' and that there is Scriptural
warrant for saying that ' whosoever shall call upon the
name of the Lord shall be saved.'[2]   Once baptized, the
new Christian was admitted to partake of the Eucharist, a
sacrament which is described as ' the meal of the Lord,' or
' the table of the Lord.'[3]   The religious life of the community is centred in its meetings for worship, and it is in
connexion with such gatherings more particularly that the
recurrent miracle is experienced of a new spiritual fellowship,
a community life in which Christ is enthroned as the Head
of a new spiritual Body.   It was in such gatherings that the
Spirit, shed forth from the Lord who was present invisibly
in the midst of His worshipping Church, was wont to be
manifested in unmistakable power.   Men prophesied, spake
with tongues, and exhibited strange new supernatural
gifts.[4]   They saw visions, they were rapt into ecstasy, they
gave utterance to psalms, hymns and inspired odes, making
melody in fervour of heart to the Lord.[5]   Beyond all question
a new and remarkable impulse of spiritual life was astir in
the little communities of devotees of the Lord Jesus which
were beginning to spring into existence in the countries of
the hellenized East.[6]

It is against this background, and in relation to the

---

[1] Rom. 10 [9], 1 Cor. 6 [11].   [2] Rom. 10 [12] *sqq.* ; cf. Joel 2 [32].

[3] Κυριακὸν δεῖπνον (1 Cor. 11 [20]), τράπεζα Κυρίου (1 Cor. 10 [21] ; cf. Mal.
1 [7, 12]).

[4] 1 Cor. 12-14.   [5] Col. 3 [16], Eph. 5 [19].

[6] For the above description, cf. Bousset, *op. cit.* pp. 84-89.

spiritual life of such a worshipping community, it is urged, that S. Paul's personal religious life as a Christian must be understood and interpreted. The objective reality and power of the unseen Lord who is worshipped and adored by the Church is the presupposition, taken for granted as a fact beyond question, of whatever is individual and personal in his thought about Christ : his Christology starts from the given fact of the worship and faith of the Church. At the same time what is thus taken for granted becomes for S. Paul only the starting-point for a further development, in which (to use the terminology of Bousset) what begins in the form of ' cult and community mysticism ' is deepened and in such fashion transformed by the intensity of S. Paul's personal experience as to pass over into the sphere of a personal and individual mysticism. It is thus, for example, that the exalted Lord who is adored by the Church becomes for the Apostle who had been so dramatically taken captive on the road to Damascus the object not merely of the Church's corporate worship, but of his own individual loyalty and love, a living and abiding Presence whose power and reality are experienced in all the relationships of life. The erstwhile persecutor has become ' Paul the slave of Jesus Christ,'[1] content to owe everything to the Lord who (in S. Paul's own phrase) 'loved him and gave Himself for him,'[2] content to belong to Him, body and soul, and to be led through the world a prisoner in the triumphal train of the victorious Christ.[3] The whole of life has in fact become for S. Paul henceforward a life which is lived mystically ' in Christ '—a phrase which implies as its background the corporate life of the Church, which for S. Paul is Christ's mystical Body.[4]

---

[1] Rom. 1 [1].   [2] Gal. 2 [20].

[3] 2 Cor. 2 [14]. I am unable to agree with Menzies (*ad loc.*) that the usual meaning of θριαμβεύω (' to lead in triumph ') is unsuitable to this passage.

[4] Bousset, *op. cit.* pp. 104 *sqq.*

So, too, with regard to the sacraments. S. Paul takes for granted, as common ground between himself and all Christians,[1] the significance of Baptism as a solemn act of initiation in which the candidate undergoes a ritual death and resurrection, in some sense representing or standing in relation to the death and resurrection of Christ ; it is regarded as probable by Bousset that he presupposes equally a popular interpretation of the Eucharist as a *mysterium tremendum* in which the Body and Blood of Christ are regarded as being eaten and drunk by the faithful. Starting from these premises S. Paul develops in each case, according to Bousset, a sacramental doctrine in some sense peculiar to himself, laying stress, in the case of the Eucharist, less upon the idea of an eating and drinking of Christ's Body and Blood [2] than upon the idea of the κοινωνία or mystical fellowship thereby established and maintained between the members of the Church as one Body with Christ who is their Head ; in the case of the initiatory sacrament of Baptism developing out of the idea of a ritual death, burial and resurrection with Christ the more mystical conceptions of a crucifixion with Christ of the ' old man, . . . that the body of sin might be done away,' and of a putting on of the ' new man,' who ' is renewed . . . after the image of Him that created him,' and is ' alive unto God.' [3]

It would be disproportionate, at the stage thus far reached, to follow out Bousset's position in further detail—to discuss, for example, the alleged parallels from the language of Hellenistic mystery cults, Gnostic systems, and magical papyri to the terminology and the general religious and

---

[1] It is noteworthy that S. Paul presupposes a sacramental view of Baptism on the part of a Church—that of Rome—which he has not as yet personally visited (Rom. 6 [3] *sqq.*).

[2] But it appears to be involved by the logic of S. Paul's analogy in I Cor. 10 [1] *sqq.* that the Eucharist is in some sense for S. Paul also βρῶμα πνευματικόν and πόμα πνευματικόν—' spiritual ' (*i.e.* supernatural) Food and Drink.

[3] Cf. Rom. 6 [6] *sqq.*, Gal. 3 [27], Col. 3 [9] *sqq.*, and Bousset, *op. cit.* pp. 107-9.

theological outlook with which we find ourselves confronted
in the surviving letters of S. Paul.   The chapter in *Kyrios
Christos* upon ' Paul ' is a decidedly brilliant piece of work,
from which much may be learnt even by those who are not
in agreement with many of the author's most characteristic
positions.   In particular, the frank recognition of the part
played in the development of Christian doctrine by the
element of *cultus*—that is to say, by the actual life and
worship of the Church—is a great advance upon much of
the doctrinaire criticism of the past.[1]   It is satisfactory to
have it admitted that S. Paul did not invent his religion
out of his own head ; on the contrary, that the presuppositions of his doctrine both of Christ and of the sacraments are
to be found in the common faith and practice of the Church
into which he was baptized, and whose fellowship of life
and worship he came to share.

The real question, however, which is at issue in Bousset's
discussion, as well as in the writings of other and less readable
representatives of the same school, is the question of the
extent to which S. Paul, in the process of working out his
theological thought, should be regarded as having remained
fundamentally a Jew, or *per contra* as having virtually
succumbed to the influences of the syncretistic Greek mind
of the period.   It is essential, as we have seen, to the theory
of Bousset, according to whom there existed from the beginning a radical divergence in respect both of worship and of
Christology between the Christianity of Palestine and that

---

[1] Cf. Deissmann, *Paulus*, 2nd ed., p. 93 : ' *Wer das Urchristentum als
Phänomen der Kultgeschichte betrachtet, protestiert damit gegen die immer
noch weitverbreitete doktrinäre Auffassung, als handele es sich im Evangelium
. . . hauptsächlich um Lehren, . . . um ein Kapitel aus der Geschichte der
antiken Reflexion.   Dieser Protest verkennt nicht, dass die Lehre eine grosse
Bedeutung hatte auch in der ältesten Zeit, aber er sieht auf ihr nicht den
Akzent der Geschichte ruhen. . . .   Unsere heilige Urgeschichte hat in Wirk-
lichkeit darin ihren inneren Fortschritt, dass die durch das Evangelium Jesu
entfesselte messianische Bewegung . . . sich zuletzt als Kult historisch
konsolidiert, als Kult Jesu als des Herrn.*'

of the Greek-speaking Church (which for Bousset means Gentile Christianity), that S. Paul should be connected, in all that concerns his life and beliefs as a Christian, exclusively with the latter. He was converted, according to Bousset, not to the Christianity of Palestine, but to the already Hellenistic and predominantly Gentile Christianity of such cities as Antioch, Damascus and Tarsus. A lingering scruple which he owed to his Jewish monotheistic inheritance and to the influence of the Old Testament prevents him from ever quite describing our Lord without qualification as ' God,'[1] and a Jewish eschatological element survives in his theology in the form of the hope of the Parousia.[2] With these exceptions S. Paul's outlook and mind are regarded by Bousset as having been virtually the outlook and mind, not of a Jew, but of an orientalized Greek.

It is difficult not to think that S. Paul himself would have been considerably astonished by such a suggestion. Indeed, the theory of Schweitzer, who would interpret S. Paul, as he had interpreted Jesus, exclusively from the standpoint of a purely Judaic eschatology, is, despite its characteristic exaggeration of emphasis, closer to the truth. Schweitzer's theory, no doubt, as it stands is accepted by no one, but his criticisms of the theories of others are frequently very much to the point. He is certainly abundantly justified in pointing out that for S. Paul there is only one true religion—to wit, Judaism—and that ' " Christianity " is for Paul no new religion, but simply Judaism with its centre of gravity shifted in consequence of the new era   His own system of thought is certainly for him no new religion. It is his belief, as fully known and worked out in its implications, and it professes to be nothing else than the true Jewish religion, in accord both with the time and with the Scriptures.'[3] It is in harmony with this view of the matter that S. Paul himself

[1] *Kyrios Christos*, 2nd ed., p. 154.   [2] *Jesus der Herr*, p. 29.
[3] A. Schweitzer, *Paul and his Interpreters* (E.T.), p. 227.

speaks of the Gospel as being ' the power of God unto salvation . . . to the Jew first,' though doubtless ' also to the
Greek';[1] that he argues habitually upon the basis of Old
Testament prophecy, even in letters addressed primarily to
Gentiles; and that he emphasizes with true Israelite pride,
as against opponents who plumed themselves on the ground
that they were Israelites, his own purely Israelite descent.[2]

It is further worthy of notice that, with the exception of
a schoolboy tag from Menander which is quoted in the first
Epistle to the Corinthians,[3] S. Paul nowhere in his Epistles
betrays any acquaintance with any work of Greek literature ;[4]
he appears, in common with most of his Jewish compatriots,
to have regarded the beings to whom the Gentiles sacrificed
as ' demons,'[5] and is certainly not likely to have wittingly
borrowed either ideas, customs or religious beliefs from such
sources ; and apart from the famous argument about Natural
Religion in the first chapter of the Epistle to the Romans
(in which he depends on the Book of Wisdom),[6] and apart
also from a few expressions and phrases which appear to
be derived ultimately from the vocabulary of populai
Stoicism,[7] he shows himself singularly innocent of any

---

[1] Rom. 1 [16].   [2] 2 Cor. 11 [22], Philipp. 3 [5].

[3] 1 Cor. 15 [33]. An anthology of ' sentences ' from the comedies of
Menander appears to have been commonly used in the Hellenistic age as
a text-book in schools.

[4] Unless the Pastoral Epistles are to be regarded as Pauline : in which
case cf. Titus 1 [12], which refers to the famous fallacy of Epimenides the
Cretan.

[5] 1 Cor. 10 [20].

[6] The argument in Rom. 1 [19] sqq. should be carefully compared with
Wisdom 13 [1] sqq. For the exploitation in Jewish apologetic and polemical
literature of arguments derived ultimately from Stoic and Academic
philosophical sources, see Wendland, Die hellenistisch-römische Kultur,
pp. 113 sqq., 150 sqq. It is probable that any acquaintance with Stoic
methods of argument which S. Paul may be supposed to have possessed
came to him mediately through Jewish Hellenistic literature and not
directly from Stoic writers. Cf. J. Weiss, Das Urchristentum, pp. 175 sqq.

[7] Among such ultimately Stoic terms and expressions may be mentioned
the words συνείδησις (frequent in S. Paul), φύσις (as used in such passages
as Rom. 1 [26], 2 [14], 1 Cor. 11 [14]), αὐτάρκης (Philipp. 4 [11]), τὸ καθῆκον (cf.

knowledge of current philosophy. According to the Acts of the Apostles, he appears once to have attempted a philosophical argument at Athens, though with conspicuous lack of success.[1] The experiment does not, in any case, appear to have been repeated. In writing subsequently to the Corinthians, S. Paul remarks that he did not come to them ' with excellency of speech or of wisdom,' but on the contrary ' determined not to know anything . . . save Jesus Christ, and him crucified,' in order that their faith should not stand ' in the wisdom of men, but in the power of God '; the ' wisdom ' which he claims indeed to possess, and which he is prepared to utter amongst those who are mature, he expressly distinguishes from the ' wisdom of this age,' which he appears to regard as being inspired by the demonic ' rulers of this age,' who are about to be destroyed.[2]

It is true, of course, that S. Paul in the latter part of his career as a Christian was called to become more particularly a preacher of Christianity to the Greeks. No doubt, like a wise missionary, he discovered ways of presenting the Gospel in such terms as were capable of making an appeal to the Gentile mind. His conception of Christ as the Son of God is in line with the Hellenistic usage according to which the term ' Son of God ' signifies primarily a supernatural Being, though the theological background of the phrase, in S. Paul's use of it, is, as we shall see, monotheistic. He employs the term ' Lord ' in accordance with what was evidently the recognized usage of Greek-speaking Christendom, and the term ' Christ ' in his Epistles is in process, as we have seen, of becoming virtually no longer a title, but rather a name.

Rom. 1 [28]), τὸ συμφέρον (1 Cor. 12 [7]). According to Norden (*Agnostos Theos*, pp. 240 *sqq.*), a Stoic doxological formula is ultimately behind such passages as Rom. 11 [36], 1 Cor. 8 [6], Col. 1 [16] *sq.*, Eph. 4 [5] *sq.*

[1] Acts 17 [22] *sqq.* The speech ascribed to S. Paul at Athens, though not likely, of course, to be a *verbatim* report of an actual speech, is regarded by J. Weiss as being ' in the higher sense not unhistorical ' (J. Weiss, *Das Urchristentum*, p. 184).

[2] 1 Cor. 2 [1] *sqq.*

He presents Christianity, moreover, to the Greeks as a religion not merely of future hope but of present redemption, after a fashion which no doubt appealed powerfully to the yearning of many Greek minds of the period for some message of super-earthly salvation which should effectively ' speak to their condition.' At the same time, it should be observed that there is not the slightest reason for supposing that S. Paul would have presented Christianity, from this point of view, under any different aspect to Jews. It was the conviction of Christians universally, despite the ' futurist ' outlook of the earliest Church, that in Jesus, who was already the Christ, God had already in some sense ' visited and redeemed His people.' S. Paul believes quite simply that the Gospel is ' the power of God unto salvation to every one that believeth,' in the case of the Jew as in the case of the Gentile.[1]

The question therefore arises whether, by those numerous critics who have concentrated their attention too exclusively upon the controversial arguments which S. Paul was led at a certain stage of his career to develop as against those of his Jewish fellow-Christians who would have imposed circumcision upon the Gentiles,[2] the whole relation of the Apostle to Judaism has not tended to be somewhat seriously misunderstood. S. Paul is the champion of Gentile freedom. He believed that the Law, which had formed the basis of the ancient covenant between God and His people, was no longer the basis of the new covenant in the blood of the Messiah.[3] The Law, in so far as it had served as a παιδαγωγός or ' nursery-tutor ' to bring men to Christ, had fulfilled its

---

[1] Rom. 1 16.

[2] That the doctrine of justification by faith is not the essence of Paulinism, but is to be understood rather as a controversial reply to Judaistic opponents, is a point which is made with characteristic directness and vigour by Wrede, who remarks truly enough that S. Paul has been read too exclusively in the light of the peculiar theological standpoint of the Reformers (W. Wrede, *Paulus*, p. 72).

[3] 1 Cor. 11 25.

divinely-intended purpose.[1] It was in a sense at an end. It was no longer the appointed basis of a man's righteousness before God, even in the case of the Jews, so that S. Paul can write that ' Christ is the end of the law unto righteousness for every one that believeth.' [2] At the same time, it was reasonable that those who were Jews born and bred, and to whom the Law was a matter of inherited religious usage and custom, should continue to observe it—' Was any man called being circumcised? let him not become uncircumcised.' [3] It is incredible that there can have been any serious foundation in S. Paul's actual conduct and teaching for the charge which appears to have been brought against him in Jerusalem to the effect that he encouraged the Jews of the Dispersion to ' forsake Moses ' and no longer to circumcise their children or to ' walk after the customs.' [4] The case of Gentiles who had been converted to Christianity, and who, as S. Paul expresses it, had ' received the Spirit ' not ' by the works of the law ' but ' by the hearing of faith,' [5] was quite different. The Law was emphatically not the completion or complement of the Gospel; on the contrary, it was the Gospel which was the divinely-intended fulfilment and end of the Law. For a converted Gentile to accept also the Law as something additional to his Christianity was in S. Paul's eyes sheer apostasy, as implying a doubt as to the sufficiency and the true character of Christian salvation. S. Paul vindicates vehemently the freedom of the Gentiles, contending not merely that they *need* not, but that they *must* not, become subject to the Law.[6] In the heat of the controversy he is capable of saying very strong things, even going to the length of apparently equating the Law with the ' element '-worship of heathenism,[7] or of taking advantage of a Jewish

---

[1] Gal. 3 [24].   [2] Rom. 10 [4].

[3] 1 Cor. 7 [18].

[4] Acts 21 [21] : cf. J. Weiss, *Das Urchristentum*, pp. 168 *sq*., 282.

[5] Gal. 3 [2].   [6] Gal. 5 [2] *sqq*., 3 [2] *sqq*.

[7] Gal. 4 [9] *sq*.

tradition to the effect that Moses received the Law through the mediation of angels to suggest that it did not directly come from God.[1]   It was part of the work of Christ to redeem men from the ' curse ' pronounced by the Law itself upon such as should fail to obey it, which He did by Himself incurring on behalf of God's people a form of death which the Law had declared to be fraught with a curse.[2]   The Law was quite impotent to enable men to become righteous ; [3] it tended rather to operate as a stimulus to its own transgression.[4] ' Justification '—that is to say, ' acquittal '— on the basis of the Law was impossible.[5]

It is nevertheless S. Paul's permanent conviction that ' the Law,' in itself, is ' holy, and the commandment holy, and righteous, and good.' [6] It was among the ' advantages ' of the Jews that they had been entrusted with the Scriptures —the ' oracles of God.' [7] ' The giving of the law ' is included along with ' the adoption, and the glory, and the covenants, and . . . the service of God, and the promises ' among the religious privileges of the Jew ; [8] and of the Jews, ' as concerning the flesh,' came eventually the Christ.[9] S. Paul's supreme heart's desire and supplication to God is for Israel, that they might be saved.[10]   The Gentiles are at best the wild branches of an oleaster, grafted into the ancient stock of the true olive tree, the Israel of God.[11]   The fact that S. Paul,

---

[1] Gal. 3 [19] sqq.   For the giving of the Law by angels, cf. Acts 7 [53] ; Josephus, Antiq. xv. v. 3 ; Jubilees, I [29], 2 [1].   In Col. 2 [14-17] the angels of the Law are apparently identified with the ' principalities and powers ' who are presumably also the στοιχεῖα of Col. 2 [8] and the ' rulers of this age ' of 1 Cor. 2 [8]—a virtual equation of the angels of the Law with the supernatural powers who in the present ' age ' of the world hold men in thrall ; a very surprising utterance on the part of S. Paul; see, however, infra, p. 148 n.

[2] Gal. 3 [13] ; cf. Deut. 11 [28], 21 [23].

[3] Gal. 3 [21], Rom. 8 [3].   [4] Rom. 7 [7] sqq.

[5] Gal. 2 [16], Rom. 3 [20].   [6] Rom. 7 [12].

[7] Rom. 3 [1] sq.   [8] Rom. 9 [4].

[9] Rom. 9 [5].   [10] Rom. 10 [1].

[11] Rom. 11 [17] sqq.

the Roman citizen and Christian Apostle, was five times ignominiously beaten in Jewish synagogues by order of the synagogue officials [1] is clear evidence that he did not regard himself on the ground of his conversion to Christianity as having ceased to be a Jew. On the contrary, he informs us himself that he became to the Jews as a Jew, that he might gain Jews [2] to the new faith, which he conceives as the true form which the Jewish religion ought now to assume ; and although in the interests of missionary work amongst Gentiles he was prepared for his own part to dispense on occasions with the observances of Judaism and to become as a Gentile,[3] it is a probable view that, apart from such occasional concessions in the interests of the special work to which in his later years he felt himself to be more particularly called, he was accustomed himself, as a Jewish Christian, to live in accordance with the traditional religious customs of his race.[4] If the Acts may be trusted, S. Paul showed anxiety to reach Jerusalem in time to keep Pentecost,[5] he had his head shorn at Cenchreae in connexion with a (presumably Jewish) religious vow,[6] and he was prepared at Jerusalem to demonstrate publicly his loyalty to Judaism by being purified in the Temple and by bearing the expenses connected with

---

[1] 2 Cor. 11 [24]; cf. Deut. 25 [3]. The reference is to a judicial punishment inflicted with due forms of law after sentence by a Synagogue court.

[2] 1 Cor. 9 [20].

[3] 1 Cor. 9 [21].

[4] Cf. J. Weiss, Das Urchristentum, p. 283.

[5] Acts 20 [16]; cf. 18 [21], where the Bezan text adds δεῖ με πάντως τὴν ἑορτὴν τὴν ἐρχομένην ποιῆσαι εἰς Ἱεροσόλυμα.

[6] Acts 18 [18]. If the 'vow' in question was, as seems probable, a Nazarite vow (cf. Num. 6 [1] sqq.), a visit to the Temple at Jerusalem was involved : in which case the Bezan reading in 18 [21] is at least a correct gloss, and the statement that after landing at Caesarea S. Paul ' went up ' and ' saluted the Church' (Acts 18 [22]) means that he ' went up' to Jerusalem, which in any case is the probable meaning of ἀναβάς in such a context (see Ramsay, S. Paul the Traveller and the Roman Citizen, pp. 262 sqq.). On S. Paul's vow see further W. L. Knox, St. Paul and the Church of Jerusalem, pp. 269, 283, who suggests that it was undertaken ' in order to remove any possible suspicion of his personal loyalty to the Jewish faith.'

the dedication of their hair by four men who were under a vow.[1]

I spoke a moment ago of the work to which S. Paul felt himself to be called ' in his later years.' It is characteristic of Semitic religious thought to see the end as implicit in the beginning, and to ante-date to the moment of crisis whatever in the light of events might appear to have been implicit in it according to the purpose of God. It is in this sense, perhaps, that S. Paul in speaking of his conversion writes that it had ' pleased God to reveal His Son ' in him, that he ' might preach Him among the Gentiles.' [2] At how early a stage in S. Paul's life as a Christian did this special vocation begin to be made definitely clear ? According to the narrative in Acts, the dramatic turning to the Gentiles, described subsequently as the opening by God of ' a door of faith unto the Gentiles,'[3] was a new and in a sense unexpected departure in the course of the mission which was organized from Antioch, and in which S. Paul was the companion of Barnabas.[4] It is important to remember that S. Paul at this time was a Christian of a dozen years' standing.[5] There are good scholars who believe that the first half of his life as a Christian, during which he appears to have worked chiefly in Syria and Cilicia,[6] was in all probability spent wholly in mission work amongst Greek-speaking Jews   It

---

[1] Acts 21 [23] sqq. The ' vow' of the four men in question, who are presumably Jewish Christians, will have been a Nazarite vow like that which S. Paul himself had taken on the former occasion. J. Weiss (op. cit. pp. 168 sq., 282 sqq.) regards the narrative of Acts 21 [20] sqq. as being in substance trustworthy, though he thinks that the statement in verse 24b that S. Paul was normally accustomed to ' walk orderly, keeping the law ' is an exaggeration, and further suggests that the words τῶν πε-πιστευκότων in verse 20 are a gloss. The ' many myriads ' whose presence in Jerusalem constituted a danger are not Jewish Christians, but non-Christian Jews, who had assembled in great numbers to keep Pentecost.

[2] Gal. 1 [16] : and so also Acts 9 [15], 22 [21].   [3] Acts 14 [27].

[4] Acts 13 [46] sqq.

[5] S. Paul was most probably converted in A.D. 35 or 36. The ' first missionary journey ' (from Antioch) may be dated about 47 or 48.

[6] Gal. 1 [21].

was during these years more particularly that he became to the Jews as a Jew, and during these years that he incurred on five several occasions the Jewish maximum penalty of 'forty stripes save one.'[1]

If this view, which appears clearly to be in harmony with the evidence of the New Testament, is correct, it would follow that the Greek-speaking Christendom in the spiritual environment of which the Christianity of S. Paul was matured was not predominantly Gentile, but predominantly Jewish. The development of a Christendom in which Gentile elements predominated has been ante-dated by Bousset, and the proper inference, if (as Bousset has so acutely divined) both the cult of the Lord Jesus and the existence of the sacraments are *presupposed* by the Christianity of S. Paul, is that the beginnings, both of sacramental theology and practice, and of the cult of the Lord Jesus, must be traced back behind Gentile Christianity to the Christianity of the original Church.[2] It is, in any case, of importance to observe that no controversy appears at any stage to have arisen between S. Paul and his predecessors in the faith with regard to the doctrine either of Christ or of the sacraments, and that he is able to claim that the Gospel which he was accustomed to preach amongst the Gentiles had been emphatically endorsed by the 'pillars' of the Church at Jerusalem.[3] It is, I think, reasonable to conclude that any fruitful examination of S. Paul's doctrine of the person of Christ must proceed upon the assumption that its presuppositions are not syncretistic and virtually pagan, but Jewish and Christian, and that the supposed cleavage in respect of Christology

---

[1] So (e.g.) J. Weiss, *Das Urchristentum*, pp. 150 *sq.*, 168 ; cf. W. Wrede, *Paulus*, pp. 14 *sq.* and p. 29.

[2] On the 'spontaneous' development of sacramentalism *auf dem Boden der Urgemeinde*, see E. Meyer, *Ursprung und Anfänge*, iii. p. 232 *n.* ; and for the equally spontaneous and immediate development of the cult of the Lord Jesus, cf. A. Deissmann, *Paulus*, 2nd ed., pp. 90, 98 *sqq.*

[3] Gal. 2 [2] *sqq.*

and worship between the Christianity of Palestine and that of the Gentile-Christian Church is a chimera. There was inevitably in early Christianity development alike in respect of doctrine and of practice. It is obvious enough that the language, the social customs, the surrounding atmosphere and the modes of thought of the Jewish Christians of Jerusalem were all widely different from those of the Gentile believers of such cities as Ephesus or Corinth. There was nevertheless here also continuity from the one to the other, and the development which took place was not an un-mediated transformation in virtue of which Christianity as it had arisen in Palestine was converted into something essentially other than itself. It was rather the beginning of that historical process of progressive self-adaptation to new environments in virtue of which Christianity through all its phases of successive change has preserved its essential self-identity from the first age until now. And that this has been so was in large measure due, under God, to the contribution which was made in the first century to the development of Christian thought and practice by S. Paul.

LECTURE V

THE CONTRIBUTION OF S. PAUL—II

SYNOPSIS

S. PAUL, the Gentile Church, and the problem of the Old Testament. The providential significance of the controversy with regard to the Law. S. Paul's great service to monotheism.

S. Paul and the doctrine of Christ. His Christology not originally independent of tradition. The significance of his baptism and membership of the Church. His probable acquaintance with the Christian tradition of our Lord's teaching and life upon earth.

Nevertheless, for S. Paul as for the Church generally the Christ is not primarily a Figure of the past, but the exalted Lord of the present and future. The significance of the term 'glory,' and of the revelation of Christ to S. Paul at his conversion as the glorified Lord.

S. Paul's doctrine of the pre-existence of Christ, derived probably in the first instance not from the thought of our Lord as the Son of God (though when once the idea of pre-existence has been brought in, S. Paul can proceed to think naturally of our Lord as having pre-existed with God as His Son) but from the identification of Christ with the Son of Man. S. Paul's eschatology implies that he accepts this identification, and the matter is made certain by a quotation which he makes from Ps. viii. The idea of our Lord as the 'second Man' who is 'from heaven' not borrowed from Gentile mythology, but derived by S. Paul from the eschatological tradition of Judaism. The 'Son of Man' in the Book of Enoch. The Hebrew doctrine of Man as being 'made in God's image.' S. Paul's doctrine of Christ as the 'image' of God.

An exposition of 1 Cor. xv. The Corinthians are concerned with a difficulty about Christians who have died. S. Paul develops a doctrine of the new 'spiritual' body, and points out that the real difficulty arises in connexion with those who survive till the Parousia with their existing bodies of 'flesh and blood.' With regard to these he proclaims to them a 'mystery.' In the course of the argument he introduces the idea of our Lord as the 'Man from heaven.' 1 Cor. xv. 45 not to be taken as meaning that he identified Christ with the Spirit.

S. Paul's doctrine of Christ as the Divine 'image' and 'glory' as (i) anticipating the later orthodox doctrine of the eternal generation of the Son, and (ii) leading on to the identification of Christ with the Divine ' Wisdom.'

The idea of our Lord as the heavenly ' Man ' who pre-exists as God's ' image and glory,' as throwing light on the interpretation of a passage in Philippians, in which S. Paul vindicates the confession and *cultus* of Jesus as ' Lord.'

LECTURE V

THE CONTRIBUTION OF S. PAUL—II

'Ο δεύτερος ἄνθρωπος ἐξ οὐρανοῦ.

The second man is from heaven.—1 Cor. 15 [47].

It was the argument of the last lecture that S. Paul's mind is to be understood as having been essentially the mind of a Jew who had come to see in Christ the fulfilment of Judaism, who had ceased to be ' as touching the law, a Pharisee,' [1] and who in the later years of his life was more particularly the missionary of Christ to the Gentiles. At the same time, we remind ourselves that it is probable that Christianity, even apart from S. Paul, would have come to be the religion eventually of a large part of the Greek-speaking world, and that the process was attended by risks. It is not difficult to conceive of the possibility that the Lord Jesus might have become the centre of a paganized cult in which the Gospel, divorced from its basis in Judaism and from the monotheistic faith of the Old Testament, would have become simply a new form of Gnosticism.

The chief safeguard of monotheism was in the first instance the Old Testament itself. The earliest missionaries appear to have been everywhere Jews. There were personal links between the Church and the Synagogue, and the Church took over from Judaism the Old Testament in the Septuagint version. But precisely here must have lurked eventually a difficulty for Gentiles. The Old Testament is a national literature. It is addressed to the Jews, and it enjoins the observance of the Law. The first non-Jewish converts to

[1] Philipp. 3 [5].

H

Christianity were drawn, as we have seen, from the class known as 'God-fearers.' They had been adherents, though not members, of the Synagogue ; they became members of the Church. But that did not mean that they accepted the Law. If the Old Testament was nevertheless to be permanently received by Gentile converts to Christianity as authoritative Scripture—if it was to be treated not merely as the Scripture of the Jews, but as the Scripture of the Church—the question must sooner or later inevitably have been raised with regard to the Law. There were in fact two questions involved which demanded an answer, and to which no answer as yet had been given. They were the questions, in the first place, of the purpose and meaning of the Law, and in the second place of the relation of Israel to the Church. The sudden demand of the Judaizing party for the circumcision of the Gentile believers—a demand which appears to have been first made at Antioch by ' certain men ' who ' came down from Judaea '[1]—had the salutary effect of precipitating a crisis which made it imperative that answers should be found.

And the answers were found by S. Paul, who developed on the one hand a doctrine of the Church as the true Israel of God,[2] in which Gentile and Jew, irrespective of circumcision or of uncircumcision,[3] were alike children of Abraham,[4] fellow-heirs, fellow-members of the body, fellow-partakers of the promise in Christ Jesus,[5] fellow-citizens with the saints in the Jerusalem above,[6] and who on the other hand developed also a constructive theory of the Law, in which a strong affirmation of its divine origin and positive significance was combined with the doctrine that its function

---

[1] Acts 15 [1].   [2] Gal. 6 [16].
[3] Gal. 5 [6], 6 [15] : Rom. 2 [25] sq.   [4] Rom. 4 [11, 16]; cf. Gal. 3 [9, 29].
[5] Eph. 3 [6].
[6] Eph. 2 [19], Gal. 4 [26]. In 1 Cor. 10 [32] we find already ' the Church of God ' as a third entity (the genus tertium of the Christian Apologists) distinct both from the ' Jews ' and the ' Greeks.'

was now at an end, and that Christians, in virtue of their
relationship to Christ, were no longer 'under law,' but
'under grace.'[1]   It is important to read S. Paul's arguments
not merely negatively, as a refusal to accept the Judaistic
demand for the circumcision of the Gentiles, but positively,
as a Christian vindication of the position of the Law in the
Old Testament.   It is probable that the Gentile Church as
a whole would not in any case have accepted circumcision,
and that what S. Paul primarily secured by his victory at
Jerusalem was simply the avoidance of an otherwise inevitable schism.   Of far greater historical importance was
the fact that S. Paul argued his case upon the basis of the
Old Testament itself, and that as a direct consequence of the
controversy he was led to work out in his own mind, and
to set down in writing, a Christian theory both of the Law
and of the Church which enabled Christians of Gentile
extraction to find themselves permanently at home with the
Old Testament.   It was a service of incalculable value to
the future monotheistic faith of the Church.

If the Judaistic controversy belongs to the later years
of S. Paul's life, the development of his Christology, at
least as regards its main outlines, must be traced farther
back.   There is a sense in which, as Johannes Weiss has
pointed out, the S. Paul of the Epistles is already mature.
The development of his mind as a Christian must be presumed
to have taken place in the period which followed his conversion—those baffling years of which nothing is known
beyond the bare facts that S. Paul visited Arabia, returned
to Damascus, went up to Jerusalem 'after three years,' and
then 'came into the regions of Syria and Cilicia,'[2] to be
sought out eventually by Barnabas, who found him at
Tarsus and brought him back in his company to Antioch.[3]
The same scholar suggests that S. Paul's statement that at

---

[1] Rom. 6 [14] *sq.*   [2] Gal. 1 [17] *sqq.*
[3] Acts 11 [25] *sqq.*

the time of his conversion he ' conferred not with flesh and blood ' [1] must be taken as the utterance of a πνευματικός and mystic who is accustomed habitually to refer both his religious beliefs and his spiritual experiences to the direct working of God through the Spirit.[2] It is probable that the mediation of man was not really so completely excluded as S. Paul in retrospect appears to imply. The real point of the argument in Galatians is to establish S. Paul's independence of the Twelve : he had not been their convert, he had never sat at their feet as a catechumen receiving instruction,[3] he had been converted by a direct ' revelation,' he had received his authority immediately from Christ. But S. Paul was certainly baptized, which implies both a baptizer (in this case Ananias of Damascus) and also a circle of disciples who receive him into their midst as a convert.[4] He must have possessed some initial acquaintance with Christianity—indeed, S. Paul knew very well what were the tenets of Christians, since he had engaged in anti-Christian polemics. He must further have possessed at least a clearly-defined mental image of the personality and character— perhaps also of the actual outward appearance [5]—of Jesus of Nazareth, in order to be able at once to identify with Jesus (as he appears without any hesitation to have done) the glorified Figure whom he believed to have appeared to him from heaven. S. Paul's Christology, in a word, must be regarded—despite his assertion that he did not receive his Gospel ' from man ' [6]—as having been determined in the first instance to a considerable extent by tradition, provided that under the head of ' tradition ' we may be allowed to

---

[1] Gal. I [16].   [2] J. Weiss, *Das Urchristentum*, p. 143.
[3] οὔτε ἐδιδάχθην (Gal. I [12]).   [4] Acts 9 [17] *sqq.*
[5] J. Weiss is disposed to infer from 2 Cor. 5 [16] that S. Paul had actually seen our Lord in the days of His flesh. There is nothing improbable in the supposition that he may have been in Jerusalem at the time of the Crucifixion (J. Weiss, *Das Urchristentum*, p. 137).
[6] Gal. I [12].

include not only such knowledge as came to S. Paul after his conversion, as the result of association with Christians, but also such knowledge as he must be presumed to have possessed *before* his conversion with regard both to the doctrinal beliefs of the Church and to the facts about Jesus.

It is to be presumed, further, that S. Paul was indebted, to a greater extent than he perhaps personally realized, for very much in the way of growing knowledge and deeper insight into the meaning of Christianity to the fact of his participation in the faith, worship, and corporate life of the Christian Society. It was because he had learnt by experience to know the meaning of Christian brotherhood, and to discover in the Eucharist the sacramental bond of a spiritual unity in Christ, that he was able at a later date to become the theologian of the Church and of the sacraments.

Nor, again, is it reasonable to suppose that he did not in time become more fully informed with regard to the Church's tradition of the teaching and life of our Lord upon earth. The Gospels were of course not yet written, but the traditions about Jesus which were later to be recorded in the Gospels must in one form or another have been current and widely received in the Church. S. Paul had visited S. Peter ;[1] he had worked as a missionary for long periods in the company of such associates as Barnabas, John Mark, and Silas, who had been members of the Church in Jerusalem ; it is absurd to imagine that he was not interested to hear from their lips what they were able to hand on of the tradition of our Lord's teaching,[2] or again of the events of His human life, or that S. Paul alone among Christian missionaries deliberately abstained from every attempt to make concrete

[1] Gal. 1 18.

[2] The authority of a saying of Jesus is for S. Paul the highest authority which he can quote ; only when he ' has no commandment of the Lord ' does he venture to give his own judgement, even though he believes himself to be inspired by the Spirit. Cf. 1 Cor. 7 10, 12, 25, 40, 9 14.

and real to his hearers by means of such illustrative material the personality of the Christ whom he proclaimed.[1] The fact that his letters contain little or nothing in the way of traditions about Jesus beyond the facts of His Crucifixion and Resurrection and the account of the institution of the Eucharist is due to the fact that his letters are not missionary preaching; they are addressed to converted believers, and are concerned either with such questions as happened to have become matters of controversy, or else with such points, whether of doctrine or of morals, as appeared to have been insufficiently grasped. It is much to be regretted that apart from the few generalized and typical speeches introduced by S. Luke into the Acts, we are totally ignorant of the Christian mission preaching of Apostolic times, nor have we any direct knowledge of the kind of catechetical instruction by which such preaching was presumably followed up in the case of those hearers who were willing to receive further teaching.

Although, however, S. Paul's Christ was thus the Christ of the Church, who was identified, by S. Paul as by others, with Jesus, his devotion was directed, like that of the Christian Church generally, not primarily towards Jesus considered as a Figure of the past, but towards Jesus the exalted Lord of the present and future ; and it is probable enough that (as has often been suggested by scholars) the actual nature of his conversion, and the precise form which it had assumed—the two facts that he had been converted to Christianity suddenly and (as he believed) ' by a revelation,' [2] and that in the moment of his conversion he had seen a vision of the risen Jesus exalted in majesty and surrounded, as the accounts in the Acts would suggest, by a radiance of white light [3]—counted for something in determining the fashion in which he was accustomed habitually to think of

---

[1] J. Weiss, *Das Urchristentum*, p. 167.

[2] δι' ἀποκαλύψεως (Gal. 1 [12]).   [3] Acts 9 [3], 22 [6], 26 [13].

the glorified Lord. 'It is God,' writes S. Paul, 'who said, Light shall shine out of darkness, who shined in our hearts, to give the light of the knowledge of the glory of God in the face of Jesus Christ.'[1]   The word δόξα, here translated 'glory,' was for any one who was accustomed to read the Old Testament in Greek peculiarly rich in religious associations.[2] Representing the Hebrew word *kabod*, it suggested on the one hand the divine splendour and majesty, believed to have been visibly manifested in real though partial fashion in the Old Testament theophanies, on the other hand the divine energy and power, and at the same time the moral and spiritual glory, of the God who was thus made manifest, and of whose true inward being and essence the visible manifestation was more and more recognized as being only a symbol.[3]   So S. Paul, though he cannot forget that what he had seen had presented itself to his outward perception as a phenomenon of bright light, as it had been the radiance of the glory of God visibly shining 'in the face of Jesus Christ,' finds instinctively in the recollection a symbol of the spiritual glory of the new creation,[4] the light of God shining in human hearts, as when God in the story of the Creation in Genesis had commanded the light to shine out of darkness.[5]   It is possible further that the phrase 'knowledge

[1] 2 Cor. 4 [6].

[2] As has been recently emphasized afresh in the late Dr. Abrahams' impressive and valuable lectures on *The Glory of God* (Oxford, 1925).

[3] Cf. Abrahams, *op. cit.*, also the article 'Glory' (by the late Dr. Gray) in *H.D.B.*, vol. ii. pp. 183 *sqq.* ; and for S. Paul's use of the term, see H. A. A. Kennedy, *St. Paul and the Mystery Religions*, pp. 190 *sqq.* The attempt of Reitzenstein (*H.M.R.*, 2nd ed., pp. 140, 166, 196) to illustrate from non-Jewish sources the meaning of δόξα in the New Testament is not very fruitful. Quotations from a magical papyrus of the third century A.D., or from a post-Christian treatise on alchemy, are no more to the point than are quotations from Philo the Jew. The single example quoted from the *Corpus Hermeticum* (*Corp. Herm.* x. 7) is not likely to be pre-Christian, and the Oxford editor of the *Corpus Hermeticum* is disposed to suspect Jewish influence in the passage in question (see W. Scott, *Hermetica*, ii. p. 244).

[4] Cf. 2 Cor. 5 [17].   [5] Gen. 1 [3].

of the glory of God ' may recall the thought of Habakkuk, who with the insight of prophecy had looked forward to a day in which the earth should be filled with the knowledge of the divine glory, ' as the waters cover the sea.' [1] The illumination given to S. Paul is not only for himself, but for the world. It constitutes a divine call to illuminate others, that they too may see the light of the knowledge of God's glory, as S. Paul has seen it himself in the face of Christ.[2]

And S. Paul thinks of the Christ who has thus been mani-fested to him in ' glory '—and this is the element in his Christology which, so far as our evidence goes, appears to be new—not simply in terms of His life upon earth, of His death and resurrection, of His subsequent exaltation to God's ' right hand,' but in terms also of the idea of His pre-existence with God since creation began. From whence did S. Paul derive this remarkable and apparently novel conception of the Christ ? It is probable, no doubt, that in Hellenistic circles the idea of pre-existence would in any case have suggested itself sooner or later in connexion with Jesus as an inference from the description of our Lord as the ' Son of God '—a title which, as we have seen, conveyed primarily to Gentiles the idea of a supernatural being, a ' divine man,' whose superhuman and supernatural character and powers were most readily to be explained by the

---

[1] Habakkuk 2 [14], where, however, the LXX has τοῦ γνῶναι τὴν δόξαν Κυρίου (as against τῆς γνώσεως τῆς δόξης τοῦ θεοῦ), so that the parallel with 2 Cor. 4 [6] is not verbally very close.

[2] See Menzies' Commentary ad loc. ; and on S. Paul's use of the word φωτισμός, see Kennedy, St. Paul and the Mystery Religions, pp. 197 sqq. The term was undoubtedly used in the language of Hellenistic religion of the ' illumination ' which was supposed to be the result of initiation into the Mysteries. Inasmuch, however, as it occurs in the LXX of Pss. 18 (19) [9] and 26 (27) [1], there is no need with Reitzenstein (H.M.R., 2nd ed., pp. 142 sqq.) to look to the Corpus Hermeticum or the Metamorphoses of Apuleius for the explanation of a metaphor which was already Biblical, and the use of which in 2 Cor. 4 [4, 6] was probably directly suggested by the form of S. Paul's experience at the moment of his conversion.

hypothesis of his supernatural origin.[1] But S. Paul was a Jew, and to the Jewish mind, as we have also seen, the phrase ' Son of God,' as applied to the Messiah, carried no such significance. It denoted rather that the Messiah was the *chosen* of God, the ' elect One,' the divinely-appointed Ruler of God's people, who at the most was divinely upheld and supernaturally endowed with the divine attributes of majesty and honour. S. Paul writes of our Lord, in accordance with this Jewish view of the matter, and in harmony with the earliest Jewish-Christian interpretation of the Resurrection and Ascension as marking the enthronement of Jesus in Messianic majesty, that He was ' born of the seed of David according to the flesh,' and ' declared to be the Son of God with power, according to the spirit of holiness ' (a phrase which perhaps means ' in accordance with the holiness of His human " spirit " '), ' by the resurrection of the dead.' [2]

It would seem probable, therefore, that it was not directly from the idea of our Lord as the Son of God that S. Paul derived, in the first instance, the idea of His pre-existence ; though of course when once the idea of pre-existence, however attained, had arisen in S. Paul's mind, and become firmly established as an integral element in his conception of Jesus, he proceeds naturally to think of the pre-existent Messiah as having been already the Son of God, not indeed in any such sense as could be akin to the pagan mythological idea of the gods as divine beings who were capable in an anthropomorphic sense of begetting offspring, but in the sense that the pre-existent Christ was the Father's Beloved, the object of His peculiar solicitude and care. It is thus that God comes to be for S. Paul in a special sense ' the God and Father of our Lord Jesus Christ,' [3] and that the Lord Jesus can be described, in relation to God, as His ' own Son,' [4]

[1] Lecture III. pp. 70 *sqq.*   [2] Rom. 1 [3] *sqq.*
[3] Rom. 15 [6], 2 Cor. 1 [3], 11 [31].   [4] Rom. 8 [3], [32] ; cf. Gal. 4 [4], 2 Cor. 1 [19].

or as ' the Son of His love ' [1]—a phrase which, in view of the analogy of the idiomatic use in the Septuagint of the word ἀγαπητός to translate in certain contexts a Hebrew word meaning ' only,' is probably meant to suggest not only the Father's love for His Son, but also the uniqueness of the sonship of Christ in relation to God.[2] Whether or not S. Paul may have been influenced in regard to this doctrine of our Lord's unique sonship by any tradition of sayings ascribed to Jesus Himself in which He was reported to have referred to Himself as ' the Son ' is a disputed point, which must be left undetermined.[3] It is not likely in any case that the specific doctrine of our Lord's *pre-existence* as Son of God was attained in this way.[4]

I would suggest rather that the obvious source of the idea of pre-existence is to be found in the identification of Jesus with the eschatological ' Son of Man,' an identification which, as we have seen, was a prominent element in the very earliest doctrine of the Church with regard to our Lord, and which almost certainly in some sense goes back behind Calvary to the historical mind of the Lord Jesus Himself.[5] The first Christians (as we may remind ourselves) thought of our Lord as the Messiah who, enthroned and exalted in

[1] Col. i 13.

[2] See Armitage Robinson, *St. Paul's Epistle to the Ephesians*, Additional Note (pp. 229 *sqq.*) on ' *The Beloved* ' *as a Messianic Title* ; and cf. the note on p. 79 *supra*. It is probable that the original meaning of ἀγαπητός in Greek was ' that wherewith one must be content,' and that the word thus came to be used of ' only ' children, and so of unique things generally. The meaning ' beloved ' follows naturally from this, since ἀγαπᾶν can mean ' to love ' as well as ' to be content with,' and what is ' unique ' becomes proportionately precious.

[3] Cf. Lecture II. pp. 50 *sqq*, and see Appended Note IV. pp. 251 *sqq*.

[4] I am not able to agree with Bishop Gore in supposing S. Paul to have been dependent upon a Johannine or quasi-Johannine tradition of our Lord's teaching with regard to Himself, supposed to have been current, but to have remained theologically inoperative, in the circle of the original disciples, and to have been understood for the first time by S. Paul, who was ' more quick than others to catch the full meaning ' of our Lord's words (so Gore, *Belief in Christ*, pp. 88-91).

[5] Cf. Lecture II. pp. 34, 49, and Appended Note III. pp. 242 *sqq*.

majesty, was destined shortly to be manifested as the Son of Man returning with power and great glory from heaven. S. Paul shared fully their outlook, as the two Epistles to the Thessalonians (but not the Epistles to the Thessalonians alone) make decisively clear. The whole setting and framework of S. Paul's theology both of the Christ and of the Christian redemption (whatever other elements it came also to include in addition to the eschatology) is cast in the eschatological mould. It is a mould which is foreign to the thought, and to a large extent foreign also to the religion, of to-day, though from the point of view both of thought and of religion it enshrines values to which it is difficult to give expression in any less frankly symbolical form, and which in one form or another it is of the utmost importance to religion to assert.[1] S. Paul, in common with his contemporaries, interprets the symbolism literally. He believes, with the author of the Ezra Apocalypse, that 'the world hasteth fast to pass away,'[2] and that he himself and the existing generation of mankind are those 'upon whom the ends of the ages are come,'[3] those, therefore, for whose benefit the Scriptures were written,[4] and within whose lifetime the prophecies are destined to be fulfilled. Nay, he believes that the time has been actually shortened,[5] that 'the night is far spent, the day is at hand,' that salvation is already appreciably nearer than when men

---

[1] The eschatological element in the Christian creed gives expression not only to the Christian conviction of the reality of the world to come, but also to the recognition (a) that the ultimate verdict upon human life and its issues is the verdict of God, (b) that the ultimate victory in the struggle between evil and good is the victory of God, and (c) that the ultimate satisfaction of the human spirit is not to be found in the sphere of things visible and temporal but in the sphere of the things eternal and invisible. It follows that human life ought to be lived from a point of view which regards the Judgment, the Kingdom of God, and the life of the world to come as being in some sense eternally 'at hand.' A religion which in such sense eschews 'otherworldliness' as to forget that 'the fashion of this world passeth away,' quickly ceases to be a religion at all and becomes mere 'savourless salt.'

[2] 2 Esdras 4 [26].   [3] 1 Cor. 10 [11].
[4] 1 Cor. 10 [11], 9 [9] *sqq.*   [5] 1 Cor. 7 [29]; cf. Mk. 13 [20], Mt. 24 [22].

first came to have faith in our Lord.[1] It is presumably this apocalyptic conviction of the imminent approach of the End which drives S. Paul with such feverish energy from province to province of the Empire, and which leads him to make far-reaching plans for a visit not merely to Rome, but to Spain,[2] in his eagerness to secure that, if possible, the whole world may be evangelized before the coming of the Lord. In the two Epistles to the Thessalonians,[3] and again in the fifteenth chapter of the first Epistle to the Corinthians,[4] he has left us a grandiose picture of the expected events of the End, based partly upon what were reported to be actual sayings of the Lord,[5] and in part also no doubt upon currently accepted apocalyptic beliefs and interpretations of Scripture.[6]

In all this it is implied that for S. Paul, as for the earliest believers in general, the Lord Jesus is identified with the mysterious 'Son of Man' of apocalyptic expectation, an identification which is not merely probable, in view of the whole character of S. Paul's eschatological outlook, but definitely certain, on the ground of his use of the eighth Psalm as a prophetic Scripture which must find its fulfilment in Christ. S. Paul grounds upon this Psalm the conviction that 'all things' must eventually be 'put in subjection' beneath our Lord's feet, and directly quotes the sixth verse of the Psalm to that effect.[7] Such a use of the Psalm could only have arisen as a result of the identification of Christ with the 'Son of Man,' who (in the words of the verse which precedes the one quoted by S. Paul) is 'made for a short time lower than the angels' in order to be 'crowned with

---

[1] Rom. 13 [12, 11].   [2] Rom. 15 [24, 28].

[3] 2 Thess. 1 [7] sqq., 2 [1] sqq. : 1 Thess. 1 [9] sqq., 4 [13] sqq., 5 [1] sqq.

[4] 1 Cor. 15 [20] sqq., [50] sqq.   [5] 1 Thess. 4 [15].

[6] The beliefs connected with the expectation of the prior coming of the Antichrist (2 Thess. 2 [3] sqq.) are especially interesting ; see Bousset, *The Antichrist Legend*, and *E.R.E.*, s.v. 'Antichrist.'

[7] 1 Cor. 15 [27].

glory and honour.'[1] It appears, therefore, probable that
S. Paul has in his mind the same thought of our Lord as the
' Son of Man ' when he writes, at a later stage of his argument
in the same chapter of 1 Corinthians, of the ' second Man '
who is 'from heaven ';[2] and there is reason to think that
S. Paul based upon the identification of Jesus with the
'heavenly Man ' of apocalyptic prophecy, regarded as a
clue to the interpretation of Scripture, far-reaching speculations with regard to the relation of our Lord both to man
and to God.

A great deal has been written in recent years with regard
to the conception of our Lord as the ' heavenly Man,' and
it has been proposed by Reitzenstein, Bousset, and others
to connect S. Paul's doctrine directly with a somewhat
widely-diffused Hellenistic myth (derived ultimately, as
it would seem, from the mythology of Persia) according to
which the origin of man—and indeed, in some systems,
of the whole existing world-order—is to be explained as
being due to the descent from heaven, through the successive
planetary spheres, of a Primal Man, who is essentially divine.[3]

---

[1] Ps. 8 [5]. The original reference of the Psalm is to man as such, who
according to the Hebrew is, despite his material insignificance by comparison with the heavens, the moon and the stars (verse 3), the spiritual
crown of God's creation, ' made but little lower than *Elohim* ' (*i.e.* than
God) ; the LXX, however, reads ἠλάττωσας αὐτὸν βραχύ τι παρ' ἀγγέλους, δόξῃ
καὶ τιμῇ ἐστεφάνωσας αὐτόν. For the Christian exegesis of the Psalm as
referring to our Lord, cf. Eph. 1 [22], Heb. 2 [5] *sqq.*

[2] 1 Cor. 15 [47], where the true reading is ὁ δεύτερος ἄνθρωπος ἐξ οὐρανοῦ.

[3] Bousset, *Hauptprobleme der Gnosis*, pp. 160 *sqq.* ; *Kyrios Christos*, 2nd
ed., pp. 140 *sqq.*, 203 *sq.* ; Reitzenstein, *Poimandres*, pp. 81 *sqq.* ; *Die
hellenistischen Mysterienreligionen*, 2nd ed., pp. 195 *sqq.* ; *Das iranische
Erlösungsmysterium*, pp. 115 *sqq.* A valuable review and discussion of the
chief documents in which the myth of the ' heavenly Man ' appears is
contained in an article on *The Heavenly Man* by the Rev. J. M. Creed in the
J.Th.S. for Jan. 1925 ; it will be observed, however, that I am disposed
to differ from Mr. Creed with regard to the exegesis of 1 Cor. 15 [47]. It
should not escape notice that the myth in the above form is adapted to
explain rather the origin of man than his redemption, and that Reitzenstein,
in his anxiety to interpret it as a myth of redemption, is obliged to assume
that the form in which it appears in the *Poimandres* text is incomplete

It is very doubtful, however, whether S. Paul was acquainted with any such non-Jewish speculations, and it is certain that the basis of his thought is not to be found in such sources, but is Hebraic, eschatological, and Biblical, going back on the one hand to the Book of Enoch and the eschatological tradition,[1] on the other hand to the description of man in the Book of Genesis as having been made in the image of God.[2] The Son of Man, as he appears in the Book of Enoch, is described as a ' being whose countenance had the appearance of a man, and his face was full of graciousness, like one of the holy angels.' The interpreting angel explains to Enoch that ' this is the Son of Man who hath righteousness . . . and who revealeth all the treasures of that which is hidden, because the Lord of Spirits hath chosen him, and whose lot hath the pre-eminence before the Lord of Spirits in uprightness for ever.'[3] He is to ' put down the kings and the mighty from their seats,' and to be the Champion and Ruler of the righteous. He is described as the ' Elect One,' and as the ' Anointed ' of the ' Lord of Spirits.'[4] We learn that ' his name was named before the Lord of Spirits ' ' before the sun and the signs were created, before the stars of the heaven were made,' and that ' he hath been chosen and hidden ' before the Lord of Spirits ' before the creation of the world and for evermore.'[5] It is further said of him

(Reitzenstein, *Poimandres*, p. 81). The point made by Dr. Bevan (see Lecture III. *supra*, p. 66) that the figure of the Redeemer in Gnosticism is in no single case demonstrably pre-Christian deserves to be borne in mind. Reitzenstein's latest work (*Das iranische Erlösungsmysterium*), which is based largely on the newly discovered Manichaean documents from Turfan, in Chinese Turkestan, should be read subject to the cautions suggested by Dr. Burkitt's *The Religion of the Manichees*, in which stress is laid on the debt of Mani's teaching to Christianity, especially as mediated by the heretical systems of Bardaisan and Marcion.

[1] The suggestion of Gressmann (*Der Ursprung der israelitisch-jüdischen Eschatologie*, pp. 340 *sq.*) that the symbolic figure ' like unto a son of man ' in Dan. 7 [13] is adapted ultimately from some traditional mythology of non-Jewish origin is probable, but for our present purposes irrelevant.

[2] Gen. 1 [27].   [3] *Eth. Enoch* 46 [1, 3].
[4] *Eth. Enoch* 49 [2, 4], 48 [10].   [5] *Eth. Enoch* 48 [3, 6].

that ' he shall be a staff to the righteous whereon to stay themselves and not fall, and he shall be the light of the Gentiles '—a justification, if any were needed, for S. Paul's Gentile mission !—' and the hope of those who are troubled of heart.' [1] He is equipped, like the King Messiah of the Old Testament, with ' the spirit of wisdom, and the spirit which gives insight, and the spirit of understanding and of might.' [2]

Here, clearly, we seem to have a clue both to S. Paul's doctrine of our Lord as the ' second Man,' who is ' from heaven,' and also the source of that idea of the pre-existence of the Messiah in virtue of which S. Paul is able to think of our Lord as the pre-existent ' Son of God.' [3] If at first sight it appears paradoxical thus to derive from the idea of our Lord as the ' heavenly Man ' the idea of His pre-existence as ' Son of God,' we may remind ourselves that for S. Paul, as a good Hebrew, the terms ' Son of God ' and ' Son of Man ' were in no way mutually exclusive, inasmuch as man was made in God's image ; and the Christ who is both ' Son of Man ' and ' Son of God ' is in fact for S. Paul precisely the pre-existent divine εἰκών or ' image,' after whose likeness, according to the story in Genesis, the first man Adam was made.[4] S. Paul believes that as we have borne the ' image ' of the earthly man, Adam, so also we shall bear the ' image ' of the heavenly Man, Christ, who Himself is the ' image ' of God. [5]

---

[1] *Eth. Enoch* 48 [4].   [2] *Eth. Enoch* 49 [3] ; cf. Is. 11 [2].

[3] Bishop Gore would demur, and attempts to get rid of the evidence afforded by the *Book of Enoch* by means of a disruptive source-criticism of that book, in which he follows Lagrange in suggesting that the passages referring to the Son of Man were interpolated in post-Christian times (see Gore, *Belief in Christ*, pp. 31 *sqq.*).   It appears to me that this is to throw away arbitrarily an illuminating clue to the interpretation of the doctrine of the Son of Man in the New Testament, and I have preferred to assume, with Dr. R. H. Charles and the majority of Biblical scholars, that the book known as the *Similitudes of Enoch* was current before the time of S. Paul in substantially the same form as that in which we read it to-day.

[4] Gen. 1 [26] *sq.*   [5] 1 Cor. 15 [49] ; 2 Cor. 4 [4], Col. 1 [15].

I proceed briefly to paraphrase the familiar, though difficult, argument with regard to the resurrection, in the course of which the conception of our Lord as the ' Man from heaven ' is introduced.[1] S. Paul, it will be remembered, is attempting to meet the difficulties of those Christians at Corinth who (no doubt starting from the presuppositions of Hellenism) are unable to make real to themselves the idea of a resurrection of departed believers, and who ask, ' With what kind of a body do they come ? ' [2] S. Paul begins his reply by drawing attention to a principle which (as he points out) may be illustrated from the processes of Nature— it is through death that the new life comes into being, as a seed when it is sown comes to life in a new form, clothed with a body which in each case is characteristic of itself (ἴδιον), but a body which is given to it by God. Even as regards bodies of flesh and blood (and ' flesh and blood,' as S. Paul proceeds later on to indicate, ' cannot inherit the kingdom of God ' [3]) it is important to remember that at least there are different *kinds* of flesh, though it is perhaps more important still to remember that there are different kinds of *bodies*; in particular there are 'heavenly' as well as 'earthly' bodies : and the glory of ' heavenly ' bodies transcends utterly the glory of bodies upon earth ; the ' heavenly ' bodies are shining, like the stars (we remind ourselves of the words of the Book of Daniel—' they that be wise shall shine as the brightness of the firmament, and they that turn many to righteousness as the stars for ever and ever ' [4]), and here, too, there are different kinds, since sun, moon and stars exhibit various degrees and distinctions of ' glory.'

---

[1] 1 Cor. 15 [35] *sqq.*

[2] Ποίῳ δὲ σώματι ἔρχονται; (1 Cor. 15 [35]). It should be noticed that the problem which distresses the minds of the Christians at Corinth is exactly the same as the problem which had distressed also the minds of the Thessalonians (1 Thess. 4 [13]). It arises from the fact that (contrary to what had been hoped and expected) there have been cases of Christians dying before the Parousia.

[3] 1 Cor. 15 [50].   [4] Dan. 12 [3]; cf. Mt. 13 [43].

Now, the new body of the resurrection is of the celestial or 'heavenly' kind : it is 'supernatural' or 'spiritual' (πνευματικόν) inasmuch as it embodies the πνεῦμα or 'spirit' (which is the principle of man's life in so far as he is inspired by the *Divine* 'Spirit,' and capable of communion with God), as the present body of flesh and blood is the embodiment of the ψυχή (the principle of man's life in so far as he is an animal). The characteristics of the new body, as contrasted with the body of flesh and blood which is destined to corruption, are incorruptibility, glory, and power. But there is a proper and due order to be observed ; the 'natural body'—the σῶμα ψυχικόν—comes first, the 'supernatural body' or σῶμα πνευματικόν comes second.[1] We cannot bear the image of the 'second Man'—Christ—who is 'from heaven,' until we have first borne the image of the first man—Adam—who was made of the dust of the ground. So far from there being a difficulty in the fact that certain Christians at Corinth have died, thereby sharing the lot of Adam, in whom (as S. Paul has already reminded his readers) 'all die,'[2] the real problem upon which further light is needed is the problem raised by the case of those who (as

---

[1] It is sometimes suggested that 1 Cor. 15 [46] is to be understood as a polemical allusion to a current speculation such as appears in Philo, who from the two accounts of the creation of man in Gen. 1 [27] and Gen. 2 [7] respectively infers a distinction between the 'heavenly' and the 'earthly' man, but who thinks naturally of the former as having been created first (so Lietzmann, *H.N.T.*, *ad loc.*, who compares Philo, *Legum allegor.* 1. 31, 49, and *De opif. mundi*, 134, 32 ; and J. Weiss, *Das Urchristentum*, pp. 375 *sq.*, who thinks that S. Paul reverses the order as between the 'heavenly' and the 'earthly' because he is thinking eschatologically, and it is as the 'last Adam,' not as the first, that the 'heavenly' Man is manifested *on earth*). I believe that the true exegesis of the passage depends upon recognizing that the expanded quotation from Gen. 2 [7] in 1 Cor. 15 [45] is a parenthesis which should be printed in brackets, and that verses 44, 46 should be read together as a continuous sentence, viz. : εἰ ἔστι σῶμα ψυχικόν, ἐστί καὶ πνευματικόν, ἀλλ' οὐ πρῶτον τὸ πνευματικόν, ἀλλὰ τὸ ψυχικόν· ἔπειτα τὸ πνευματικόν. The reference all through is to the antithesis between the 'natural' and the 'spiritual' *body*, not to the contrast between the 'earthly' and the 'heavenly' Man.

[2] 1 Cor. 15 [22].

I

S. Paul believes) will still be alive in their present mortal and perishable bodies at the time of the Parousia of the Lord. With regard to these S. Paul believes that he is in a position to make known to the Corinthians a μυστήριον or ' secret ' of God. They cannot, of course, enter the Kingdom of God as they are, but they will be miraculously ' changed ' —' in a moment, in the twinkling of an eye, at the last trump '; they will be transformed without passing through death.[1] In all this S. Paul shows himself to be both literal-minded in respect of his view of the resurrection, and at the same time characteristically Jewish.[2]

It is in the context of this general argument that S. Paul introduces, by way of scriptural ' proof,' a quotation from Genesis which has been made the theme of a good deal of discussion : ' So also it is written, the first man Adam became a living soul,' or (as it has been proposed to translate the words, with a slight correction of the text), ' So also it is written, Man—the first Adam—became a living soul.'[3] In their Old Testament context the words are meant to explain how it was that man, who according to the story was formed by God of the dust of the ground, became a living and animate being : it was because God had ' breathed into his nostrils the breath of life.'[4] S. Paul not only glosses ' man ' as ' the first Adam,' but he adds also the words ' the last Adam a life-giving Spirit '—an addition which he appears to treat as an integral part of the Old Testament quotation. The late Dr. Burney suggests that S. Paul may have been following a midrashic expansion of the text, already current in Christian circles, and ' drawn from a collection of O.T.

---

[1] Cf. Philipp. 3 [21].

[2] Jewish parallels of varying degrees of closeness to the thought of S. Paul are collected and considered by H. St. J. Thackeray (*The Relation of St. Paul to Contemporary Jewish Thought*, pp. 114 sqq.).

[3] Cf. Gen. 2 [7] (LXX). The suggestion that in the text of 1 Cor. 15 [45] we should read and punctuate ἐγένετο ὁ ἄνθρωπος—ὁ πρῶτος Ἀδὰμ—εἰς ψυχὴν ζῶσαν is due to Reitzenstein (*H.M.R.*, 2nd ed., p. 198).

[4] Gen. 2 [7a].

Testimonia, composed with the object of meeting Rabbinic Judaism upon its own ground.'[1] It is equally possible that S. Paul in rabbinical fashion is making his own *midrash* upon the text, that the idea of the 'life-giving spirit' was suggested to his mind by the reference in Genesis a sentence earlier to the 'breath of life' breathed by God into man's nostrils, and further that the ideas of the 'last Adam' and of the 'life-giving Spirit' appeared to him to be implicit by way of antithesis in the scriptural terms 'man' and 'living soul.' If this be so, then it follows that the phrase 'life-giving spirit' in I Corinthians was determined indirectly by the wording of the passage in Genesis, and ought not to be made the basis of an argument to the effect that S. Paul directly identified our Lord with the Spirit.[2] The true meaning of the expanded quotation from Genesis in its Pauline connexion is that as the first Adam is the source of the principle of life—that is to say, of the 'natural' life —in his descendants, so Christ, the 'last Adam,' is the source of the 'life-giving Spirit,' on whose presence and activity in believers S. Paul bases his assurance that they shall one day be clothed with the new 'spiritual' body.[3] The words in their context throw light, not directly upon S. Paul's conception of Christ, but upon his conception of the new life of the resurrection, and of the means by which God brings it about.[4] For S. Paul's conception of Christ we

---

[1] Burney, *The Aramaic Origin of the Fourth Gospel*, p. 46.

[2] On 2 Cor. 3 [17], see Lecture VI. p. 155, *n.* 6.

[3] The curious Greek expression ἐγένετο . . . εἰς ψυχὴν ζῶσαν, κ.τ.λ., is not easy to render in English. The words in their O.T. context describe of course how man, who is supposed to have been already formed out of dust, but who as yet was no more than a lifeless clay figure, 'came to be' (as a result of the inbreathing of the Divine breath) 'a living' (*i.e.* animate) 'soul.' In their Pauline context I think the most natural meaning of the words is the one suggested above, viz.: that men are indebted to Adam for the 'living soul' and to Christ for the 'life-giving Spirit' (*i.e.* the 'becoming' of Adam is 'with a view to the living soul,' that of Christ is 'with a view to the life-giving Spirit ').

[4] The best commentary is to be found in Rom. 8 [11]—' If the Spirit of

are thrown back upon the idea of the heavenly 'Man,' who is elsewhere identified with the divine 'image.'[1]

And this idea of the divine 'image' is very important for S. Paul's thought both about Christ and about man. In a curious passage which is concerned with the subject of dress, and from which we learn that there were Christian women at Corinth who had outraged contemporary notions of decency by appearing in the Christian assembly unveiled, S. Paul writes of man that he is the 'image *and glory*' of God, and of woman that she is the 'glory of man'—on the ground, as it would seem, that according to the story in Genesis the first woman was *derived from* the first man (though of course it is also true that man comes into existence 'through woman,' and that 'all things' in the last resort come into existence 'from God'[2]). The passage appears certainly to suggest that in the mind of S. Paul the idea of the divine 'image' was closely associated with the idea of the divine 'glory,' and further that just as the idea of an 'image' carried with it the idea of an original of which the 'image' was a copy, so also the conception of 'glory' carried with it the idea of derivation, as from a source. The Christ, therefore, who as the heavenly 'Man' was from the beginning of the Creation the 'image and glory' of God and at the same time the 'Son of His love,'[3] must be regarded both as deriving His being from God, and also as reflecting, like an 'image' seen in a mirror, the divine 'glory,' as Christians in turn are to reflect with unveiled face the 'glory' of the Lord Jesus.[4] S. Paul, in other words, if we have rightly interpreted his thought, has approximated with singular closeness to precisely that idea of a co-essential

---

Him that raised up Jesus from the dead dwelleth in you, He that raised up Christ Jesus from the dead shall quicken also your mortal bodies by His Spirit that dwelleth in you ' (reading διὰ του ἐνοικοῦντος αὐτοῦ Πνεύματος ἐν ὑμῖν).

[1] 2 Cor. 4 [4], Col. 1 [15].   [2] 1 Cor. 11 [7-12]; cf. Gen. 2 [21] *sq.*
[3] Col. 1 [13].   [4] 2 Cor. 3 [18].

yet derivative Godhead which for later Church orthodoxy was expressed by the doctrine of the eternal generation of the Son.

It appears, moreover, to be probable that it was the same identification of our Lord with the divine ' image ' and ' glory ' which served as the link in S. Paul's mind with yet a further Old Testament conception—that of the pre-existent personified ' Wisdom,' the ' master-workman ' of God in the creation of the world.[1]   In the *Book of Wisdom* (which was certainly read by S. Paul [2]) the Divine Wisdom is described both as ' a clear effluence ' of God's '*glory*' and also as an '*image*' of His ' goodness.' [3]   In the thinking of S. Paul's period the transition from the personal to what we should call the impersonal, and *vice versa*, was less difficult than we should find it to-day ; [4] abstract conceptions were readily personified, and conversely S. Paul is able (as it would seem, without being conscious of any difficulty) to identify Christ with what to our minds might appear to be an abstract conception or principle—the personified ' Wisdom ' of God.   The passage from *Wisdom*, with other passages from the Old Testament, became the basis for S. Paul of those elements in his Christology in which our Lord is conceived as having been in some sense the intermediary in creation, the divine principle of the created universe, the Christ in whom ' all things consist.' [5]

The consideration in detail of S. Paul's ' Wisdom ' Christology must be reserved for the next lecture.   I would draw attention, in conclusion, to-day to the light which I believe to be thrown by S. Paul's conception of our Lord

---

[1] Proverbs 8 [30].

[2] For S. Paul's dependence on *Wisdom*, see Thackeray, *The Relation of S. Paul to Contemporary Jewish Thought*, p. 223, where reference is made to the investigation of the subject by Grafe in *Theologische Abhandlungen C. von Weizsäcker . . . gewidmet* (Freiburg i. B., 1892).

[3] Wisdom 7 [25] *sqq.*

[4] Cf. J. Weiss, *Das Urchristentum*, p. 331.

[5] Col. 1 [17],

as the heavenly 'Man,' who from the beginning of the creation pre-exists as God's 'image and glory,' upon the great Christological passage in the Epistle to the Philippians.[1] S. Paul is in process of exhorting his readers to 'lowliness of mind,' and to this end he appeals to the example and 'mind' of our Lord Jesus Christ, of whom we have seen reason to believe that he habitually thinks as the new Man, the second 'Adam' from heaven. S. Paul elsewhere bids Christians be 'transformed by the renewing' of their 'mind'; [2] they are to live no longer according to the 'old man,' [3] for they have 'put on the new man, which is renewed after the image of him that created him.' [4] I am driven to suspect that this familiar antithesis between the 'old man' and the 'new' underlies what he writes to the Philippians The 'old man'—namely, Adam—was tempted by the Serpent, who suggested to Eve that the eating of the fruit of the magic tree would not really bring death, but would make man the equal of God : ' God doth know that in the day ye eat thereof, then your eyes shall be opened, and ye shall be as Gods.' [5] Of Adam that was true which S. Paul (without mentioning Adam) points out was *not* true of Christ, namely, that he ' counted equality with God as a prize at which to snatch.' [6] The 'mind' of the first Adam was the mind of self-deification ; the mind of the second Adam was the mind of humility and lowliness. Pre-existent as God's 'image' in the glory of the Father—or, as S. Paul here

---

[1] Philipp. 2 [5] *sqq.* [2] Rom. 12 [2].

[3] Rom. 6 [6], Col. 3 [9], Eph. 4 [22]. [4] Col. 3 [10] ; cf. Eph. 4 [24].

[5] Gen. 3 [5].

[6] This explanation of the difficult words οὐχ ἁρπαγμὸν ἡγήσατο τὸ εἶναι ἴσα θεῷ appears preferable to that of Dibelius, who in *H.N.T.*, 1st ed., *ad. loc.*, suggests an allusion by way of contrast to the pride of Satan, or to other legends in which spiritual or heavenly beings were supposed to have been envious of God. (In the 2nd ed. of *H.N.T.*, Dibelius abandons the idea of an antithetical allusion altogether, and reverts to the patristic view that the meaning is simply that our Lord did not regard His position of equality with God as a prize to be enjoyed : so also Lightfoot.)

expresses it, in God's ' form ' [1]—He had ' made Himself of
no account,' [2] and assumed deliberately a different ' form '
—the ' form ' of a ' servant ' or ' slave ' (δούλου) ; [3] He
had become ' like man ' (ἐν ὁμοιώματι ἀνθρώπων) [4] in the
ordinary sense, that is to say, in outward appearance or
' fashion ' (σχήματι) : He had stooped in lowly obedience
to death, even to the death of the Cross. ' Ye shall not
surely die,' said the Serpent ; [5] and the first Adam had
succumbed to the temptation. The second Adam, as the
climax of His lowliness and of His submission to the will
of God, was willing even to die ; and for that reason—
precisely on the ground of His submission to death—God
exalted, nay, more than exalted Him,[6] even to the point of
bestowing upon Him ' the name that is above every name,'
the Divine title of ' Lord.' It is in fact by means of a
worship in which Jesus is invoked by that title that the
prophecy of Isaiah is to be fulfilled,[7] and the whole universe
brought to acknowledge the One God of the Old Testament

---

[1] 'Εν μορφῇ θεοῦ is an expression found only here in the N.T., and the
phrase is a puzzling one. It is possible that S. Paul uses it for the sake
of rhetorical antithesis, since he goes on to speak of the μορφὴν δούλου as
being assumed by our Lord. Dibelius refers to Corp. Hermet. i. 14, in
which it is said that the Primal Man ' showed ' to ' Nature ' τὴν καλὴν τοῦ
θεοῦ μορφήν. It is worth noticing, however, that in Num. 12 [8] it is said
of Moses that he shall behold the ' form ' of the Lord, and that the LXX
in the passage in question paraphrases ' the form of the Lord ' by δοξὰν
Κυρίου. It seems possible that S. Paul, like the translators of the LXX
version, understood by the ' form ' of God the Divine δόξα or ' glory,' and
that he means that our Lord pre-existed in the ' glory ' of God.

[2] The R.V. rendering ' emptied himself ' translates ἐκένωσεν ἑαυτόν too
literally.

[3] Is there an allusion to the 'ebed Jahweh of Deutero-Isaiah ? Or is
δοῦλος the correlative of Κύριος ? Does S. Paul mean that our Lord was
given the position of a ' Lord ' because He had assumed the position of a
' slave ' ?

[4] As the Divine ' Glory ' appeared in the form of ' a likeness as the
appearance of a man ' to Ezekiel (Ezek. 1 [26], where the LXX has ὁμοίωμα
ὡς εἶδος ἀνθρώπου).

[5] Gen. 3 [4].   [6] ὁ θεὸς αὐτὸν ὑπερύψωσε (Philipp. 2 [9]).

[7] Is. 45 [23], a text which S. Paul apparently read in the form Ζῶ ἐγώ,
λέγει Κύριος, ὅτι ἐμοὶ κάμψει, κ.τ.λ. (Cf. Rom. 14 [11].)

Scriptures. Every knee is to bow, every tongue to confess Jesus as Lord, not as though there could be any rivalry between Jesus and God—that is to say, not to the prejudice of monotheism—but ' to the glory of God the Father.' It is thus that S. Paul vindicates the cult of the Lord Jesus, not as a pagan might vindicate it from the standpoint of polytheism, but as a Jew, from the standpoint of monotheism, and upon the basis of the Old Testament faith.

LECTURE VI

THE CONTRIBUTION OF S. PAUL—III

SYNOPSIS

THE eschatological hope and the belief in the renewal of the creation. Jewish pessimism with regard to the existing world-order. Creation as marred by sin, and by the consequent prevalence of death. The present ' Age ' as controlled by angelic ' principalities and powers ' who are regarded as being virtually evil. The heathen worship of the ' elements.' A Jewish theory of idolatry. The future judgment of the ' angels ' and the impending παλιγγενεσία or ' restoration of all things.'

The eschatological background of the coming redemption as conceived by S. Paul. The future ' redemption of our body.' The final judgement, and the subdual of ' principalities and powers.' Nevertheless, they are already defeated in principle—God has ' triumphed over them ' in Christ. They are from henceforth mere ἀσθενῆ καὶ πτωχὰ στοιχεῖα.

The Pauline doctrine of *present* salvation—' we *have* our redemption.' The forgiveness of sins as the primary marvel. The Divine paradox of the crucifixion of Jesus. The Pauline conception of Atonement. The Cross as the supreme manifestation of the Divine love towards sinners. The wide contrast between S. Paul's doctrine of salvation through Christ and the Hellenistic idea of an assurance of immortality and of deliverance from troubles as the semi-magical result of the initiation into the mysteries of a ' saved god.'

The doctrine of the new supernatural life. Its connection with Baptism and with the gift of the Spirit. The term ' regeneration ' not used by S. Paul. The new life in the Spirit. The Spirit for S. Paul is the source (a) of supernatural χαρίσματα of a quasi-miraculous kind, (b) of the ' fruit ' of a new type of character, and (c) of a new inward principle of life, destined ultimately to be manifested in ' glory ' at the coming of Christ.

S. Paul's ' Christ-mysticism,' his use of the phrases ' in the Spirit ' and ' in Christ,' and the relation of Christ to the Spirit. S. Paul's ' mysticism ' not to be exaggerated : it is in any case not individualistic, but bound up with the conception of membership in the Church as Christ's ' Body ' ; and the distinction between Christ and the believer is always maintained. Nor, again, does it appear likely that S. Paul either interprets the Spirit materialistically or identifies Christ with the Spirit. If he does not invariably discriminate precisely between the idea of the Spirit and the idea of the indwelling Christ, his real thought is that Christ indwells His Church through the Spirit. S. Paul's doctrine, if not always explicitly Trinitarian, is Trinitarian in tendency, and expresses those elements in the Christian experience of God which were to render a Trinitarian theology inevitable.

The doctrine of Christ and the renewal of the creation. S. Paul thinks of creation as being capable of being reconstituted in Christ, because he believes that it was in Christ that creation originally had its beginning. The Christology of Colossians—to be understood as being essentially a ' Wisdom ' Christology, and as having been based by S. Paul upon Scripture. The late Dr. Burney and the doctrine of Christ as the ' Firstborn.' S. Paul's doctrine of the ' fulness of Godhead ' as dwelling in Christ.

LECTURE VI

THE CONTRIBUTION OF S. PAUL—III

Giving thanks unto the Father, who made us meet to be partakers of the inheritance of the saints in light; who delivered us
out of the power of darkness, and translated us into the Kingdom
of the Son of his love: in whom we have our redemption, the
forgiveness of our sins: who is the image of the invisible God,
the firstborn of all creation: for in him were all things created
. . . and in him all things consist . . . who is the beginning, the
firstborn from the dead.—Col. 1 [12-18].

Wherefore if any man is in Christ, there is a new creation: the
old things are passed away; behold, they are become new.

2 Cor. 5 [17] (R.V., mg.).

THE belief in a renewal of the creation of God was bound
up with the Jewish eschatological hope. The Jew of
S. Paul's day may be said virtually to have shared, though
on different grounds, the prevailing Greek pessimism with
regard to the existing world-order. The world that now is
was a world 'full of sadness and infirmities,' fast hastening to
pass away.[1] S. Paul's statement in the second Epistle to
the Corinthians that ' the things that are seen are but for
a time ($\pi\rho\acute{o}\sigma\kappa\alpha\iota\rho\alpha$), the things that are not seen are eternal,' [2]
was no utterance of Greek philosophy, but a conviction
derived from the Jewish apocalyptic tradition.[3] The present
' age ' was predominantly evil. The good creation of God [4]
had been marred by the entry of sin, and by the prevalence
of death, which according to Jewish belief was the penalty
of sin.[5] The very ground had been cursed for man's sake,[6]

[1] 2 Esdras 4 [26] sq.   [2] 2 Cor. 4 [18].
[3] Cf. 2 Baruch 44 [8-11], 51 [8].
[4] Gen. 1 [31].
[5] Rom. 5 [12].
[6] Gen. 3 [17].

and the creation 'subjected to vanity.'[1] The created universe had been delivered over to ' the bondage of corruption,' so that S. Paul can write that ' the whole creation groaneth and travaileth in pain together until now.'[2] Or again, it was taught that the world was comparable to a woman who had grown old, and was past the strength of her youth.[3] ' The youth of the world is past,' we read in the *Apocalypse of Baruch*, ' and the strength of the creation is already exhausted.'[4]

It was, moreover, among the beliefs of late Judaism—at least in the more pessimistic of its moods—that the control of the universe had for the period of this present ' age ' been entrusted by God to subordinate agencies—angels, ' principalities,' spirits of the ' elements,' ' thrones,' ' dominions ' and ' powers '[5]—a vast complicated hierarchy of supernatural existences who, though created by God and subject ultimately to His judgement, are by no means regarded as being predominantly good.[6] On the contrary, it was believed that very much that was amiss in the existing state of the universe was to be assigned to the sin of the angels as to its ultimate cause, that the ' world-rulers '[7] had virtually set themselves up in opposition or rivalry to God, and that there were ' spiritual agencies of wickedness in the regions of the heavens.'[8] It was a Jewish theory of idolatry that the heathen had mistaken God's subordinates for God—as, for example, in the case of the current pagan

---

[1] Rom. 8 20.

[2] Rom. 8 22.

[3] 2 Esdras 5 55.

[4] 2 *Baruch* 85 10.

[5] 1 Cor. 15 24 ; Rom. 8 38 ; Col. 1 16, 2 10, 15 ; Eph. 1 21, 3 10, 6 12.

[6] On the whole subject, see H. St. J. Thackeray, *The Relation of St. Paul to Contemporary Jewish Thought*, pp. 142 *sqq.* : W. Bousset, *Die Religion des Judentums*, 2nd ed., pp. 368 *sqq.*; M. Dibelius, *Die Geisterwelt im Glauben des Paulus, passim.*

[7] Eph. 6 12 ; cf. 1 Cor. 2 6.

[8] τὰ πνευματικὰ τῆς πονηρίας ἐν τοῖς ἐπουρανίοις. (Eph. 6 12.)

worship of the 'elements.'[1] As the writer of the *Book of Wisdom* expressed it,

> 'From the good things that are seen they gained not power to know him that is,
> Neither by giving heed to the works did they recognize the artificer :
> But either fire, or wind, or swift air,
> Or circling stars, or raging waters, or luminaries of heaven,
> They thought to be gods that rule the world.'[2]

According to Judaism, the beings thus worshipped by the heathen, and by them thought to be 'gods that rule the world,' were in reality angels : there were angels of the 'elements,' of the 'circling stars,' and of the 'luminaries of heaven,' as there were angels of the hoar-frost and of the snow,[3] of the heights and of the depths,[4] of the firmament,[5] and of the various nations of mankind ;[6] and both as being thus, from the point of view of Judaism, the real objects of the mistaken worship of the heathen, and also as being the 'rulers' of the existing evil world-'age,'[7] the 'principalities and powers' who were responsible for the existing order— or disorder—of the universe tended to be regarded as being evil. If the Gentiles practised idolatry, it was either because evil angels had led them astray,[8] or because they had been tempted to idolatry by demons ;[9] and the things which the Gentiles sacrificed, they sacrificed to demons and not to God ;[10] the 'principalities and powers,' if not actually identical with the 'demons' in question,[11] were at least in

---

[1] Gal. 4[9]; Col. 2[8].   [2] Wisdom 13[1] *sq.*   [3] *Eth. Enoch* 60[17] *sq.*

[4] 2 *Baruch* 54[3] ; cf. Rom. 8[39].   [5] 2 Esdras 6[41].

[6] Deut. 32[8] (LXX) ; Dan. 10[13, 20] ; Ecclus. 17[17].

[7] 1 Cor. 2[6].   [8] *Eth. Enoch* 19[1].

[9] *Jubil.* 11[4], 19[28].   [10] 1 Cor. 10[20] ; Deut. 32[17] (LXX).

[11] The 'demons,' who instigate to idolatry, and who actually benefit by the sacrifices of the heathen, are perhaps to be distinguished both from the 'dumb idols' (1 Cor. 12[2]) and from the 'gods many and lords many' (1 Cor. 8[5]) of heathenism. The heathen sacrifices are intended for these latter by their offerers, but in practice they are intercepted and enjoyed by the 'demons' (so Dibelius, *op. cit.* pp. 67 *sqq.*).

extremely bad company. Or again, it was explained that the present afflictions and adversities of the people of God and the sufferings endured by the righteous, were the result of the misuse of their powers by the ' world-rulers ' to whom God had entrusted the temporary government of His world.[1]

Upon all these beings there was destined eventually to be a judgement, even 'the great eternal judgement' wherein God would 'execute vengeance amongst the angels '; [2] and it would seem from a passage in the first Epistle to the Corinthians that it was concluded from the Book of Daniel that in this judgement of the angels, as in the judgement of the world generally,[3] the 'saints' should be granted the privilege of taking part.[4] At the same time the existing ' Age ' should be brought to an end, and the existing 'creation' should pass away. ' The first heaven shall depart and pass away, and a new heaven shall appear.' [5] It was ordinarily taught that there should be not only new heavens, but a new earth.[6] ' The Mighty One' would 'renew his creation.' [7] There should be a παλιγγενεσία—a new Beginning [8]—a 'restoration of

---

[1] Cf. *Eth. Enoch* 89 ⁶¹ *sqq.*   [2] *Eth. Enoch* 91 ¹⁵.

[3] 1 Cor. 6 ²; cf. Wisdom 3 ⁸.   [4] 1 Cor. 6 ³.   [5] *Eth. Enoch* 91 ¹⁶.

[6] Is. 65 ¹⁷, 66 ²²; 2 Pet. 3 ¹³ ; Rev. 21 ¹.   [7] *Apoc. Baruch* 32 ⁶.

[8] The word παλιγγενεσία was used by the Stoics of the periodical renewal (ἀποκατάστασις) of the world-order, which according to their theory supervened upon its periodical ἐκπύρωσις or destruction by fire: cf. Philo, *De incorr. mundi*, 14, οἵ τε τὰς ἐκπυρώσεις καὶ τὰς παλιγγενεσίας εἰσηγούμενοι τοῦ κόσμου : M. Antonin. *Ad semet ipsum*, xi. 1, τὴν περιοδικὴν παλιγγενεσίαν τῶν ὅλων. It is used further by Philo of the life after death (*De legat. ad Caium*, 41: *De cherub.* 32), and of the recovery of the world after the Flood (*De vita Moys.* ii. 12) ; by Cicero of his restoration from exile (*Ad Att.* vi. 6) ; and by Josephus of the recovery which followed the return of the Jewish exiles from Babylon (*Antiq.* xi. 3, 9). Liddell and Scott refer also to Plutarch and Clem. Alex. as having used it in connexion with the idea of the transmigration of souls. The word means properly *not* ' new birth ' but ' new beginning ' or ' renewal.' It is used in Mt. 19 ²⁸ as the nearest Greek equivalent for the Hebrew idea of the renewal of the creation: and it is not improbable that the same idea underlies the phrase ' bath of renewal ' (λουτρὸν παλιγγενεσίας) in Tit. 3 ⁵, the renewal of human nature in Baptism being regarded as part and parcel of the general process of the

all things,' [1] as at the first. ' Behold, I make the last things like the first things, saith the Lord.' [2] The creation should be restored to its original perfection and glory, as in the day when ' God saw everything that he had made, and behold, it was very good.' [3] Meanwhile it was taught that the ' age to come' was not destined to be subjected to angels [4]—that the authority and power of the ' world-rulers ' was limited to the present evil world-' age.' The ' world-rulers,' in the vigorous phrase of S. Paul, were essentially ' rulers of this age,' who were ' coming to nought.' [5]

It was this characteristically Jewish world-outlook, with its sharply-defined eschatological dualism, and its doctrine of the renewal of the creation of God, which provided the intellectual background of S. Paul's doctrine of Christian redemption.   There is a sense in which, for S. Paul as for the earliest disciples, salvation, in the full and proper meaning of the word, was regarded as being still in the future.   S. Paul can write that ' by hope were we saved : but hope that is seen is not hope : for who hopeth for that which he seeth ? But if we hope for that which we see not, then do we with patience wait for it.' [6] In what is not improbably the

renewal by God of His creation.   There is no evidence that the word was ever used in a sacramental sense in any form of pagan religion : on the other hand, it is used in Libellus xiii. of the *Corpus Hermeticum* to denote the effect of illumination by *gnosis*.   It is not likely that *Corp. Hermet.* xiii. is of early date : the date suggested by Scott is towards the end of the 3rd century A.D.   The writer may have derived the term παλιγγενεσία from the vocabulary of Stoicism, or from general Greek usage : but it is at least equally possible that he derived it from Christianity, and that he is in effect deliberately opposing a doctrine of ' renewal' by *gnosis* to what he understood to be the sacramental theology of the Church.   Presumably he would have said to his Christian acquaintances that what men needed was not Christian baptism with water, but (in the phrase of an earlier Hermetic writer) to ' dip themselves in the bath of Mind ' (cf. *Corp. Hermet.* iv. 4).

[1] Acts 3 21.

[2] ἰδού, ποιῶ τὰ ἔσχατα ὡς τὰ πρῶτα.   The words are quoted, with an introductory ' Λέγει δὲ Κύριος,' in the Epistle of Barnabas (*Ep. Barn.* 6 13) : the source from which ' Barnabas ' derived them is unknown.

[3] Gen. 1 31.   [4] Hebr. 2 5.   [5] 1 Cor. 2 6.   [6] Rom. 8 24 *sq.*

earliest of his extant writings—the first Epistle to the Thessalonians—S. Paul describes his converts as those who have ' turned unto God from idols, to serve a living and true God, and to wait for his Son from heaven ' :[1] but the thought is in no way confined to his earliest writings ; it recurs in the Epistle to the Philippians—a 'captivity' Epistle [2]—in which S. Paul writes that ' our citizenship is in heaven : from whence also we wait for a Saviour, the Lord Jesus Christ : who shall fashion anew the body of our humiliation, that it may be conformed to the body of his glory, according to the working whereby he is able even to subdue all things unto himself.'[3] Salvation in this full sense, as involving what S. Paul calls ' the redemption of our body '[4] (by which he means the transformation of our present bodies of flesh and blood into the likeness of the glorified ' spiritual ' body of the risen and exalted Saviour), can be consummated only at the Parousia or ' Coming ' of the Lord : an event which is to S. Paul's mind the object of eager hope and of ' earnest expectation ' on the part of the whole ' creation,' which in its present state of subjection to ' vanity ' looks forward with groaning and travail-pangs to the day which shall witness the final ' revealing ' or ' manifestation ' of the sons of God.[5] In the meantime ' we that are in this tabernacle do groan, being burdened ' ;[6] for the ' spirit of adoption ' which we have ' received '[7] does not mean that we have entered upon our inheritance ; on the contrary, we are still ' waiting for our adoption.'[8] The ' good work ' which God ' began ' in us has yet to be

---

[1] 1 Thess. 1 [9] *sq.* It is perhaps the most generally accepted view that 1 Thessalonians is the earliest in date of the Pauline Epistles ; but the theory that 2 Thessalonians was written earlier has also found advocates, and there are some scholars who think that Galatians was actually the earliest Epistle.

[2] Philipp. 1 [13].

[3] Philipp. 3 [20] *sq.*

[4] Rom. 8 [23].

[5] Rom. 8 [19] *sqq.*

[6] 2 Cor. 5 [4] ; cf. Wisdom 9 [15].

[7] Rom. 8 [15].

[8] Rom. 8 [23].

perfected 'until the day of Jesus Christ.'[1] The work of redemption has not yet been fully accomplished : the triumph of the Lord Jesus is not yet fully made complete. The final Judgement—'the day of wrath and revelation of the righteous judgement of God'[2]—remains still in the future ; the concluding act of the great world-drama has yet to take place ; and there are 'enemies' still to be subdued, of whom 'the last enemy that shall be abolished is Death'[3]—it is possible that S. Paul, who here personifies Death as a kind of demon, would have agreed in the last resort with the writer to the Hebrews in thinking rather of 'him that had the power of death, that is, the devil.'[4]

A final reckoning, moreover, has still to be made with the various types of angelic 'rule and authority and power,'[5] for the 'world-rulers of this darkness' are still active—there is need for the Christian to 'put on the panoply of God' for his 'wrestling' against them, bearing in mind that these are antagonists more formidable than mere 'flesh and blood.'[6] Nevertheless, it is to be remembered that they are in principle already defeated—that God has 'triumphed over them in Christ, made a show of them openly, and despoiled them.'[7] They had failed to understand the Divine 'wisdom,' and in their ignorance 'crucified the Lord of glory.'[8] In so doing they had made, from their own

---

[1] Philipp. 1 [6].

[2] Rom. 2 [5] : cf. 1 Thess. 1 [10].

[3] 1 Cor. 15 [26].

[4] Heb. 2 [14].   [5] 1 Cor. 15 [24].

[6] Eph. 6 [12]—the Epistle to the Ephesians, whether actually Pauline or not, is sufficiently in S. Paul's vein to be quoted in this connexion.

[7] Col. 2 [14] *sq.* I assume (*a*) that the subject of the sentence is 'God,' (*b*) that ἀπεκδυσάμενος means 'having despoiled,' and not 'having stripped off from himself,' and (*c*) that ἐν αὐτῷ means 'in Christ.'

[8] 1 Cor. 2 [7] *sqq.* It was a theory of later Gnosticism that the ἄρχοντες failed to recognize our Lord because He had come to earth in disguise : thus in the (2nd century ?) work known as the *Ascension of Isaiah*, the Redeemer, in order to escape recognition in the course of His descent to earth through the various successive 'heavens,' assimilates His outward appearance to that of the dwellers in each region in turn as He passes through.

point of view, a most fatal mistake, for the crucifixion of Jesus had signalized the beginning of their downfall, and of the final victory of God. The 'world-rulers' are from henceforth mere ἀσθενῆ καὶ πτωχὰ στοιχεῖα—'weak and beggarly elements' [1]—bereft of their power, and under sentence of doom. They must submit and be reconciled to their lot, for it was God's good pleasure through Jesus 'to reconcile all things unto himself.' [2] There can be no exceptions to the recognition of His lordship, which is to be acknowledged by the dwellers in the heavens, as by the dwellers on earth and the dwellers under the earth.[3] He is destined to 'reign, till he hath put all his enemies under his feet'; [4] and in the meantime S. Paul is 'persuaded that neither death, nor life, nor angels, nor principalities, nor things present, nor things to come, nor powers, nor height, nor depth, nor any other creature,' shall be able to separate Christians from the love of God, which is in Christ Jesus their Lord.[5]

For S. Paul, despite his futurist outlook, proclaims none the less emphatically the doctrine of a *present* salvation in Christ. He can write of the Father, 'who delivered us out of the power of darkness, and translated us into the Kingdom of the Son of his love.' [6] He can write that in Christ 'we *have* our redemption, the forgiveness of our sins,' [7] that we have 'received the reconciliation,' [8] that we

---

Dibelius and Bousset assume, surely gratuitously, that a similar myth of the descent of the Redeemer *incognito* through a succession of heavens is presupposed by S. Paul (so Dibelius, *Die Geisterwelt im Glauben des Paulus*, pp. 92 *sqq.*, and Bousset, *Hauptprobleme der Gnosis*, p. 242).

[1] Gal. 4 [9]. I assume the identity of the στοιχεῖα with the ἄρχοντες του αἰῶνος τούτου of 1 Cor. 2 [6]. It would seem further that in Gal. 4 [1] *sqq.* the angels of the Law are to all intents and purposes equated practically with the στοιχεῖα τοῦ κόσμου—presumably on the ground that the Law, as having been an essentially temporary provision for the discipline and training of the people of God until the coming of the Messiah, belongs by its very nature to this present 'Age,' which is under the στοιχεῖα.

[2] Col. 1 [20].　　[3] Philipp. 2 [10].　　[4] 1 Cor. 15 [25].

[5] Rom. 8 [38] *sq.*　[6] Col. 1 [13].　　[7] Col. 1 [14].　　[8] Rom. 5 [11].

'were bought with a price,'[1] that 'God was in Christ reconciling the world unto himself.'[2]   Despite the fact that 'redemption' for S. Paul is a wider term than 'forgiveness'[3] —for he thinks of our Lord as the Deliverer not merely from sin, but from death and corruption,[4] from creaturely weakness and misery,[5] from the 'curse' of the Law,[6] and from all that is involved in the idea of 'this present evil world-age'[7]—it is none the less clear that forgiveness is the primary marvel, in which everything else is in a manner comprised. As S. Paul himself expresses it, 'He that spared not his own Son, but delivered him up for us all, how shall he not also with him freely give us all things?'[8] S. Paul cannot adequately do justice to the miracle of the Divine Love in Christ Jesus   In some moods he can regard the whole Gospel as being summed up in 'the word of the Cross.'[9] It is the perpetual ground of his glorying,[10] the central burden of that which he ironically describes as the 'foolishness' of the Christian 'preaching.'[11] The Divine paradox of a crucified Messiah, which to S. Paul in the days before his conversion had presumably constituted the essential blasphemy of Christianity, has become for him the very kernel of his message.

S. Paul was not in the proclamation of this Gospel a pioneer : he describes the conviction that 'Christ died for our sins according to the Scriptures' as being part of the tradition which he had 'received.'[12] We have seen reason to think that the Church very early interpreted the mystery of our Lord's death in the light of the passages referring to the

---

[1] I Cor. 6 20, 7 23.   [2] 2 Cor. 5 19.

[3] 'Die Erlösung ist nach Paulus, kurz und doch genau gesagt, Erlösung von dieser ganzen gegenwärtigen Welt. Jede andere Fassung, etwa Erlösung von der Sünde, wäre schliesslich zu eng' (Wrede, Paulus, 2nd ed., p. 56).

[4] Rom. 8 21.   [5] Rom. 7 24 sq.
[6] Gal. 3 13.   [7] Gal. 1 4.
[8] Rom. 8 32.   [9] I Cor. 1 18.
[10] Gal. 6 14.   [11] I Cor. 1 21.
[12] I Cor. 15 3.

Servant of the Lord in the second part of the Book of Isaiah.[1]
It is very remarkable that S. Paul in his extant epistles has
barely an allusion to this conception,[2] though it is no doubt
probable that for him, as for others, the ' Scriptures ' in
accordance with which our Lord died ' for our sins '[3] may
have included the passages in question. It would seem,
however, that S. Paul normally preferred to dwell less upon
the description in Old Testament prophecy of the sufferings
endured by God's innocent Servant than upon the love which
had been manifested in the willing acceptance of death on
behalf of mankind by God's Son. It is probable that the
thought of the Passion as being before all things a manifestation of the Divine Love towards sinners was more
vividly and personally realized by S. Paul, who had once
been an ' enemy,'[4] than it was by the original Apostles,
who had been our Lord's ' friends.'[5] It has been noticed
that S. Paul is unique among Apostolic writers in specifically
applying the idea of our Lord's self-oblation on behalf of
mankind to himself as an individual—' He loved *me*, and
gave himself up for *me*.'[6]

A full discussion of S. Paul's doctrine of the Atonement
cannot here be attempted. It is a difficult doctrine, and
one which is to a large extent worked out—like much else
in S. Paul—in terms of ideas and conceptions which are
foreign to the mind of to-day. For example, S. Paul seems
to regard our Lord's death as being in some sense the
voluntary acceptance on behalf of mankind of a penalty
due to the demands of the personified Law. The Law had
enjoined death as the penalty of sin, and the penalty had
not been in the full sense enforced. ' Because of the passing

---

[1] Lecture II. p. 45.

[2] Unless μορφὴν δούλου λαβών in Philipp. 2 [7] is to be taken as such (see
Lecture V. p. 135), the only probable allusion to Is. 53 in S. Paul is Rom. 4 [25].

[3] 1 Cor. 15 [3] has, however, ὑπὲρ τῶν ἀμαρτιῶν ἡμῶν as against διὰ τὰς
ἀμαρτίας ἡμῶν in the LXX of Is. 53 [5].

[4] Cf. Rom. 5 [10].　　　　[5] Lk. 12 [4]; Jn. 15 [14] *sq*.　　　　[6] Gal. 2 [20].

over of the sins done aforetime, in the forbearance of God,'
God must now ' shew his righteousness,' which He had done
by ' setting forth ' Jesus Christ as a ' propitiation.'[1] It is
easy to rebel against such a conception, but on the other
hand it is foolish to complain of a first-century writer on
the ground that his mind is not modern. It is far more
profitable to recognize that the real core of S. Paul's doctrine
of Atonement, as distinguished from its particular forms,
is to be found in the principle that in relation to God man can
be only a recipient, not a giver,[2] and must be content to
have that done for him which he is unable to do for himself.
Thus, if it is a question of ' righteousness,' man, who is
impotent to make himself ' righteous,' must be content to
receive ' righteousness ' as a free gift from God.[3] If it is a
question of ' justification ' or ' acquittal,' God alone can
' acquit ' the ungodly [4]—the sinner can never *merit* acquittal,
and his forgiveness must be the free act of the mercy of God.
If it is a question of satisfaction, regarded as being due to
the claims of the Law, God alone can provide the satisfaction
in question—and God has done so, at infinite cost.[5] If (as
contemporary religion, both Jewish and pagan, assumed)
there was need of propitiation and sacrifice for sin, it was the
peculiar paradox of the Gospel that ' propitiation ' was the
concern, not of man, but of God.[6] S. Paul's main doctrine
of the Passion, is, in fact, simply to the effect that it is an
amazing act of the Divine Love. Christ died for us ; [7] God

---

[1] Rom. 3 [25].

[2] Cf. Wrede, *Paulus*, 2nd ed., p. 76 : ' *Das eigentlich Religiöse in der
Religion . . . ist der Gedanke, dass der Mensch Gott gegenüber ganz der Empfan-
gende, Gott allein der Gebende ist.*'

[3] Rom. 1 [17].   [4] Rom. 3 [24].

[5] Gal. 3 [13], 4 [5].

[6] Rom. 3 [25]. Deissmann, who points out that the word ἱλαστήριον
occurs in Greek inscriptions of the Imperial period in the sense of ' a pro-
pitiatory gift,' a ' votive-offering,' would have us understand Rom. 3 [25]
as meaning that ' the crucified Christ is the votive-gift of the Divine Love
for the salvation of men ' (Deissmann, *Bible Studies*, E.T., pp. 124 *sqq.*).

[7] Rom. 5 [6].

sent His own Son in the likeness of the flesh of sin, and as a sin-offering.[1] 'There is therefore now no condemnation to them that are in Christ Jesus.' [2]

Despite all superficial analogies, it would be difficult to imagine a doctrine more really remote than this Pauline conception of Atonement from the Hellenistic idea of an assurance of immortality and of deliverance from troubles as the semi-magical result of initiation into the mysteries of a 'saved god.' [3] It is true that (if a quotation from the Pastoral Epistles may be allowed) S. Paul can think and write of the Lord Jesus as having 'abolished death, and brought life and immortality to light through the Gospel,' [4] but his main emphasis does not lie here. What is central for S. Paul is the doctrine that ' Jesus our Lord . . . was delivered up for our sins, and was raised for our justification.' [5] His Gospel is concerned with the thought of the love and of the redemptive activity of God ; the death of Christ is a sacrifice freely offered for sinners by One who is sinless, and S. Paul believes that ' God was in Christ reconciling the world unto Himself.' [6] There are no pagan analogies to such an idea. In Reitzenstein's words, ' the tremendous emphasis upon the preaching of sin and atonement is lacking in Hellenism,' and the Christian Gospel of the forgiveness of sins is essentially ' new.' [7]

[1] Rom. 8 [3] : the phrase περὶ ἁμαρτίας is used in the LXX as a Greek rendering of the Hebrew word for a ' sin-offering ' (e.g. Lev. 16 [5]).

[2] Rom. 8 [1].

[3] Cf. the fragment quoted (from the Attis ritual ?) by Firmicus Maternus (De err. prof. relig. 23) :

Θαρρεῖτε μύσται τοῦ Θεοῦ σεσωσμένου.
ἔσται γὰρ ὑμῖν ἐκ πόνων σωτηρία.

The Christian Redeemer is not regarded by Christians as being ' saved. He is the Saviour of others, at cost to Himself (cf. Mk. 15 [31]).

[4] 2 Tim. 1 [10]. The Pastoral Epistles are doubtfully Pauline.

[5] Rom. 4 [24] sq.

[6] 2 Cor. 5 [19].

[7] Dass diese Erlösung . . . zunächst eine Vergebung der Sünden ist, scheint mir das Neue. Der furchtbare Ernst der Predigt von der Schuld und Versöhnung fehlt, soweit ich sehe, dem Hellenismus (Reitzenstein, Poimandres, p. 180 n.).

The correlative of forgiveness, which looks towards the past, and has reference to 'the passing over of the sins done aforetime,'[1] is the doctrine of the new supernatural life. The new life is primarily a fact of experience. S. Paul has seen men's lives changed.[2] He has known very ordinary sinners enabled by the power of the Spirit to bring forth the fruits of a type of character which was manifestly Christlike,[3] and which in relation to the standards of the corrupt pagan life of the period was manifestly new. S. Paul regards the new life as being mediated by Baptism and membership of the Church [4]—of course, upon the basis of faith [5]—in connexion with which the Spirit was bestowed. He can describe Christian Baptism, by a somewhat violent metaphor, as a 'putting on' of Christ,[6] or as a 'growing together' into organic unity with Him.[7] It is interesting to notice that he does not use the metaphor of regeneration, for which parallels can be quoted from the language of the Mysteries,[8] and which became naturalized in the vocabulary of the

---

Cf. also Schweitzer, who points out that if we are to use language accurately, the so-called 'redeemer-gods' of the Mysteries have no title to be so described, since in no pagan mystery-cult does it appear to have been taught that a Divine Being so loved mankind as to come into the world and to consent freely to die for man's sake (Schweitzer, *Paul and his Interpreters*, E.T., p. 193; and see Appended Note VI. pp. 270 *sqq.*).

[1] Rom. 3 25.

[2] Cf. especially 1 Cor. 6 9-11.

[3] The description of the 'fruit of the Spirit' in Gal. 5 22 should be carefully compared with the portrait of our Lord's human character as reflected in the Gospels.

[4] 1 Cor. 12 13.   [5] Gal. 3 2.   [6] Gal. 3 27.

[7] σύμφυτοι γεγόναμεν (Rom. 6 5).

[8] Cf. Apuleius, *Metamorph.* xi. 21: '*quodam modo renatos*'; Sallustius, Περὶ Θεῶν καὶ Κόσμου, iv. : 'Then comes the cutting of the tree and the fast . . . after that the feeding on milk, *as though we were being born again* (ὥσπερ ἀναγεννωμένων)' : the reference in Apuleius is to the Isis cult, in Sallustius to the cult of Attis. See further Tertullian, *De bapt.* v. : '*certe ludis Apollinaribus et Eleusiniis tinguuntur idque se in regenerationem et impunitatem periuriorum suorum agere praesumunt.*' There is late inscriptional evidence (not earlier, apparently, than the 4th century A.D.) for the use of the formula *renatus in aeternum* in connexion with the ceremony of the *taurobolium*. On the word παλιγγενεσία see the note *supra*, pp. 144 *sq.*

Church before the end of the New Testament period as a term vividly descriptive of the significance of the new life.[1] S. Paul prefers to speak rather of a new creation,[2] of being buried with Christ [3] and 'raised together' with Him,[4] of being dead to sin and alive unto God,[5] of being no longer 'in the flesh,' but 'in the Spirit.' [6]

It would appear that, if modern exegesis is right,[7] S. Paul conceives of the new life imparted by the Spirit extremely literally : that he thinks of the Spirit not simply as the source of supernatural χαρίσματα or 'gifts' of an apparently miraculous kind,[8] or again of those graces of Christian character, supreme among which is charity, which to S. Paul's mind are 'more excellent' and no less supernatural than they,[9] but as the source also of an actual, though hidden, supernatural life, which is the inward principle of the new manhood : a life which, concealed for the present beneath the outward integument of the mortal and perishable body, is destined hereafter to be manifested in visible glory at the Parousia of the Lord. 'Wherefore,' writes S. Paul, ' we faint not ; nay, though our outward man is decaying, yet our inward man is renewed day by day. For our light affliction, which is for the moment, worketh for us more and more exceedingly an eternal weight of glory.' [10] ' Ye died,' he writes, ' and your life is hid with Christ in God. When Christ, who is our life, shall be manifested, then shall ye

---

[1] Cf. 1 Pet. 1 ³, 2 ² ; Jn. 3 ³ sqq. ; James 1 ¹⁸.

[2] 2 Cor. 5 ¹⁷ ; Gal. 6 ¹⁵.

[3] Rom. 6 ⁴.

[4] Col. 3 ¹.

[5] Rom. 6 ¹¹.

[6] Rom. 8 ⁹. There is, of course, an obvious and literal sense in which Christians are still for the time being ' in the flesh,' as S. Paul recognizes (Gal. 2 ²⁰).

[7] Cf. (e.g.) Gunkel, Die Wirkungen des heiligen Geistes, pp. 85 sqq.; J. Weiss, Das Urchristentum, pp. 405 sqq.

[8] 1 Cor. 12 ¹ sqq.

[9] 1 Cor. 12 ³¹ sqq.

[10] 2 Cor. 4 ¹⁶ sq.

also with him be manifested in glory.'[1]   Or again : ' But if the Spirit of him that raised up Jesus from the dead dwelleth in you, he that raised up Christ Jesus from the dead shall quicken also your mortal bodies through his Spirit that dwelleth in you.'[2]   For the Spirit, according to the thought of S. Paul, is ' the Spirit of life,' in a sense which is opposed not merely to sin, but to death : [3] and the possession of the Spirit is already an ' earnest '[4] of the future inheritance of the saints.

A great deal of discussion has been lavished in modern times upon what it has become customary to describe as S. Paul's ' Christ-mysticism,' as well as upon the two closely-related problems of the precise meaning of the Pauline formula ' in Christ,' and of the exact relation, in S. Paul's system of thought and belief, of the exalted Christ to the Holy Spirit.[5]   On the ground partly of a misunderstanding of a passage in the second Epistle to the Corinthians,[6] but still more on the ground that in S. Paul's uses of them the phrases ' in Christ ' and ' in the Spirit ' are to a large extent parallel, and that the same functions in relation to the spiritual life of believers can be ascribed with apparent

---

[1] Col. 3 [3] sq.

[2] Rom. [8] [11].

[3] Rom. 8 [2].

[4] Eph. 1 [14]; 2 Cor. 1 [22], 5 [5].

[5] For what follows, cf. especially Deissmann, *Die neutestamentliche Formel ' in Christo Jesu,'* and the same writer's *St. Paul* (E.T.), pp. 125 *sqq.* ; W. Bousset, *Kyrios Christos,* 2nd ed., pp. 110 *sqq.* ; J. Weiss, *Das Urchristentum,* pp. 355 *sqq.* ; W. Morgan, *The Religion and Theology of Paul,* pp. 24 *sqq.* ; H. J. Holtzmann, *Lehrbuch der neutestamentlichen Theologie,* ii. pp. 79 *sqq.* ; T. Rees, *The Holy Spirit,* pp. 100 *sqq.*   But the literature of the subject is enormous.

[6] In 2 Cor. 3 [16] *sq.,* verse 16 is a reference (in part paraphrase and in part free quotation) to Ex. 34 [34] ; verse 17 is S. Paul's comment, and means ' Now ὁ Κύριος, in the passage which I have just quoted, denotes the Spirit : and where the Spirit of the Lord is, there is liberty.' So the majority of the Greek Fathers interpret the passage (see the references in Lebreton, *Les Origines du Dogme de la Trinité,* p. 567, *n.* 2) ; and it is difficult to regard any other interpretation as doing anything but violence to the context.

indifference either to the Spirit or to Christ,[1] it has been maintained that in the theology of S. Paul the exalted Christ and the Holy Spirit, notwithstanding the occurrence of passages in which they are distinguished,[2] are essentially identical. It has been maintained, further, that the preposition ' in ' in such phrases as ' in Christ ' and ' in the Spirit,' must be understood in a sense rigidly literal and local :[3] that the Spirit-Christ is conceived as a kind of quasi-material atmosphere or fluid [4]—Christians, according to this view, are in a quite literal sense ' in ' Christ, as conversely Christ,[5] or the Spirit,[6] can be regarded as being ' in ' them : in the words of Johannes Weiss, ' the clear outlines of the form of the heavenly Lord fade away, and he is merged in the element of the spirit which envelops and flows into all Christians.'[7] According to Bousset, we have here the beginnings of a ' Christ-mysticism,' or doctrine of the mystical indwelling of the faithful in Christ, and of Christ in them, out of which at a later stage there was destined to be developed a corresponding ' God-mysticism,' such as makes its appearance for the first time in Christian literature in certain passages of the Fourth Gospel, and in the first Epistle of S. John.[8]

[1] Thus Deissmann compares Gal. 3 [26] etc. with 1 Cor. 12 [9] ; 2 Cor. 5 [21] etc. with Rom. 14 [17] ; Gal. 2 [17] with 1 Cor. 6 [11] ; 1 Cor. 1 [30] etc. with Rom. 8 [9] ; Philipp. 4 [1] etc. with Philipp. 1 [27] ; Philipp. 3 [1] etc. with Rom. 14 [17] ; Rom. 6 [23] with 1 Cor. 12 [9] ; Rom. 8 [39] etc. with Col. 1 [8] ; Philipp. 4 [7] with Rom. 14 [17] ; 1 Cor. 1 [2] with Rom. 15 [16] ; Eph. 1 [13] etc. with Eph. 4 [30] ; 2 Cor. 2 [17] etc. with 1 Cor. 12 [3] ; Col. 2 [10] with Eph. 5 [18] ; Rom. 12 [5] with 1 Cor 12 [13] ; Eph. 2 [21] with Eph. 2 [22] (Deissmann, *St. Paul*, E.T., pp. 126 *sq.*).

[2] Cf. Rom. 8 [10] *sq.*, 15 [16, 30] ; 1 Cor. 6 [11], 12 [3] ; 2 Cor. 1 [21] *sq.* ; Eph. 1 [17]; 2 Cor. 13 [14], 1 Cor. 12 [4-6] ; 2 Thess. 2 [13].

[3] Deissmann, *Die neutestamentliche Formel ' in Christo Jesu,'* pp. 81 *sqq.*

[4] For the theory of the materiality of the Spirit see especially Gunkel, *Die Wirkungen des heiligen Geistes*, pp. 43 *sqq.*

[5] Gal. 2 [20] ; Rom. 8 [10] ; Col. 1 [27].

[6] Rom. 8 [9] ; 1 Cor. 3 [16], 6 [19].

[7] J. Weiss, *Christ : the Beginnings of Dogma*, E.T., pp. 92 *sq.*

[8] Jn. 14 [23], 17 [21] *sqq.* ; 1 Jn. 4 [16] ; Bousset, *Kyrios Christos*, 2nd ed., pp. 113 *sqq.*, 177 *sqq.*

With regard to this latter point, something no doubt turns upon what precisely is to be understood by the term 'mysticism.' There is a sense in which such expressions as 'Christ in you, the hope of glory,' [1] or 'I live ; and yet no longer I, but Christ liveth in me,' [2] may be described as being mystical phrases, and it is certainly an important element in S. Paul's teaching that Christ indwells His Church through the Spirit in such a fashion that believers, in virtue of their common participation in the Spirit, are knit together into one body, [3] which, because Christ is at once its Lord and its Head, [4] can be described as being 'the body of Christ.' [5] Nevertheless, I am disposed to believe with Johannes Weiss that there has been a tendency of late to overestimate the extent to which S. Paul may be rightly described as a mystic. [6] The parallels quoted by Bousset from the *Corpus Hermeticum* and other sources are not strictly parallel, as Bousset himself is constrained to admit. [7] For one thing, S. Paul's mysticism is not individualistic—the proper correlate of Christ, as Bousset remarks, is strictly speaking not the individual believer, but the whole body of believers, that is, the Church. [8] For another thing, the distinction between believers and Christ is invariably maintained : S. Paul can use the language of mutual indwelling : he never uses the language of pantheistic absorption. He has no

[1] Col. 1 [27].   [2] Gal. 2 [20].
[3] Rom. 12 [4] *sqq.* ; 1 Cor. 12 [12] *sqq.* ; Eph. 4 [4].
[4] Col. 1 [18].
[5] I am disposed still to adhere to the suggestion put forward by Dr. R. G. Parsons and myself in *Foundations* (pp. 184 *sq.*) to the effect that the origin of this very remarkable phrase, as applied to the Church, is not impossibly to be found in the use of the same phrase in connexion with the Eucharist (cf. 1 Cor. 10 [17]).
[6] J. Weiss, *Das Urchristentum*, pp. 359 *sqq.*
[7] *Es unterliegt nun keinem Zweifel, dass Paulus, mit seiner Formel des ἐν Χριστῷ εἶναι eine diesen Auschauungen gegenüber singuläre Stellung annimmt* (Bousset, *Kyrios Christos*, 2nd ed., p. 115).
[8] *Als das eigentliche Korrelat zu Christus erscheint bei dem Apostel streng genommen nicht der einzelne Gläubige, sondern die Gemeinde, das σῶμα Χριστοῦ* (Bousset, *op. cit.* p. 116).

sooner written the words, ' I live ; and yet no longer I, but Christ liveth in me,' than he proceeds to qualify and interpret their meaning—' the life which I now live in the flesh I live in faith, the faith which is in the Son of God, who loved me.' [1] He remains true to what German writers call the ' I and thou ' type of religion : his *ego* is never merged in the *ego* of Christ.[2]

So again I am unable to convince myself that S. Paul ever really identifies Christ with the Spirit, any more than that he interprets the Spirit materialistically. The Spirit, in the theology of S. Paul, is not the quasi-material *anima mundi* of the Stoics, but the Biblical ' spirit which is from God.' [3] The fundamental idea is that of the Spirit of God as set forth in the Old Testament, more particularly as the Spirit destined to be ' poured out ' in the ' last days,' [4] the ' Holy Spirit of promise,' [5] whereby believers are ' sealed unto the day of redemption.' [6] At the same time, inasmuch as it was in virtue of the new filial relationship to God which was established in Christ and made effectual through Baptism into His Name [7] that the Spirit, in the sense in which the Spirit was the distinctive endowment of Christians, was bestowed, it was possible in a secondary sense to regard Christ Himself as the bestower of the Spirit, and to speak of the Spirit as being not only ' the Spirit of God ' but ' the Spirit of Christ ' ; [8] or again, the Spirit can be described by S. Paul as ' the Spirit of God's Son,' ' sent forth ' by God into men's ' hearts,' whereby they are enabled to cry ' Abba,

---

[1] Gal. 2 [20].

[2] J. Weiss, *Das Urchristentum*, p. 361.

[3] Τὸ πνεῦμα τὸ ἐκ τοῦ Θεοῦ (1 Cor. 2 [12]). Canon Lacey goes so far as to suggest the idea of a deliberate allusion by way of contrast to the Stoic conception in the words ἡμεῖς δὲ οὐ τὸ πνεῦμα τοῦ κόσμου ἐλάβομεν, which immediately precede those just quoted (T. A. Lacey, *The One Body and the One Spirit*, pp. 62, 244).

[4] Acts 2 [16] *sqq.* ; Joel 2 [28].

[5] Eph. 1 [13].

[6] Eph. 4 [30].

[7] 1 Cor. 6 [11].

[8] Rom. 8 [9].

Father.' [1] Recalling to the Corinthians the significance of their baptism, S. Paul can write that ' in one Spirit were we all baptized into one body, whether Jews or Greeks, whether bond or free : and were all made to drink of one Spirit,' [2] but it is clear that these last words are to be understood as being simply a strong, vivid metaphor ; it would be absurd to infer from them that S. Paul thinks of the Spirit as being literally or semi-literally a fluid! On the contrary, the Spirit for S. Paul is essentially active, creative, life-giving ; the sustaining, animating principle of the new life in Christ Jesus : the helper of human infirmity, who inspires Christian prayers, and who can be regarded as Himself making intercession for the saints. [3] S. Paul can speak of ' the mind of the Spirit, [4] as he can speak elsewhere of Christians as ' having the mind of Christ.' [5] If he is not invariably careful to discriminate precisely between the idea of the Spirit and the idea of the indwelling Christ, it is, I believe, much truer to maintain that he regards the one as being the medium of the other than that he identifies the two. The risen Christ indwells His Church through the Spirit—that is S. Paul's real thought. The Spirit, as it were, actualizes in the hearts of believers and in the fellowship of the Christian Society the presence of Christ, who, except in so far as He is thus operative in the Church through the Spirit, is regarded as being ' seated on the right hand of God.' [6] If S. Paul's language is not always explicitly Trinitarian—and it would be absurd to expect to find in his writings a technical statement of the doctrine of the Trinity—his theology is nevertheless in a general sense Trinitarian in tendency, and in the passage in which he writes of ' the grace of the Lord Jesus Christ and the love of God and the fellowship of the Holy Spirit ' [7] he has given classical expression to precisely those

[1] Gal. 4 [6] ; cf. Rom. 8 [15].   [2] 1 Cor. 12 [13].   [3] Rom. 8 [26] sqq.
[4] Rom. 8 [6, 27].   [5] 1 Cor. 2 [16].
[6] Col. 3 [1].   [7] 2 Cor. 13 [14].

elements in the Christian experience of God which were in the long run to render a Trinitarian theology inevitable.[1]

I referred at the beginning of this lecture to the doctrine of the future renewal of the creation. If I return to it in closing, it is in order to point out that if there is a sense in which for S. Paul the creation is still ' subjected to vanity,' [2] there is a sense also in which the renewal of the creation of God has already begun. It began with the resurrection of Christ, who is ' the beginning, the firstborn from the dead.' [3] It is continued in Christians, who in Christ are made new— ' if any man is in Christ, there is a new creation : the old things are passed away : behold, they are become new.' [4] It is destined to be consummated in Christ, in whom it is God's good pleasure ' to sum up all things,' [5] ' that in all things he might have the pre-eminence.' [6]

It would, moreover, appear that S. Paul is thus able to think of the creation as being destined, according to the

---

[1] It will be clear from the foregoing discussion that I regard as untenable the theory of Deissmann that the preposition ' in,' in such phrases as ' in Christ Jesus,' ' in Christ,' ' in the Lord,' ' in the Spirit,' etc., is to be interpreted with literal-minded rigidity in a uniformly local and quasi-mystical sense. For a valuable note criticizing Deissmann and discriminating a variety of different meanings in which S. Paul makes use of the expression ' in Christ,' see J. Weiss, *Das Urchristentum*, pp. 359 *sqq.* According to Deissmann's calculation (which excludes from consideration not only the Pastoral Epistles but also the Epistles to the Ephesians and Colossians), the formula ' in Christ' with its cognates occurs 164 times in the writings of S. Paul. Despite Deissmann's opinion, it appears probable that it was not coined by S. Paul, but was already in current use in the Church. It is perhaps idle to speculate as to its original meaning. It can be used quasi-mystically, or more conventionally to denote simply the fact of being a Christian, of having been ' baptized into Christ ' and become a member of the Messianic Community. Or again, it can be used as the antithesis of being merely ' in Adam.' The phrase ' in the Spirit' should be interpreted differently. It denotes (at least in some cases) the condition of being *possessed* or *inspired* by the Spirit (so especially of the φανέρωσις or ' manifestation ' of the Spirit in the more ecstatic types of χαρίσματα referred to in 1 Cor. 12).

[2] Rom. 8 [20].
[3] Col. 1 [16].
[4] 2 Cor. 5 [17] (R.V., marg.).
[5] Eph. 1 [10].
[6] Col. 1 [18].

purpose of God, to be renewed, summed up afresh, and reconstituted in Christ, for the reason that he believes that it was in Christ that the creation originally had its beginning. He can write of the ' one Lord Jesus Christ, through whom are all things, and we through him.' [1] He can write of the ' Son of God's love,' in whom ' we have our redemption,' that He is ' the image of the invisible God, the firstborn of all creation : for in him were all things created, in the heavens and upon the earth, things visible and things invisible, whether thrones or dominions or principalities or powers : all things have been created through him and unto him : and he is before all things, and in him all things consist.' [2] It is clear that S. Paul here thinks of our Lord as being not only the ' image ' or derivative reflection, the manifested counterpart, or in Lightfoot's phrase the ' visible manifestation,' of the invisible God : he thinks of Him also as standing in relation to the creation of God as the ' firstborn ' who is at the same time the first principle of all things, the archetype of the created universe, the intermediary of God in creation, the source, goal and sustainer of the world as created.

Analogies have been sought for this very remarkable conception of Christ both in the Logos doctrine of Philo [3]

---

[1] 1 Cor. 8 [6].   [2] Col. 1 [13] sqq.

[3] ' Hier steht nun Christus genau an der Stelle, an der . . . bei Philo der Logos steht ' (J. Weiss, Das Urchristentum, p. 369).   Philo's Logos, from one point of view equivalent, in Bishop Lightfoot's phrase, to ' the Divine mind energizing,' is from another point of view a mediating principle between God and the world, identified by Philo both with the ' archetypal seal,' impressed by God on the created universe, and also with the κόσμος νοητός wherein are contained, already implicit as a rational system, the ' ideas ' which in the creation of the world are actualized (cf. Philo, De opif. mundi, 5 : εἰ δέ τις ἐθελήσειε γυμνοτέροις χρήσασθαι τοῖς ὀνόμασιν, οὐδὲν ἂν ἕτερον εἴποι τὸν νοητὸν εἶναι κόσμον ἢ Θεοῦ Λόγον ἤδη κοσμοποιοῦντος . . . Δῆλον δ'ότι καὶ ἡ ἀρχέτυπος σφραγὶς ὃν φάμεν εἶναι κόσμον νοητὸν αὐτὸς ἂν εἴη τὸ ἀρχέτυπον παράδειγμα, ἰδέα τῶν ἰδεῶν, ὁ Θεοῦ Λόγος).   The statement in Col. 1 [16] that ' in him were all things created ' appears to mean similarly that the creation of all things was implicit in the bringing into existence of the ' firstborn,' who stands uniquely related both to the created universe and to God.   It is idle to ask whether S. Paul thinks of our Lord Himself as being in the last resort a ' creature '

and in the world-soul or world-Reason of Stoicism.[1] It
has been pointed out that the affinities of the phrase ' in
him all things consist ' are with the vocabulary of current
philosophy rather than with that of the Septuagint.[2] The
type of doxology represented by such phrases as ' of him and
through him and unto him are all things ' [3] as applied either
to Christ or to God [4] has been shown to have been not
original in Christianity, but adapted—perhaps mediately
through Greek-speaking Judaism [5]—from the already existing use by Stoic writers of the same type of phraseology to
express what, according to their system, was conceived to be

of God, or as having had a beginning in time. That was an issue which
was destined to be raised at a later date by the Arians. S. Paul thinks as a
Jew, to whom it does not occur to ask what happened before the ' beginning.' He could have spoken of our Lord as having been ' begotten of the
Father before all worlds ' ; beyond that he does not go.

[1] According to Stoic doctrine the Universe was a living being (ζῷον)
informed by Reason as by a kind of soul : cf. Diog. Laert. vii. 138 : τὸν
δὴ κόσμον διοικεῖθαι κατὰ νοῦν καὶ πρόνοιαν—εἰς ἅπαν αὐτοῦ μέρος διήκοντος τοῦ νοῦ,
καθάπερ ἐφ᾿ ἡμῶν τῆς ψυχῆς ; Cicero, *Academ.* ii. 37 : *hunc mundum esse
sapientem, habere mentem, quae se et ipsum fabricata sit et omnia moderetur,
moveat, regat* ; and Verg. *Aen.* vi. 724 *sqq.* :

> *Principio caelum et terras camposque liquentes
> lucentemque globum lunae Titaniaque astra
> spiritus intus alit, totamque infusa per artus
> mens agitat molem et magno se corpore miscet.*

[2] ' Πάντα ἐν αὐτῷ συνέστηκε. *Cette expression appartient à la langue
philosophique beaucoup plus qu'à la langue biblique* ' (Lebreton, *Les Origines
du Dogme de la Trinité*, p. 369, *n.* 2). J. Weiss quotes from the anonymous
work Περὶ Κόσμου (ch. 6), ἀρχαῖος μὲν οὖν τις λόγος καὶ πάτριος πᾶσιν
ἀνθρώποις, ὡς ἐκ θεοῦ πάντα καὶ διὰ θεοῦ ἡμῖν συνέστηκεν : from Pap. Par.
f. 20 pp. 1748 *sqq.*, ἐξ οὗ τὰ πάντα συνέστηκεν : and from Pap. Leid. ii.
32 *sq.*, διὰ σὲ συνέστηκεν ὁ πόλος καὶ ἡ γῆ (J. Weiss, *Das Urchristentum*,
pp. 369 *sq.*). The nearest parallel in the LXX appears to be *Ecclus.* 43 [26],
which has ἐν λόγῳ αὐτοῦ συγκεῖται πάντα.

[3] Rom. 11 [36].

[4] In Rom. 11 [36] the formula is applied wholly to God ; in Col. 1 [16] *sq.*
it is applied wholly to Christ ; in 1 Cor. 8 [6] it is divided between Christ
and the Father.

[5] So Norden, who quotes with approval a remark of Harnack's with
reference to S. Paul, viz. : ' *nichts Hellenisches hat er sich anzueignen
versucht, was nicht bereits Anknüpfungspunkte in der ihm vertrauten religiösen
und theologischen Überlieferung besass* ' (Harnack, *Sitzungsber. d. Berl.
Akad.*, 1911, p. 162, quoted by Norden in *Agnostos Theos*, p. 244, *n.* 1).

the relation of the universe, regarded as a whole, to the Divine Reason.[1]

Nevertheless, it would appear that here also the foundations of S. Paul's doctrine are Jewish. It has been pointed out by the late Dr. Burney, in an article posthumously published in the *Journal of Theological Studies*,[2] that the conception of Christ in the Epistle to the Colossians as the ' firstborn ' or first-begotten of creation can be directly derived from the Old Testament on the basis of the identification of Christ, as the ' image ' of God, with the Divine Wisdom, described in the *Book of Wisdom* as God's ' image,' [3] and in the Book of Proverbs as having been ' begotten ' by God ' as the beginning of His way, the antecedent of His works, of old.' [4] It has been pointed out further by Burney that the remainder of the passage quoted from Colossians, not excluding the use made of the prepositional phrases ' in him ' and ' through him ' and ' unto him,' could have been derived, by a *tour de force* of the kind of rabbinical exegesis in which S. Paul had been trained, from the first word of the first chapter of the Book of Genesis—the word which in our English versions is translated ' in the beginning '— interpreted in the light of the conception of Christ as the ' beginning ' of creation, and expounded in all the various conceivable meanings which the expression in Hebrew might be taken to bear.[5] It appears to be probable that if S. Paul has adapted and applied to our Lord, whether consciously or (as upon the whole is more likely) unconsciously, a type

---

[1] E. Norden, *Eine stoische Doxologie bei Paulus. Geschichte einer Allmachtsformel*, in *Agnostos Theos*, pp. 240 sqq.

[2] C. F. Burney, *Christ as the APXH of Creation*, in the *Journal of Theological Studies*, vol. xxvii. pp. 160 sqq.

[3] Or, more strictly, as ' an image of his goodness ' (Wisdom 7 [26]).

[4] I adopt Dr. Burney's revised translation of Prov. 8 [22].

[5] Col. 1 [15-18] is according to Burney an elaborate exposition of the various possible meanings of the word *Bĕrêshîth* in the Hebrew text of Gen. 1 [1]. ' Three explanations are given of the preposition *bĕ* ; then four explanations of the substantive *rêshîth* : and the conclusion is that, in every possible

of formula which was current in Stoicism, it was because he believed himself to be able to justify his use of it from Scripture. ' We speak,' he writes elsewhere, ' God's wisdom in a mystery, even the wisdom that hath been hidden . . . which things also we speak, not in words which man's wisdom teacheth, but which the Spirit teacheth.' [1] S. Paul could have written in like terms to the Colossians, and I submit that the hypothesis of his conscious dependence upon what he would doubtless himself have described as the ' wisdom of this world ' is unthinkable.

S. Paul was arguing, in his letter to the Colossians, against certain false teachers, whom he describes as attempting to ' make spoil of ' his converts by means of a ' philosophy and vain deceit ' which was ' not after Christ.' [2] It seems probable that the false teachers in question were disposed to place Christ upon a level with other mediating beings as together with them making up the Divine *pleroma* or ' fulness.' S. Paul will have none of such doctrine. He will tolerate no rival to Christ. He asserts confidently that in Him dwells the entire ' fulness ' of Godhead σωματικῶς—a rare word which is perhaps best translated ' in concrete actuality.' [3] S. Paul believes the entire ' fulness ' and plenitude of the Divine Being to reside concretely embodied in Christ, because he believes that it is God's good pleasure ' that in Him

---

sense of the expression, Christ is its Fulfiller. . . . Putting the argument in tabular form for the sake of lucidity, it appears as follows :—

Prov. 8 [22] *sqq.*, where Wisdom (i.e. Christ) is called *rêshîth*, gives the key to Gen. 1 [1], " *Běrêshîth* God created the heavens and the earth."

Běrêshîth = " in *rêshîth* "—ἐν αὐτῷ ἐκτίσθη τὰ πάντα, κ.τ.λ.
Běrêshîth = " by *rêshîth* "—πάντα δι' αὐτοῦ ἔκτισται.
Běrêshîth = " into *rêshîth* "—πάντα εἰς αὐτὸν ἔκτισται.
Rêshîth = " Beginning "—αὐτός ἐστι πρὸ πάντων.
Rêshîth = " Sum-total "—τὰ πάντα ἐν αὐτῷ συνέστηκε.
Rêshîth = " Head "—αὐτός ἐστιν ἡ κεφαλὴ τοῦ σώματος, κ.τ.λ.
Rêshîth = " First-fruits "—ὅς ἐστιν ἀρχή, πρωτότοκος ἐκ τῶν νεκρῶν.
Conclusion : Christ fulfils every meaning which may be extracted from Rêshîth—ἵνα γένηται ἐν πᾶσιν αὐτὸς πρωτεύων.' (C. F. Burney, *loc. cit.*)

[1] 1 Cor. 2 [7, 13].   [2] Col. 2 [8].   [3] Col. 2 [9].

should all the fulness dwell.'[1] He believes that Christ
is the absolute Mediator, in whom the entire 'fulness'
dwells, but on the other hand that the Being of Christ, and
the plenitude of Godhead which He shares, is derivative
from the Being and from the Godhead of the Father, who
has bestowed His own attributes, rank, and Divine plenitude of Being upon the Son.

[1] Col. 1 [19].

LECTURE VII

MEDIATOR, HIGH PRIEST, LIVING ONE

SYNOPSIS

THE Pastoral Epistles in their canonical form are probably later than the time of S. Paul. They exhibit a tendency, more marked than in the writings of the authentic S. Paul, to exploit in the interests of the Christian propaganda the religious terminology of Hellenism. The terms σωτήρ, ἐπιφάνεια, φιλανθρωπία—their Hellenistic associations, and their deepened meaning in Christianity. The Christian ' Saviour ' contrasted with pagan ' saviours.'

The redactor of the Pastorals a traditionalist, who belongs to the second generation of Christianity. His doctrine of God and of Christ. His emphasis upon the reality of our Lord's manhood.

The Epistle to the Hebrews, of unknown authorship, addressed probably not to ' Hebrews ' but to Christians of Greek culture, perhaps at Rome, who were personally known to the writer. The recipients of the letter more probably of Gentile than of Jewish extraction, but assumed to be amenable to an argument drawn from the Old Testament. They are warned against apostasy from ' the living God.' They have not grasped the full meaning of Christianity as the ' absolute ' religion. The argument presupposes the relative worth of the Old Testament revelation, in order to exhibit its fulfilment (and supersession) in Christianity. The writer does for the Old Testament Law as a system of worship what S. Paul had done for the Law as a system of ordinances governing every-day life.

The writer interprets religion primarily as *worship*. In Christianity worship is perfected on a basis of reality, as against the shadows and types of the Old Testament. The Platonic strain in the writer's thought—he combines the doctrine of the two Ages with a doctrine of two Worlds. Judaism was of this Age and of this Cosmos—essentially temporal and transient : Christianity is not of this world ; it is essentially eternal.

The writer's doctrine of *faith* as a conviction of unseen realities, an insight into the eternal world of real worship. In that world Christ as the eternal Priest eternally offers the one true sacrifice, which is ' the sacrifice of Himself.' With some incongruity of imagery He is conceived both as being seated in majesty as King and as perpetually ministering as High Priest. The writer would suggest at once the finality of His sacrifice and its eternal character and efficacy.

169

Modern criticism of the writer's doctrine on the ground that he is still enmeshed in Old Testament conceptions, and that he believes in the necessity of sacrifice and mediation and in the mysterious potency of blood. But the writer himself provides at least the beginnings of a rationalization of the idea of sacrifice—it is ultimately the offering of a dedicated life in obedience to the will of God—and it is not depth but shallowness of spiritual insight which can see no appropriateness in the idea ot a Mediator on behalf of sinners. The influence of the Epistle to the Hebrews on Christian eucharistic theology and on the language of Christian worship.

The Christology of the Epistle in the narrower sense. The writer conceives of Jesus as ' Lord,' ' Son of Man ' and ' Son of God,' as the Mediator of creation, and as the ' Image ' of God's Being. It is implied that he may rightly be addressed as ' God.' He is superior to Moses and to the angels, but in His life on earth He was made ' lower than the angels ' and was emphatically human. In combining a ' Wisdom ' Christology with a strong emphasis upon the human life of Jesus the writer anticipates the Fourth Gospel.

The writer of the Apocalypse—a Christian prophet and seer who thinks in pictures and who in a time of persecution and impending tribulation sets forth the triumph of Christ over evil in a riot of imagery and symbolism. Rome as the ' woman drunken with the blood of the saints.' The legend of the returning Nero—who is identified with the Antichrist. Christ as the Divine Warrior whose name is ' the Word of God '—the first occurrence of the title ' Word ' in Christian literature.

The Christology of the book is otherwise expressed in a variety of terms and images. The special significance of the designation of Christ as ' the Lamb.' The Lamb, who alone can open the sealed Book of the Future, is adored by the heavenly host.

LECTURE VII

MEDIATOR, HIGH PRIEST, LIVING ONE

For there is one God, one mediator also between God and man, himself man, Christ Jesus.—1 Tim. 2 [5].

Named of God an high priest after the order of Melchizedek.
Hebr. 5 [10].

I am the first and the last, and the Living One.—Rev. 1 [17] *sq*.

THE two Epistles to Timothy and the Epistle to Titus, conventionally grouped together under the title of the Pastoral Epistles, are regarded by the majority of critical scholars as being, in their present form, not directly the work of S. Paul, though it is believed that they may in places incorporate fragments of letters which were actually written by him. From the point of view of Christology they exhibit a tendency, more strongly developed than in the undoubtedly Pauline Epistles, to exploit, in the interests of the missionary propaganda of the Gospel, the religious terminology of Hellenism. The term σωτήρ or Saviour, prominent later in Gnosticism as well as in the orthodox writing of the Church, is used once by S. Paul in a passage in the Epistle to the Philippians, in which in an eschatological context he speaks of our Lord as the Deliverer or Saviour for whom Christians wait.[1] In the Pastorals the title is more frequent. It is used both of Christ [2] and of God.[3] It is combined with the characteristically Greek term ' epiphany ' in connexion both with the original manifestation or ' epiphany ' of Christ and with the hope of His future return. We read of the ' grace which was given us in Christ Jesus before times eternal,

---

[1] Philipp. 3 [20] ; cf. also Eph. 5 [23].
[2] 2 Tim. 1 [10], Tit. 1 [4], 2 [13], 3 [6].
[3] Tit. 1 [3], 3 [4].

but hath now been manifested by the " epiphany " of our Saviour Christ Jesus, who abolished death, and brought life and incorruption to light through the Gospel.' [1] We read, in a remarkable verse which it is difficult to think could have been written by S. Paul, of the 'blessed hope and "epiphany" of the glory of our great God and Saviour Jesus Christ ' [2]— a description of our Lord which has been variously interpreted, and which is no doubt capable of being reconciled with orthodoxy,[3] but which it is tempting to regard as having been in the first instance Hellenistic and popular ; there must have been many Greek converts for whom our Lord was thus simply the ' great God and Saviour ' of Christians. The writer further makes use, in connexion with the idea of the ' epiphany ' of our Saviour, of the term φιλανθρωπία to describe the Divine attitude towards mankind as displayed in Christ Jesus [4]—God has shown himself to be ' kindly,' that is to say ' benignantly disposed,' towards men.

It is impossible in reading such passages to avoid being reminded of current Greek usage. The term φιλάνθρωπος was applied to such deities as Asklepios the Healer, acknowledged gratefully, on the basis of benefits received, as being a ' lover of men.' The title σωτήρ was applied equally to Asklepios, as being the ' deliverer ' of men from disease, and to the deified Emperors, as being the ' saviours ' of society from the miseries of misgovernment and strife. The term ' epiphany ' was used regularly to denote the appearance or manifestation of a divine being upon earth.

At the same time, it is clear that the writer of the Pastorals,

---

[1] 2 Tim. 1 [9] sq.   [2] Tit. 2 [13].

[3] Thus, it has been proposed either to translate ' the " epiphany " of the glory of our great God and of our Saviour Jesus Christ ' (a very unnatural rendering of the Greek), or (with Hort, Parry, and Gore) to regard ' glory ' as a Christological term, and to understand the words as meaning ' the " epiphany " of Him who is the Glory of our great God and Saviour, viz. : Jesus Christ.'   [4] Tit. 3 [4].

if he has taken over certain terms from the usage of Hellenism, has deepened their meaning. The divine or deified 'saviours' of Hellenism were the helpers of men in the distresses and troubles of life here upon earth, the bestowers of such temporal blessings as physical health, settled order and peace —it is of interest, for example, to observe that the title ' saviour ' was not commonly borne in the period of the New Testament by the gods of the mysteries, whose religion was concerned with the hope of the life after death.[1] The salvation mediated by Christ was of a different order, at once super-earthly and spiritual. It was concerned, in so far as it had its beginning here and now upon earth, with deliverance, not from outward and temporal afflictions—on the contrary, it is 'through many tribulations' that men must ' enter into the Kingdom of God '[2]—but from sin and estrangement from God. It was destined to be consummated hereafter in life everlasting. So again in like manner the ' kindness of God our Saviour, and his love toward man,' which had ' appeared ' in Christ Jesus,[3] were not *in pari materia*, despite the existence of ' gifts of healings ' and ' workings of miracles ' in the Church [4] and the healing miracles ascribed to our Lord, with the type of benefits for which men had been wont to give thanks to the Greek god of healing ; and the ' epiphany ' of Jesus the Saviour was conceived as being no mere casual theophany, but the manifestation in actual ' flesh '[5] of the one true ' mediator between God and men, himself man, Christ Jesus, who gave himself a ransom for all,'[6] and who could be described—in

---

[1] ' *Wenn Bousset, Kyrios Christos, 295, " zum Beweise dafür, dass Mysteriengötter auch in früherer Zeit den Titel σωτήρ erhalten haben," eine Inschrift aus der Zeit des Ptolemaeos IV. anführt Σαράπιδι καὶ Ἴσιδι Σωτῆρσιν, so ist in keiner Weise erweisbar, dass diese Götter hier als Mysteriengötter angerufen werden und dass der Beiname etwas anderes bedeutet als bei so zahlreichen anderen Götter, die ihn auch erhalten* ' (E. Meyer, *Ursprung und Anfänge des Christentums*, iii. p. 393 *n*.).

[2] Acts 14 [22].　　　　[3] Tit. 3 [4].　　　　[4] 1 Cor. 12 [9] *sq.*
[5] 1 Tim. 3 [16].　　　　[6] 1 Tim. 2 [5] *sq.*

words quoted, perhaps, from some early liturgical hymn—
as having been ' justified in the spirit, seen of angels, preached
among the nations, believed on in the world,' and ' received
up in glory.' [1]

The impression which upon the whole is created by the
Pastoral Epistles is to the effect that the writer—or, at
least, the redactor—belongs not to the first but to the second
generation of Christians, for whom Christianity is already a
traditional faith. There is a ' deposit ' to be guarded,[2] a
' pattern of sound words ' to be jealously maintained and
preserved.[3] There are ' faithful sayings ' which are already
proverbial.[4] There is not only a hierarchy of Church
officers,[5] but an organized order of Christian ' widows.' [6]
There are ' heretics ' also,[7] who can be described as having
' made shipwreck concerning the faith ' [8]—we hear of ' endless genealogies,' [9] and of ' oppositions of the knowledge
which is falsely so called,' [10] and are reminded of certain
of the tenets of second-century Gnosticism. The mind,
moreover, of the writer is that of the typical traditionalist.
He believes in meeting false teaching, not with argument,
but with ' admonition,' [11] apart from which he is content to
fall back simply upon the reaffirmation of the orthodox belief.

Nevertheless, there are fine things in the Pastorals. The
writer has the gift of being able to formulate clearly and
impressively the ' sound doctrine ' [12] of which he is so ardent
a champion. He can write of God that He is ' the living
God,' [13] one only,[14] who is ' the Saviour of all men, especially
of them that believe,' [15] the ' blessed and only Potentate, the
King of kings, and Lord of lords ; who only hath immortality,

---

[1] 1 Tim. 3 [16].
[2] 1 Tim. 6 [20] (R.V., mg.) ; 2 Tim. 1 [14].   [3] 2 Tim. 1 [13] ; cf. 2 Tim. 3 [14].
[4] 1 Tim. 1 [15], 3 [1], 4 [9] ; 2 Tim. 2 [11] ; Tit. 3 [8].
[5] 1 Tim. 3 [1] *sqq.* ; Tit. 1 [5] *sqq.*
[6] 1 Tim. 5 [3] *sqq.*   [7] Tit. 3 [10].   [8] 1 Tim. 1 [19].
[9] 1 Tim. 1 [4] ; Tit. 3 [9].   [10] 1 Tim. 6 [20].   [11] Tit. 3 [10].
[12] ἡ ὑγιαίνουσα διδασκαλία (1 Tim. 1 [10] ; 2 Tim. 4 [3] ; Tit. 1 [9], 2 [1]).
[13] 1 Tim. 4 [10].   [14] 1 Tim. 1 [17].   [15] 1 Tim. 4 [10].

dwelling in light unapproachable ; whom no man hath seen, nor can see.'[1] If he can write of Christ as ' our great God and Saviour,' or—according to another but less probable interpretation—' the Glory of the great God who is our Saviour,'[2] he has at the same time a firm grasp upon the historical reality of His manhood. He lays emphasis upon the fact that the ' one mediator between God and men ' is Himself also ' man,'[3] ' of the seed of David,'[4] the Messiah who ' before Pontius Pilate witnessed the good confession,'[5] and who ' gave himself a ransom for all.'[6] He believes that ' Christ Jesus came into the world to save sinners,'[7] and he is sure that the ' doctrine which is according to godliness '[8] is also ' the good doctrine,'[9] that to be a Christian is to ' war the good warfare,'[10] and that the ' house of God, which is the Church of the living God,' is ' the pillar and ground of the truth.'[11] If there is little that is new in the theology of the Pastoral Epistles, they at least bear witness to the existence in the second generation of Christians of a type of Christianity, sane, sober and quietly confident, which looked still for the hope of the Saviour's appearing,[12] but which in the meantime was content to hold fast the tradition ;[13] a Christianity in contact with Hellenism, but still not radically hellenized ; in conflict with heresy, and developing Church order and discipline, but proclaiming still the free mercy of God towards sinners, and the Divine will for the salvation of all men ;[14] ready if need be to suffer hardship in the service of Christ ;[15] and believing the ' end of the charge ' which had been committed to the Church to be ' love out of a pure heart and a good conscience and faith unfeigned.'[16]

[1] 1 Tim. 6 [15] sq.
[2] Tit. 2 [13].
[3] 1 Tim. 2 [5].
[4] 2 Tim. 2 [8].
[5] 1 Tim. 6 [13].
[6] 1 Tim. 2 [6].
[7] 1 Tim. 1 [15].
[8] 1 Tim. 6 [3]; Tit. 1 [1].
[9] 1 Tim. 4 [6].
[10] 1 Tim. 1 [18].
[11] 1 Tim. 3 [15].
[12] Tit. 2 [13].
[13] 1 Tim. 6 [20]; 2 Tim. 1 [13] sq.
[14] 1 Tim. 1 [15], 2 [4].
[15] 2 Tim. 2 [3] sqq.
[16] 1 Tim. 1 [5].

The Epistle to the Hebrews, which next claims our attention, is a document of a different order altogether. Of unknown authorship,[1] and belonging probably (like the Pastoral Epistles in their present form) to the second generation of Christianity rather than to the first [2]—for long regarded, despite early hesitations of mind on the subject, as the work of S. Paul, and yet manifestly non-Pauline in respect both of contents and of literary style—the Epistle has been described as being ' in many respects the riddle of the New Testament,' as standing ' solitary and mysterious ' among early Christian writings, ' " without father, without mother, without genealogy," like that Melchizedek on whom its argument turns.' [3] It is not even probable that it was addressed to the ' Hebrews.' The culture of the writer was certainly Greek, not Semitic, and it is unlikely that Aramaic-speaking Christians of Palestine would have been able to make much of his argument. It is tempting to think rather of Rome, where the Epistle is first quoted,[4] as the place of destination,[5] and of Ephesus (on the somewhat conjectural ground that the writer's theology is in some respects transitional between the work of S. Paul and the point of view of the Fourth Gospel) as the place of composition. It has been suggested that the Epistle may have been addressed, in the first instance, not to the Roman Church as a whole, but to a particular group or assembly of Christians at Rome who were personally known to the writer. They have apparently become somewhat dis-

[1] The final word of wisdom on the subject of the authorship of Hebrews is contained in a sentence of Origen's which is quoted by Eusebius—τίς δὲ ὁ γράψας τὴν ἐπιστολήν, τὸ μὲν ἀληθὲς θεὸς οἶδεν (Origen apud Euseb., H.E. vi. 25).

[2] Heb. 2 [3] sq.

[3] E. F. Scott, The Epistle to the Hebrews, p. 1.

[4] In the Epistle of Clement of Rome, circa A.D. 96 ; cf. A. J. Carlyle in The New Testament in the Apostolic Fathers, pp. 44 sqq.

[5] Cf. Heb. 13 [24], which implies certainly that the Epistle was written either from or to some place in Italy.

couraged, and are in danger of apostasy. The apostasy, however, which is dreaded is not a relapse into Judaism. It is a 'falling away from the living God,'[1] a relapse into wilful, deliberate sin,[2] a doing 'despite unto the Spirit of grace,'[3] a crucifixion of Jesus afresh.[4] It is unlikely that the readers of the Epistle were Jews, though the fact that the main argument of the writer turns largely upon the contrast between the two 'covenants' appears early to have suggested this notion, and to have given rise to the traditional description of the Epistle as being addressed 'to the Hebrews.' The writer himself may have once been a Jew—a Jew, perhaps, of the Alexandrine school, at once Biblical theologian and Platonist. He assumes, no doubt rightly, that his circle of readers will be amenable to an argument drawn from the Old Testament Scriptures. They have not grasped the full worth and significance of their religion, they have failed to appreciate the finality, or, to use a modern expression, the 'absoluteness,' of the revelation of God in His Son, and the writer says to them, in effect—to quote Moffatt—' Come back to your Bible, and see how fully it suggests the positive value of Jesus.'[5] In a sense the main argument of the writer is strikingly modern. He is dealing—despite the fact that he is precluded by his presuppositions from the recognition of any pre-Christian revelation beyond that which is contained in the Old Testament—with what is essentially the problem of comparative religion; and he argues for the finality and absolute worth of the revelation of God in Christ Jesus on the ground primarily of the intrinsic finality and absoluteness of the relationship to God which it mediates. ' He seeks ' (I again quote from Moffatt) ' to show from the Septuagint how the Christian faith alone fulfils the conditions of real religion; and as he knows

---

[1] Heb. 3 [12].   [2] Heb. 10 [26] *sqq.*
[3] Heb. 10 [29].   [4] Heb. 6 [6]; cf. 10 [39]
[5] Moffatt, *The Epistle to the Hebrews* (I.C.C.), p. xxv.

no other religion than the earlier phase in Israel, he takes common ground with his readers on the Septuagint record of the first διαθήκη, in order to let them see even there the implications and anticipations of the higher.'[1]

Presupposed by the whole argument of the Epistle is the assumption of the validity and relative worth of the Old Testament revelation. The Jewish religion had not been mistaken. It was divinely ordained. The Old ' Covenant ' was essentially valid. It had been appointed by God. But it had been essentially provisional, imperfect, prophetic and transitory. The Jews under the Law had possessed only ' a shadow of the good things to come,' and ' not the very image of the things.'[2] The Law had ' made nothing perfect.'[3] Its sanctuary—for ' even the first covenant ' had possessed 'ordinances of divine service'—had been only ' a sanctuary of this world.'[4] Its priests—for there had been priests too under the Old Covenant—were mere erring and fallible men.[5] Its sacrifices, continually repeated,[6] had been mere sacrifices of beasts, ' bulls and goats,' whose blood could not possibly take away sins.[7] In all these respects the New Covenant was ' better.'[8] It was alone final and adequate. It was that, moreover, to which the ordinances of the Old Covenant—' carnal ordinances,' imposed only ' until a time of reformation '[9]—had all along been prophetically pointing. The Old Testament law had been truly appointed by God, but not meant to be final. It was ' a parable for the time now present,'[10] and in its literal significance it belonged to the past. ' The priesthood being changed '—and it is the cardinal doctrine of the Epistle that there *has* been a change of the priesthood— ' there is made of necessity a change also of the law.'[11] The

---

[1] Moffatt, *op. cit.* p. xxvi.   [2] Heb. 10 [1].

[3] Heb. 7 [19].   [4] Heb. 9 [1].

[5] Heb. 5 [2] *sq.*, 7 [27], 9 [7].   [6] Heb. 10 [1] *sqq.*

[7] Heb. 10 [4].   [8] Heb. 8 [6].

[9] Heb. 9 [10].   [10] Heb. 9 [9].   [11] Heb. 7 [12].

writer of Hebrews in effect may be said to have done for
the Law upon its sacrificial side—that is to say, as a divinely-
enjoined system of worship—what S. Paul had done for the
Law as a system of injunctions and commands regulating
everyday life : he has at once powerfully vindicated its
place in the Old Testament, and at the same time provided
a theoretical justification of the fact that it had been in
practice abandoned by exhibiting its fulfilment in Christ.

It has been pointed out recently that it is in a special
sense characteristic of the mind of this writer that he thinks
of religion as consisting primarily in *worship*.[1]   It is as a
divinely-revealed system of worship that he interprets the
Old Testament law, and it is as the religion in which the
perfected reality of worship is for the first time made fully
possible for sinners that he interprets Christianity.   To
' draw near to God '[2] in the ' full assurance of faith,'[3]
believing both ' that he is, and that he is a rewarder of them
that diligently seek him,'[4] to ' serve the living God ' with a
conscience cleansed ' from dead works,'[5] to ' offer service
well-pleasing to God with reverence and awe '[6]—it is in
phrases like these that the writer sums up what is meant
by religion.   And it is through Christ that it has been made
possible, as it had not been possible before, inasmuch as
the Law, as we have already seen, had ' made nothing
perfect ' ;[7] its sacrifices had been only of typical significance,
and not ultimately real or efficacious ; its sanctuary had been
only ' a sanctuary of this world.'[8]   The writer, influenced
partly by Platonism and partly, perhaps, by the Apocalyptic
tradition of Judaism, which believed already in the existence
of a ' heavenly Jerusalem ' and of a celestial worship rendered
by angels in the immediate presence of the Most High,

---

[1] E. F. Scott, *op. cit.* pp. 30, 78 *sqq.* ; Moffatt, *op. cit.* pp. xliii. *sqq.*
[2] Heb. 7 [25] ; cf. 4 [16], 10 [1], [22].
[3] Heb. 10 [22] (R.V., marg.).   [4] Heb. 11 [6].
[5] Heb. 9 [14].   [6] Heb. 12 [28].
[7] Heb. 7 [19].   [8] Heb. 9 [1].

combines with the Jewish and Christian doctrine of the two Ages a doctrine, essentially philosophical in its colouring, of two Worlds. Fundamental in his thought is the belief that the world of things seen and temporal is at best only a provisional replica, a mere transient copy and symbolical representation, of the true world which is eternal and unseen. The Jewish religion was essentially of this Age and of this Cosmos, which as a whole is destined to vanish utterly away. Christianity is not of this world. It is ' eternal, just as it shall be everlasting, and . . . all else is only this, that the true heavenly things of which it consists thrust themselves forward on to this bank and shoal of time, and took cosmical embodiment, in order to suggest their coming everlasting manifestation.' [1] Profoundly influenced by this philosophical and platonizing conception is the writer's doctrine of faith—of the faith which had at all times characterized the people of God, which was exemplified in the heroes of the Old Testament and of Jewish tradition, and which has been perfected in Jesus, ' the great Believer,' [2] the Pioneer of our faith, who was at the same time faith's perfect embodiment. [3] The writer defines faith in a famous verse as ' the sure confidence of what we hope for, the conviction of the reality of things unseen.' [4] It is the capacity to ' endure as seeing him that is invisible,' [5] the faculty of insight into that eternal world wherein is ' the true tabernacle, which the Lord pitched, not man.' [6] In that eternal world is the true reality of worship, the worship which is offered in the immediate presence of the Most High in the ' more perfect tabernacle,' [7] of which the ' pattern ' was shown to Moses ' in the mount.' [8] Into that sanctuary Christ as

---

[1] A. B. Davidson, quoted by Moffatt, *op. cit.* p. xxxi.

[2] Moffatt, *op. cit.* p. xliv.

[3] τὸν τῆς πίστεως ἀρχηγὸν καὶ τελειωτὴν Ἰησοῦν (Heb. 12 [2]).

[4] Heb. 11 [1]. I believe with Moffatt that the rendering given above conveys substantially the true meaning of this difficult verse.

[5] Heb. 11 [27].   [6] Heb. 8 [2].   [7] Heb. 9 [11].   [8] Heb. 8 [5].

our ' forerunner ' (πρόδρομος) has entered, ' having become
a high priest for ever after the order of Melchizedek.' [1]
But since ' every high priest is appointed to offer both gifts
and sacrifices . . . it is necessary that this high priest also
have somewhat to offer.' [2] It is explained that what He
offers is ' the sacrifice of himself,' [3] ' his own blood,' [4] once
poured out for sinners—that is to say, His own offered and
dedicated life which had been ' perfected ' through sufferings and death,[5] and which is the true inner reality of sacrifice,
the ' one offering,' eternal in its significance and efficacy,
whereby He is able to ' perfect for ever them that are
sanctified.' [6] Guided by his ' Melchizedek ' analogy from
the Old Testament,[7] the writer thinks of our Lord as being
at once High Priest and King, and with a certain incongruity
of imagery conceives of Him both as being seated in majesty
as a King,[8] and also as exercising perpetually the mediatorial
ministry of a Priest in the ' true tabernacle,' [9] wherein He
' abideth a priest continually,' [10] ever living to make intercession for sinners.[11] In effect he takes over from primitive
Christianity the conception of our Lord as having been
enthroned, as the sequel to His ascension into the heavens,
on the ' right hand ' of God, and makes use of it in order to
suggest vividly the finality of the one sacrifice once offered,[12]
while at the same time making use of the idea of the eternity
of Christ's priesthood to suggest also the perpetual character
of His sacrifice and the eternal significance of the redemption
which He has won.[13] ' It is in the heavenly sanctuary,' says
a modern writer, summing up the argument, ' that Christ
exercises his office. This is apparent, not only from the
prophetic Psalm which described him as sitting at God's
right hand, but from the very fact that he was excluded

---

1 Heb. 6 [20].   2 Heb. 8 [3].   3 Heb. 9 [26].
4 Heb. 9 [12].   5 Heb. 2 [9] sq.   6 Heb. 10 [11].
7 Ps. 110 [4]; Gen. 14 [18] sqq.   8 Heb. 8 [1], 10 [12].
9 Heb. 8 [2, 6] ; cf. 7 [3, 24].   10 Heb. 7 [3].
11 Heb. 7 [25].   12 Heb. 10 [12].   13 Heb. 9 [12].

from an earthly priesthood. For if the prerogative granted to the sons of Levi was withheld from this greater Priest, the reason could only be that he was destined to minister on a far grander scene.[1] He was to pass through the veil that separates the invisible world from the visible, and to appear before God in the eternal sanctuary. Not only so, but he was to enter that heavenly sanctuary to abide there for ever. The earthly priest remained standing in the divine presence, as one who enjoyed a mere transitory privilege, but the Priest of whom the Psalm was written is to "sit down at God's right hand."[2] His ministry is a perpetual one, and so long as it continues those for whom he ministers have an access to God which cannot be interrupted. They have the assurance at all times that they are God's people, who may come freely to the throne of grace.'[3] 'Wherefore,' says the writer of the Epistle, 'holy brethren, partakers of a heavenly calling, consider the Apostle and High Priest of our confession, Jesus.'[4] . . . 'Having therefore, brethren, boldness to enter into the holy place by the blood of Jesus, by the way which he dedicated for us, a new and living way, through the veil, that is to say, his flesh ; and having a great priest over the house of God : let us draw near with a true heart in fulness of faith, having our hearts sprinkled from an evil conscience, and our body washed with pure water : let us hold fast the confession of our hope that it waver not : for he is faithful that promised.'[5]

It has been argued by modern scholars to whom the ideas of priesthood and sacrifice, even as spiritualized and interpreted in terms of the doctrine of this Epistle, are uncongenial, that it is a limitation in the thought of the writer that he still clings to the ideas of the Old Testament. 'The

---

[1] Heb. 8 4.   [2] Heb. 10 11 sq.
[3] E. F. Scott, op. cit. pp. 134 sq.
[4] Heb. 3 1.   [5] Heb. 10 19 sqq.

fundamental idea,' writes E. F. Scott, ' in this whole argument is the same in essence as that which must underlie
every attempt to affirm the absolute claim of Christianity.
If our religion is indeed the final and all-sufficing one, we
must have some guarantee that it lifts us out of the domain
of half-truths into that of reality.   .   It is one of the
writer's chief services to religious thought that he has so
clearly drawn the distinction between type and reality—
a distinction which must be recognized before any spiritual
form of worship is possible.   But the weakness of his argument consists in this—that while he shows the inadequacy
of the old ritual conceptions, he never definitely escapes
from them.   He cannot rid himself of the belief that the
substance must in some manner be of the same nature as
the type.   The true worship must conform to that of the
tabernacle, with the difference that it is offered in heaven
instead of on earth, and has therefore a higher validity.' [1]
It is pointed out that the writer takes over without criticism
from primitive religion—or to put the matter more accurately,
from the Scriptural teaching of the Book of Leviticus—the
idea of the mysterious atoning efficacy of consecrated blood.
It is argued that he thinks of the priesthood of Christ as
being exercised in a literal and not merely figurative sense,
in a sanctuary which literally exists, though it is not upon
earth.   It is complained that he assumes as an axiom that
there can be no access to God without a mediator, and again
that there can be no access to God without the offering in
some form of a sacrifice or sacrifices to take away sins, and
that there is no attempt made in the Epistle to rationalize
or explain these conceptions.   ' Without shedding of blood
there is no remission,' writes Moffatt ; ' we ask, Why ?   But
the ancient world never dreamt of asking, Why ?   What
puzzles a modern was an axiom to the ancient.' [2]

[1] E. F. Scott, *op. cit.* pp. 136 *sq.*
[2] Moffatt, *op. cit.* p. xlii.

I cannot think that this criticism is very profound. It is no doubt the case that to the ancient world the ideas of sacrifice and priesthood were immediately intelligible conceptions, which could be taken for granted as hardly requiring an explanation : and it is true, no doubt, that to-day they do need explanation, in default of which they are seriously liable to be misunderstood. But it does not appear to me to be true to suggest that even the writer of this Epistle has provided no explanation at all. He is perhaps more bound to the letter of the Old Testament typology than we should be to-day—he does believe quasi-literally in the potency of blood. Nevertheless, he supplies at least a hint of an interpretation in the passage in which, after pointing out, in the very spirit of rationalism, that ' it is impossible that the blood of bulls and goats should take away sins,' [1] he proceeds to quote from the fortieth Psalm—

' Sacrifice and offering thou wouldest not,
But a body didst thou prepare for me :
In whole burnt-offerings and sacrifices for sin thou hadst
    no pleasure :

' Then said I, Lo, I am come
(In the roll of the book it is written of me)
To do thy will, O God.' [2]

To this writer the will of God, which our Lord was appointed to do, was no doubt the offering of His life as a sacrifice. Nevertheless, by the emphasis which he lays upon the idea of the doing of the Divine will, and by his accompanying criticism of the inherent irrationality of the sacrifices of animals, he at least may be held to suggest that the true inward meaning of sacrifice is to be found—when once the transition has been made from the sacrifices which were typical to the sacrifice which is real—not in the last resort

---

[1] Heb. 10 [4].   [2] Heb. 10 [5] *sqq.* ; Ps. 40 [6-8].

in the merely literal outpouring of blood (though it is true that he probably regarded the literal outpouring of blood as being in some sense essential),[1] but in the offering of a deliberately dedicated and consecrated will. He proclaims, not obscurely, that the essence of Christ's sacrifice lies in the fact that it was ' the sacrifice of himself.' [2]   If he believes —as he does believe—that there is no access to God without a mediator, and no access to God for sinners without a sacrifice to take away sins, he is on the one hand giving expression, as even Scott recognizes, to a doctrine which ' has grown out of . . . Christian experience ' and ' which in one aspect or another must ever belong to the very substance of Christianity,' the doctrine, namely, ' that through Christ we have been brought near to God,' and that ' men have learned through him that they are God's people, that their sins have been forgiven, that they can now come boldly before the throne of grace';[3] and on the other hand, by the use which he makes of the fortieth Psalm he suggests (without developing further) the beginnings of a theory of sacrifice which may appeal to us still. ' Not the knife, but the flame,' it has been said, ' is the symbol of sacrifice '—the central idea is that of the offering and dedication of life. The true and ultimate meaning of the doctrine of this Epistle with regard to the High Priesthood and sacrifice of Christ is only grasped when we interpret sacrifice so. On the one hand, access to God is not simply to be taken for granted—there is a true sense in which sinners, in the presence of the Divine holiness, are rightly afraid, and it is shallowness, and not depth, of religious and spiritual insight which can see no appropriateness in the idea of a mediator. On the other hand, ' God, who at sundry times and in divers manners spake in time past unto the fathers by the prophets, hath in these last days spoken unto us by his Son,'[4] thus

[1] Heb. 9 [22].
[2] Heb. 9. [26].
[3] E. F. Scott *op. cit.* p. 139.
[4] Heb. 1 [1].

providing a Mediator, human like ourselves, and 'in all things
. . . made like unto his brethren,'[1] save only in respect of
sin,[2] the ideal Representative of man before God, who as
High Priest has offered the ultimate sacrifice, which is 'the
sacrifice of himself.'[3]

That 'the Son of man came not to be ministered unto,
but to minister, and to give his life a ransom for many,' is
a saying which in the Gospels is ascribed to our Lord.[4]
The writer of Hebrews would express the same truth—it is
Christ's life of flawless obedience, made perfect in death,
and utterly consecrated to God on behalf of His brethren,
which is at once the means of man's reconciliation with God
and the ground of his confidence.   It is not without
significance that the theology and modes of expression of
this Epistle have so deeply influenced not only the eucharistic
theology of Christendom but also the actual language of
Christian liturgies and hymns.   As Scott expresses it, 'in
their actual approach to God, men have been constrained
to fall back on its conception of the High Priest who offered
up himself and makes intercession for them in the heavenly
temple,' because—whatever difficulties may be raised by
modern thinkers from the side of theology—'the spirit of
Christian devotion in all ages has found a truth in it to which
it has responded.'[5]

A few words may be added from the point of view of
Christology in the narrower sense of the word.   The writer
starts simply from the tradition of the Church.   He thinks
of our Lord as being at once Lord, Son of Man, and Son of
God.   Because Jesus is Lord, he regards himself as being
entitled to quote Psalm cii., which makes use of this title, as
though it were addressed not to God, but to Christ, with the
result that the words, 'Thou, Lord, in the beginning hast laid
the foundation of the earth,' become Scriptural evidence,

[1] Heb. 2 17.   [2] Heb. 4 15.   [3] Heb. 9 26.
[4] Mk. 10 45; Mt. 20 28.   [5] E. F. Scott, op. cit. p. 141.

to his mind, that our Lord was concerned in the work of creation.[1] Because Jesus is Son of Man, he can quote, like S. Paul, the eighth Psalm as being prophetic of Jesus.[2] So also the use made of Psalm cx. is in like manner traditional, and goes back, as we saw in an earlier lecture, to primitive Christianity, and perhaps actually to Jesus Himself,[3] though the special development by this writer of the doctrine of the Melchizedek priesthood is probably original and new ; and the second Psalm, together with the Divine promise to the house of David from the second Book of Samuel, are quoted as Scriptural ' proof-texts ' for our Lord's Divine Sonship.[4]

At the same time, he has himself a more developed doctrine of the Divine Sonship ; he thinks of our Lord, as we have seen, as having been concerned in the work of creation : he has taken over—more probably from S. Paul than from Philo [5]—a ' Wisdom ' type of Christology, and can speak of the ' Son,' whom God has ' appointed heir of all things,' as being at the same time the ' Son . . . through whom also he made the worlds,' who ' upholds all things by the word of his power,' and who is the ' effulgence ' of God's ' glory,' and the ' express image ' of His ' being.' [6] He implies by quotations from the Old Testament that the

---

[1] Heb. 1 [10], Ps. 102 [25].

[2] Heb. 2 [6] *sqq.* ; Ps. 8 [4] *sqq.*

[3] Mk. 12 [35] and parallels ; see Lecture II. pp. 31 *sq.*

[4] Heb. 1 [5] ; cf. Ps. 2 [7], 2 Sam. 7 [14].

[5] There are, of course, close verbal parallels in the writings of Philo which can be quoted as illustrating the thought of the Epistle to the Hebrews at a number of points : e.g. Philo's doctrine of the Logos—itself influenced by the Old Testament doctrine of ' Wisdom '—is closely akin to the ' Wisdom ' Christology of Hebrews, the figure of Melchizedek is allegorized by Philo and identified with the Logos, and the Logos is further identified with the High Priest and regarded as mediating between God and mankind. It is probable that the writer of Hebrews was in general familiar with the language and standpoint of Jewish Alexandrian theology, that as Moffatt expresses it he had ' breathed the Philonic atmosphere.' But it is improbable that he was directly dependent in a literary sense upon Philo.

[6] Heb. 1 [2] *sq.* ; cf. Wisdom 7 [26].

Son may be addressed rightly as ' God.' [1]   It is not impossible that there may be a polemic against some kind of contemporary *cultus* of the angels, or against some doctrine of mediating angels such as that which had been attacked by S. Paul in the Epistle to the Colossians. The writer is certainly at pains to establish from Scripture the superiority of the Son not only to Moses, who as the mediator of the Old Covenant had been ' faithful ' in God's ' house as a servant,' [2] but to the angels, who are at most only ' ministering spirits,' [3] to whom ' the world to come ' is not subjected, [4] and none of whom had been addressed by God as His ' Son.' [5] On the contrary, the angels are commanded to ' worship ' God's Son, [6] who as His ' firstborn ' [7] and ' heir ' [8] is supreme over His ' house.' [9]   In His human life upon earth He had been ' made for a short time lower than the angels,' but that was in order that on the ground of His suffering of death He might be crowned subsequently with ' glory and honour,' that by the grace of God His tasting of death might be on every man's behalf. [10]   Like the author of the Pastoral Epistles, the writer of Hebrews combines a strong emphasis upon the Divinity of Christ with the conviction that the ' one mediator . . . between God and men ' must be Himself also ' man.' [11]   He is to succour not angels, but the offspring of Abraham ; He must be in all things ' made

---

[1] Heb. I [8] (=Ps. 45 [6]) : it is possible also that Heb. I [9] [b] should be translated, ' therefore, O God, thy God hath anointed thee, etc.' In Heb. 3 [4] the words ὁ δὲ πάντα κατασκευάσας θεός are ambiguous : they are perhaps only, as Moffatt suggests, an ' edifying aside,' viz. : ' He that established all things is God ' ; but the logic of the immediate argument might be held to support the translation, ' He that established all things (i.e. Christ) is divine.'

[2] Heb. 3 [2] *sqq.*   [3] Heb. I [14].
[4] Heb. 2 [5].   [5] Heb. I [5].
[6] Heb. I [6].   [7] Heb. I [6].
[8] Heb. I [2].   [9] Heb. 3 [6].
[10] Heb. 2 [9]. I assume that the *textus receptus* is right, and that the alternative reading χωρὶς θεοῦ for χάριτι θεοῦ is to be rejected.
[11] I Tim. 2 [5].

like unto his brethren.'[1] The writer lays emphasis upon
the human life of our Lord, upon His birth from the tribe
of Judah,[2] His 'prayers and supplications with strong
crying and tears unto him that was able to save him from
death '[3]—a passage in which it is impossible not to see an
allusion to the story of Gethsemane—His obedience, learnt
through the things which He suffered,[4] His temptations—
it is affirmed that He was 'in all points tempted like as we
are, yet without sin,' and is thereby qualified to be 'a
merciful and faithful high priest,' 'touched with a feeling'
of human 'infirmities' and 'able to succour them that are
tempted '[5]—His patient endurance of the gainsaying of
sinners,[6] His crucifixion outside the gates of Jerusalem.[7]
In combining a 'Wisdom' Christology with so strong an
insistence upon the importance of the human story of our
Lord's life the writer of Hebrews may be regarded as having
anticipated, and perhaps actually influenced, the theology of
the Fourth Gospel. For the rest, he holds fast to the primitive
eschatology, believing that there shall be yet but 'a very
little while' and 'He that cometh shall come,'[8] and that
Christ 'having been once offered to bear the sins of many,
shall appear a second time, apart from sin, to them that
wait for him, unto salvation.'[9]

The Epistle to the Hebrews is in some sort the work of a
theologian. Of interest precisely because it is not the work
of a theologian, but of a man who is accustomed to think
vividly in pictures, and whose sublime confidence in the
future victory of Christ and the final overthrow of everything that is evil is expressed in what to us is the somewhat
bizarre form of a riot of apocalyptic imagery and symbolism,

[1] Heb. 2 [16] sq. For ἐπιλαμβάνεσθαι as meaning 'to succour,' cf.
Ecclus. 4 [11] (Moffatt).
[2] Heb. 7 [14].   [3] Heb. 5 [7].   [4] Heb. 5 [8].   [5] Heb. 4 [15], 2 [17] sq.
[6] Heb. 12 [3].   [7] Heb. 13 [12].   [8] Heb. 10 [37].   [9] Heb. 9 [28].

is the Christology of the Apocalypse. The author of the Book
of Revelation is a Christian prophet and seer, steeped in
the literature of the apocalyptic convention and in the
language and imagery of the Old Testament prophets, who
in a time of persecution and suffering, when men's hearts were
failing them for fear and for expectation of the things which
were coming on the earth,[1] writes to communicate to the
Christians of the seven churches of the Roman province of
Asia the contents of a vision, or of a series of visions, which
he has seen, and of a message, or series of messages, with
which he believes himself to have been entrusted by the
Spirit. The Empire has declared definitely against the
Church. There have already been martyrdoms in Asia,[2] and
there are worse things in prospect. It is believed by Dr.
Charles that the writer looks forward to the martyrdom,
literally universal, of the whole of the Church upon earth.[3]
Already Rome is the mystic Babylon, the woman drunken
with the blood of the saints.[4] It is being whispered darkly
in the bazaars of Asia Minor that Nero has returned from
the realms of the dead and is about to lead the Parthians
against Rome. The seer identifies him with Antichrist:
his death and reported resurrection [5] are a diabolical parody
of the death and resurrection of Christ : his ' number '—
666, a Hebrew anagram upon the name ' Nero Caesar '—is
the ' number of the Beast.' [6] There are riders upon horses
—the ' four horsemen of the Apocalypse '—who symbolize
respectively foreign invasion, carnage, famine and pestilence.[7]
There are ' woes ' which are coming upon the earth.[8] There
is also another Rider—' And I saw the heaven opened ; and
behold, a white horse, and he that sat thereon, called Faithful
and True ; and in righteousness he doth judge and make

[1] Lk. 21 [26].   [2] Rev. 2 [13].
[3] R. H. Charles, *Revelation* (I.C.C.), vol. ii. pp. 113, 456.
[4] Rev. 17 [6].
[5] Rev. 13 [3, 12].   [6] Rev. 13 [18].
[7] Rev. 6 [1] *sqq.*   [8] Rev. 8 [13], 9 [12], 11 [14].

war. And his eyes are a flame of fire, and upon his head are many diadems; and he hath a name written, which no one knoweth but he himself. And he is arrayed in a garment sprinkled with blood : and his name is called The Word of God.'[1] It is noted by Lebreton that the Word of God is conceived in a passage of the Book of Wisdom as a Divine Warrior—' Thine all-powerful Word leaped from heaven,' we read, ' out of the royal throne, a stern warrior, into the midst of the doomed land, bearing as a sharp sword thine unfeigned commandment; and standing it filled all things with death ; and while it touched the heaven it trode upon the earth.'[2] It is certainly not without interest to observe that the title ' Word ' is applied to our Lord for the first time in Christian literature in the context of an apocalyptic vision, and in a passage of which the inspiration is emphatically Jewish.[3]

For the rest, the Christology of the Apocalypse is expressed in a series of images which for the most part call here for no detailed discussion. The writer thinks of our Lord as being essentially the regnant and exalted Redeemer, the Living One,[4] faithful and true,[5] who was dead, and behold, He is alive for evermore, and who has the keys of death and of Hades.[6] He is described both as ' the firstborn of the dead '[7] and as ' the beginning of the creation of God '[8]— phrases based probably upon the doctrine of S. Paul as set forth in the Epistle to the Colossians.[9] He is ' the faithful witness '—a phrase derived possibly from a Messianic passage in the eighty-ninth Psalm.[10] He is ' the ruler of the kings of the earth,'[11] the ' King of kings, and Lord of

---

[1] Rev. 19 [11] sqq.
[2] Wisdom 18 [15] sq. The reference in Wisdom is to the plagues of Egypt.
[3] Lebreton, Les Origines du Dogme de la Trinité, pp. 435 sq.
[4] Rev. 1 [18].   [5] Rev. 19 [11].
[6] Rev. 1 [18].   [7] Rev. 1 [5].
[8] Rev. 3 [14].   [9] Cf. Col. 1 [15, 18]; and see Lecture VI. pp. 160 sqq.
[10] Rev. 1 [5] : cf. Ps. 89 [35-37].   [11] Rev. 1 [5].

lords.'[1] If He is described by such Messianic titles as 'Lion of the tribe of Judah' and 'Root of David,'[2] He is at the same time the Son of God with flaming eyes, whose countenance is as the sun shining in his strength,[3] and who is the Alpha and the Omega, the Beginning and the End—a description which the writer applies once to our Lord,[4] but in two other passages to God.[5] So too in the account of the seer's opening vision in the first chapter of the book the Figure 'like unto a son of man, clothed with a garment down to the foot '[6] is described in terms which are derived partly from the description in the Book of Daniel of God Himself as the 'ancient of days';[7] and there are other instances also of the transference to our Lord by this writer of Divine functions and attributes which in the Old Testament are ascribed only to God.[8]

Of particular interest is the frequent description of our Lord as 'the Lamb,'[9] a term used, on the one hand, in a sense derived from the literature of Jewish Apocalyptic,[10] to denote our Lord as the leader and shepherd of His people,[11] the Messiah who as a Divine Warrior can fight and overcome,[12] and who as the assessor of God at the Judgement can manifest 'wrath,'[13] and on the other hand, in a sense distinctively Christian, influenced probably by the fifty-third chapter of

[1] Rev. 19 16.
[2] Rev. 5 5.
[3] Rev. 1 14, 16, 2 18, 19 12.
[4] Rev. 22 13.
[5] Rev. 1 8, 21 6; cf. Is. 41 4, 44 6.
[6] Cf. Dan. 7 13; Ezek. 9 2; Dan. 10 5 (LXX).
[7] Rev. 1 13 sqq.; cf. Dan. 7 9.
[8] R. H. Charles compares Rev. 2 18 with Jer. 17 10, Ps. 7 9; Rev. 5 6 with Zech. 4 10; Rev. 19 13 with Is. 63 1 sqq.; Rev. 17 14 with Deut. 10 17.
[9] The description of our Lord as 'the Lamb' occurs 29 times in the Apocalypse.
[10] Cf. Eth. Enoch 89 44 (where Samuel is the 'sheep whose eyes were opened,' and Saul and David in the immediate context are indicated as 'rams'), Eth. Enoch 90 9, 12 (where the Maccabaean leaders, and especially Judas Maccabaeus, are symbolized as horned lambs).
[11] Rev. 7 17.
[12] Rev. 17 14.
[13] Rev. 6 16 sq.

Isaiah,[1] to denote our Lord as the Lamb offered in sacrifice, the 'Lamb . . . slain'[2] for the redemption of sinners, in one passage described, in a phrase probably meant to express the eternal character of the Christian salvation as having been foreordained from the beginning in the counsels of God, as 'the Lamb that hath been slain from the foundation of the world.'[3] As Dr. Charles expresses it, 'under the designation of "the Lamb" there lie the ideas of sacrifice and triumphant love. . . . The Lamb who conquers is the Lamb who has given Himself up as a willing sacrifice. But the principle of love going forth in sacrifice is older than the world—the Lamb was slain from its foundation.'[4]

In the great symbolic vision which is described in the fifth chapter of the Apocalypse the seer beholds 'in the midst of the throne and of the four living creatures, and in the midst of the elders, a Lamb standing, as though it had been slain, having seven horns and seven eyes, which are the seven Spirits of God, sent forth into all the earth.'[5] The seven horns are the symbols of power : the seven eyes, representing the seven Spirits of God, are the symbols of omniscience, such as in the Old Testament is the prerogative of God.[6] According to the thought of the writer, the Messiah has attained by the avenue of absolute self-sacrifice to a position of omniscience and absolute power. 'The Lion that is of the tribe of Judah, the Root of David, hath overcome.'[7] The Lamb who was slain yet stands ; that is to say, the sacrifice has been offered, and He by whom it was offered is not dead, but alive. To Him alone it is assigned

---

[1] Is. 53 ⁷, where, however, the LXX has ἀμνός : the word used in the Apocalypse is invariably ἀρνίον.

[2] Rev. 5 ¹².

[3] Rev. 13 ⁸. This appears on the whole to be the most probable interpretation : so Charles, following Bede, Eichhorn, and Alford. Contrast Rev. 17 ⁸, where ἀπὸ καταβολῆς κόσμου connects with γέγραπται.

[4] R. H. Charles, op. cit. i. p. cxiv.

[5] Rev. 5 ⁶.   [6] Zech. 4 ¹⁰.

[7] Rev. 5 ⁵.

as His prerogative to open the sealed book of the future, the roll wherein are contained the Divine decrees with regard to 'the things which must come to pass hereafter.'[1] The Lamb takes the book 'out of the right hand of him that sat on the throne,'[2] and forthwith adoration is offered to Him by the four Living Creatures, and by the four and twenty Elders, and by an innumerable company of angels, and by every created thing, and there is sung in heaven a 'new song' to His glory—'Worthy art thou to take the book, and to open the seals thereof: for thou wast slain, and didst purchase unto God with thy blood men of every tribe, and tongue, and people, and nation. . . . Worthy is the Lamb that hath been slain to receive the power, and riches, and wisdom, and might, and honour, and glory, and blessing. . . . Unto him that sitteth upon the throne, and unto the Lamb, be the blessing, and the honour, and the glory, and the dominion, for ever and ever.'[3]

There could be no better summary of the Christology of the Apocalypse.

---

[1] Rev. 5 [1] sqq., 4 [1].   [2] Rev. 5 [7].   [3] Rev. 5 [8] sqq.

LECTURE VIII

THE INCARNATION OF THE WORD

SYNOPSIS

THE critical problem of the Fourth Gospel. It will be assumed in this lecture that the book was written in Greek at Ephesus by a Palestinian Jew well acquainted with Jerusalem and originally Semitic in culture ; that the writer was ' John the Presbyter ' ; that he had known John the son of Zebedee (the ' Beloved Disciple ') personally, and that he had also himself probably as a boy at Jerusalem seen our Lord in the flesh. It will be assumed that the writer was indebted to the Beloved Disciple for certain ' eye-witness ' details, but that the identification of the Beloved Disciple with the Evangelist rests on a mistake (and that therefore Jn. 21 24 is an early addition to the text, embodying an erroneous conjecture as to authorship).

It will be assumed that for the materials of his Gospel the writer depended on oral and written tradition, which he handled with considerable freedom. He uses Mark and Luke, but appears some-times to correct the Synoptic tradition. Nevertheless, his main purpose is to produce faith in our Lord as the Son of God. He writes ' a doctrinal work in the form of a Gospel,' neither an allegory nor a merely naïve history. He believes the episodes which he narrates to be historical ; he produces a vividly realistic account, and the Christ whom he describes is true Man. But the book is doctrinal, interpretative and mystical. The Evangelist seeks to set forth the Lord Jesus to cosmopolitan Hellenists as the Saviour of the world, and his narrative is governed by this purpose. His theory of miracle.

The theology which in the Synoptic tradition is implicit is in this Gospel made explicit and ascribed to our Lord : and our Lord talks in the Evangelist's style. The Gospel as the work of a πνευματικός—' Hear what the Spirit saith. . . . These are true words of God.'

Our Lord in this Gospel—in strong contrast with the Synoptic tradition—is represented as proclaiming Himself in the first person singular. The theories of Norden and Wetter about this. A more natural explanation.

' The Word became flesh.' It is assumed that the title ' the Word ' is familiar. Its possible associations and meanings, both Jewish and pagan. It does not govern the Gospel, but is confined to the Prologue, unless it be held to govern the thought of the

Gospel indirectly, as paraphrased by the doctrines of Life and of Light. The Jewish background of these. The Evangelist takes over the actual term ' Word ' from current usage at Ephesus and employs it to express the same type of essentially ' Wisdom ' Christology which had been developed by S. Paul and by the writer of Hebrews. An exposition of the Prologue.

The Fourth Gospel—doctrinally the crown of the New Testament—contains also quite primitive Christology. The titles, ' Messiah,' ' Son of God ' (in the primitive sense of ' Messiah '), ' Prophet ' (like unto Moses), and ' Son of Man.' The title ' Lord,' except as a form of address, is not prominent, but Bousset is probably wrong in suggesting that the Evangelist disliked it.

The theory of Bousset that the type of religion expressed in the Gospel is non-Jewish. The alleged doctrine of ' deification by means of the vision of God,' illustrated (a) by the ἐποπτεία of the mysteries, (b) by the ' astral mysticism ' of contemporary astronomers, and (c) by the use of the terms ' life ' and ' light ' in the literature of Gnosticism (including the *Corpus Hermeticum*). The strength and weakness of Bousset's position. It is possible that some Greek readers might interpret the Gospel as he suggests, but improbable that the Evangelist deliberately so meant it to be interpreted. The doctrine of eternal life in this Gospel. The double meaning of the eschatological ideas.

The doctrine of Christ as the Son of God. The theory of Wetter. The Evangelist's theological interpretation of the Divine Sonship in the interests of monotheism. ' Salvation is from the Jews.'

Concluding remarks. The Christological doctrine of the New Testament was developed with remarkable rapidity, and assumes within the period covered by the New Testament itself a remarkable variety of forms. What is constant throughout is (a) the cult of the Lord Jesus, (b) the insistence on monotheism, and (c) the conviction, implicit in the most primitive assertion of the Messiahship, that the person of Jesus is of absolute and final significance. Presupposed from beginning to end is the doctrine of the self-revealing and redemptive activity of the living God, who is the God of the Old Testament. The significance of the ' Wisdom ' type of Christology— it is ultimately an assertion of the identity of the God of religion with the God of creation. The affirmation of Nicene orthodoxy, viz. that our Lord, in His essential being, is one with God, is required ultimately as the intellectual justification of the New Testament faith.

LECTURE VIII

THE INCARNATION OF THE WORD

The Word became flesh, and dwelt among us.—John 1 [14].

THE Gospel according to S. John is notoriously the most difficult to estimate of all the New Testament books. It has been approached and interpreted from almost every conceivable point of view, the relevant literature is enormous, and there is neither agreement nor the likelihood of agreement among scholars with regard to the majority of the questions involved. Nevertheless, there are certain conclusions which I propose to assume. I assume, in the first place, that the book is not a translation, but that it was originally written in Greek, and at Ephesus, as tradition affirms.[1] I assume, in the second place, that the writer was a Jew, who possessed more than a pilgrim's acquaintance with Jerusalem, whose original home had been in Palestine, and whose native idiom of thought and of speech was Semitic, and not Greek.[2] I assume, in the third place, that the writer was not John the son of Zebedee, but another John, whom I am disposed with Streeter and others to identify with John the Presbyter, who is mentioned by Papias,[3] and who was perhaps, as Streeter suggests, a disciple and admirer of John the son of Zebedee, to whose ' witness ' it is probable that in one passage he

---

[1] The thesis of the late Dr. C. F. Burney that the Gospel was originally written in Aramaic, and at Antioch, as set forth in his book, *The Aramaic Origin of the Fourth Gospel* (Oxford, 1922), does not appear to have carried conviction to the minds of the majority of Semitic scholars.

[2] The demonstration of this fact is the really permanent gain which may be said to have resulted from Dr. Burney's book.

[3] Papias, *apud* Euseb., *H.E.* iii. 39. 4.

appeals,[1] and whom it is natural to identify with the ' Beloved
Disciple ' of the Gospel itself.[2] If we assume, further, that
John the Presbyter, the author of the Gospel and of the
three Johannine Epistles,[3] had himself, as a boy at Jerusalem,
seen our Lord in the flesh, this will explain both certain
claims which he apparently makes,[4] and also the veneration
in which he was held by a later generation, and the description of him by Papias as having been, like Aristion, a ' disciple
of the Lord.'[5] In this limited sense the Evangelist may have
been an eye-witness—an eye-witness of Christ, but not an
eye-witness of all, and perhaps not of any, of the events
which he describes. It is not necessary to assume that his

---

[1] Jn. 19 ³⁵. I incline to the view that ἐκεῖνος in this verse means our
Lord (cf. 1 Jn. 2 ⁶, 3 ³, ⁵, ⁷, ¹⁶., 4 ¹⁷), and that ὁ ἑωρακώς is the Beloved
Disciple, from whom the Evangelist may have had this particular story.

[2] Jn. 13 ²³, 19 ²⁶, 20 ², 21 ⁷, ²⁰. It is, of course, necessary, on the hypothesis adopted above, to regard Jn. 21 ²⁴ as being a later addition to the
text of the Gospel, embodying an erroneous assumption with regard to the
authorship. The twenty-first chapter as a whole is no doubt in some sense
an appendix : it is suggested that the last two verses may be an addition
to the twenty-first chapter. Cf. Streeter, *The Four Gospels*, p. 430.
The addition must be presumed to have been very early ; and the identification thus made between the author of the Gospel and the Beloved Disciple
rendered inevitable the identification of the Evangelist with the son of
Zebedee—an identification which appears in Irenaeus (cf. Iren. *Adv. Haeres.*
I. ix. 2, 3, where the Fourth Evangelist, whom Irenaeus describes usually
as ' John the disciple of the Lord,' is twice designated ' the Apostle ').

[3] R. H. Charles (*Revelation*, i. pp. xxxiv sqq.) appears to have shown
conclusively that the Fourth Gospel and the three Epistles of S. John are
by one and the same author. The Apocalypse is of course by a different
writer, a man of a wholly different cast of mind, who moreover is marked
off from every other New Testament author by the extraordinary character
of the ' pidgin-Greek ' which he writes.

[4] In 1 John 1 ¹ sqq., Jn. 1 ¹⁴, the impression is created that the writer
is the still surviving spokesman of those who had actually seen and known
our Lord in the flesh.

[5] εἰ δέ που καὶ παρηκολουθηκώς τις τοῖς πρεσβυτέροις ἔλθοι, τοὺς τῶν πρεσβυτέρων
ἀνέκρινον λόγους, τί Ἀνδρέας ἢ τί Πέτρος εἶπεν ἢ τί Φίλιππος ἢ τί Θωμᾶς ἢ Ἰάκωβος
ἢ τί Ἰωάννης ἢ Ματθαῖος ἤ τις ἕτερος τῶν τοῦ κυρίου μαθητῶν ἅ τε Ἀριστίων καὶ ὁ
πρεσβύτερος Ἰωάννης, οἱ τοῦ κυρίου μαθηταί, λέγουσιν (Papias, *loc. cit.*). The
change of tense from εἶπεν to λέγουσιν appears to imply that the Apostles
(including ' John ') were dead when Papias was making his enquiries, but
that ' Aristion ' (otherwise unknown) and ' the presbyter John ' were still
alive.

acquaintance with John the son of Zebedee had been lengthy
or exceptionally intimate. He may have derived from him
certain details—the fact, for example, that at the Last
Supper S. John had leaned on his Master's breast, the story
of the lance-thrust and of the issue of water and blood, in
which he appears to have seen a symbolic significance.[1] Apart
from such details it is sufficient to assume that he remembered
and idealized S. John as the Apostle with whom he had had
personal associations,[2] and to whom, perhaps, he may have
originally owed his Christianity. It appears to have been
his habitual practice, for example, to think and to speak
of S. John not by name, but as ' the disciple whom Jesus
loved.' He is always so described in the Gospel, and the
name ' John,' in the usage of this writer, denotes always
the Baptist. It is not altogether surprising that posterity
identified the Evangelist himself with the Beloved Disciple,
but on the other hand such a description is not really natural,
and would hardly have been in good taste, as a self-
designation.

For the materials of his Gospel it is to be presumed that
the writer depended in the main, like the other Evangelists,
upon Church tradition, whether oral or written   He makes
some use, as it would seem, of the Gospels according to
S. Mark and S. Luke ; his acquaintance with the Gospel according to S. Matthew is possible, but less certain.[3] At the
same time, he does not regard himself as being in any way
tied down to a slavish reproduction of his sources. On the
contrary, the story is retold with considerable freedom. It
is probable that at certain points the writer believed himself to be in a position deliberately to correct the Synoptic

---

[1] Jn. 19 [35] ; cf. 1 Jn. 5 [6]. Is there an implicit contrast with John the
Baptist, who came ' with the water only ' ? In any case it is probable
that the Water and the Blood are regarded as being typical respectively of
Baptism and of the Eucharist.

[2] Cf. Streeter, *op. cit.* p. 433.

[3] Streeter, *op. cit.* pp. 395 *sqq.*

tradition—thus, for example, in suggesting that our Lord visited Jerusalem repeatedly he is almost certainly right,[1] and it is probable that he is right also in respect of the date of the Crucifixion in relation to the Passover.[2] Nevertheless, it was not his main purpose to correct, or to supersede, the Synoptic tradition, but to produce faith in our Lord as the Son of God.[3] His book has been described by a modern Catholic writer as ' a doctrinal work in the form of a Gospel.' [4] It has been regarded by Loisy and others as a pure allegory, divorced from all reference to history—a view which is quite certainly false, since the main thesis of the writer that ' the Word became flesh ' is destroyed unless it be assumed that the Evangelist himself was convinced that the Incarnation had actually happened, and that the Christ whom he portrays was an historical Person.[5] The Gospel is rooted in history in the same sense in which the other Gospels are rooted in history—the writer is drawing upon the tradition of the Church, that is to say, upon the large fund of reminiscence about Jesus which was available,[6] and he believes the episodes which he narrates to be episodes which had actually occurred. He had been in contact, like S. Mark, with first-hand traditions about Jesus, and also, no doubt, with traditions which were not quite first-hand. He is

---

[1] The Synoptic tradition is unintelligible as it stands, since it does not explain why our Lord, as He goes up to Jerusalem for the last Passover of His life, knows in advance that the city will reject Him, or why, when He arrives there, He finds in Jerusalem and the surrounding villages not only enemies, but friends. Cf. Scott Holland, *The Philosophy of Faith and the Fourth Gospel*, pp. 127 *sqq.*

[2] According to the Synoptic tradition, the Last Supper was the Passover Meal (Mk. 14 [2], Lk. 22 [7]) : according to the Fourth Gospel, the Crucifixion took place on the day of the Preparation of the Passover (Jn. 19 [14]). For a discussion of the historical problems involved, see my edition of *The Gospel according to S. Mark* (Westminster Commentaries), pp. 262 *sqq.*

[3] Jn. 20 [31].

[4] ' *Lehrschrift in der Form des Evangeliums* ' (Tillmann, quoted by Lagrange, *Évangile selon S. Jean*, p. lxvii).

[5] Cf. Streeter, *op. cit.* pp. 388 *sq.*

[6] Jn. 20 [30].

familiar with Jewish customs, with the geography of
Palestine, and with the topography of Jerusalem. He
possesses, like S. Mark, a vivid power of realistic narration
and the capacity to visualize a scene as he describes it.
The Jesus, moreover, whose portrait he sets before his
readers is—despite the assertions of eminent critics—neither
a lay figure nor a theological abstraction. If He is the only-
begotten Son of God and the Word made flesh, He is also
emphatically true Man. He sits weary by the well,[1] He
weeps tears of human sorrow by the grave of His friend,[2]
He is troubled in soul,[3] He is distressed by the impending
treachery of Judas,[4] He thirsts upon the Cross.[5] The Gospel,
like the Johannine Epistles,[6] is anti-Docetic ; as Streeter
justly remarks, in the early Gentile Church, and especially
in Asia, it was the reality of our Lord's manhood that most
needed emphasis, and stress is laid in this Gospel, to an
extent which is unparalleled in the Synoptists, upon ' the
susceptibility of Christ to purely physical and simple human
experience.' [7]

The reason why these points have been to a large extent
missed or ignored by so considerable a number of scholars
is that their minds have been impressed by the difference
of atmosphere between the Fourth Gospel and the other
three Gospels. The difference of atmosphere is undoubted.
The Fourth Gospel is interpretative and mystical, selective
and deliberately doctrinal in its representation of our Lord.
The Evangelist, if we like to express it so, has put more of his
own subjectivity into the writing. He is a conscious artist,
and he writes with a deliberate purpose. What he is seeking
to do is to set forth the Lord Jesus to the cosmopolitan
Hellenists of Ephesus as the Saviour of the World [8]—to

---

[1] Jn. 4 [6].
[2] Jn. 11 [35].
[3] Jn. 12 [27].
[4] Jn. 13 [21].
[5] Jn. 19 [28].
[6] 1 Jn. 4 [2] sq.; 2 Jn. [7].
[7] Streeter, op. cit. p. 387.
[8] Jn. 3 [16] sq., 4 [42]; 1 Jn. 4 [14].

enable the 'Greeks' to 'see Jesus,'[1] and to believe that He is truly the Son of God [2]—and his writing is adapted throughout to this particular end. He is not content to record simply and without comment what Clement of Alexandria described as 'the bodily facts'; he is concerned to draw out and to make clear their doctrinal significance.[3] He has a special theory, for example, with regard to our Lord's miracles. The miracles manifest Christ's 'glory.'[4] They are 'works,' wrought by the Son in the name of His Father,[5] or by the Father indwelling the Son [6]—the 'works which the Father gave him to accomplish, that they might bear witness that the Father had sent him.'[7] They are meant to produce faith [8]—even though it be conceded that the faith which depends upon 'signs and wonders' is not faith at its highest [9] —so that at least 'for the very works' sake' men may believe on the Son of God.[10] At the same time the miracles are 'signs'—so the Evangelist characteristically describes them [11]—signs of Christ's Godhead, and symbols of spiritual truth. The Evangelist selects for narration by preference such stories of miracle as may best serve to illustrate the leading themes of his Gospel—Christ the Life and the Light of the world,[12] the Son of God,[13] the living Bread which came

---

[1] Jn. 12 21.   [2] Jn. 20 31.

[3] τὸν μέντοι Ἰωάννην ἔσχατον συνιδόντα ὅτι τὰ σωματικὰ ἐν τοῖς εὐαγγελίοις δεδήλωται, προτραπέντα ὑπὸ τῶν γνωρίμων, πνεύματι θεοφορηθέντα, πνευματικὸν ποιῆσαι εὐαγγέλιον (Clem. Alex. apud Euseb., H.E. vi. 14. 7).

[4] Jn. 2 11.   [5] Jn. 10 25.
[6] Jn. 14 10.   [7] Jn. 5 36.
[8] Jn. 2 11 : contrast Jn. 12 37.
[9] Jn. 4 48, 20 29.   [10] Jn. 14 11.
[11] Jn. 2 11, 23, 3 2, 4 54, 6 2, 14, 7 31, 9 16, 11 47, 12 18, 37, 20 30.

[12] The raising of Lazarus (cf. Jn. 11 25) : the healing of the man who was born blind (Jn. 9 1 sqq. ; cf. Jn. 8 12, 9 39 sqq.).

[13] The story of the healing of the impotent man at the pool of Bethesda (Jn. 5 2 sqq.). A discourse follows on the functions and prerogatives of the Son ; it is explained that His beneficent activities, like those of the Father, know no Sabbath rest or interruption ; He is 'equal with God,' and yet subordinate to the Father, inasmuch as He 'can do nothing of himself' (Jn. 5 17 sqq.).

down out of heaven [1]—and the doctrinal significance of the miracles is represented as being drawn out by the Saviour Himself.

Throughout this Gospel the theology which in the first three Gospels is implicit becomes explicit—and moreover it is ascribed to our Lord. The Jesus of this Gospel confutes the Jews, discusses with them the theology of His own Person, argues with them in a detached kind of fashion about the Law of Moses—' Yea, and in your Law it is written ' [2]—as though He Himself were no longer a Jew. He speaks in a different style from that of the Jesus who is the utterer of the sayings which have come down to us in the Synoptic tradition, and the style in which He speaks is identical with that of the Evangelist. It requires frequently keen observation to detect at what points, according to the scheme of the Gospel itself, the sayings of our Lord are intended to be regarded as having ended and the comments of the Evangelist as having begun.[3] The impression is created that the Evangelist himself hardly distinguishes even in his own mind—if indeed he distinguishes at all—between such sayings as perhaps formed part of the historical tradition of our Lord's words, and such other sayings as were the fruit rather of his own or of others' meditations—utterances not literally of Jesus Himself in the days of His flesh, but of the Spirit whom the Father had sent in Christ's name to be the teacher and guide of the Church, even ' the Spirit of truth ' [4] It has been suggested that the Evangelist

---

[1] The feeding of the multitudes (Jn. 6 [1] sqq.), followed by a discourse on our Lord as the Bread of Life (Jn. 6 [26] sqq.) and on the meaning of the Eucharist (Jn. 6 [51] sqq.).

[2] Jn. 8 [17], 10 [34].

[3] It was an excusable mistake on the part of the compilers of the ' comfortable words ' in the Anglican Prayer Book to treat Jn. 3 [16] as being, according to this Gospel, an utterance of Jesus, though it is probable that the Evangelist actually means the discourse with Nicodemus to be regarded as having ended at Jn. 3 [15], and that what follows is meant to be read as his own commentary.　　　　　[4] Jn. 14 [26], 16 [13], 14 [17].

himself may have been by temperament and gifts in a conspicuous degree a πνευματικός—a 'man of the Spirit,' a
Christian prophet [1]—and that in effect he is saying (like the
writer of the Apocalypse), 'Hear what the Spirit saith to the
Churches. . . . These are true words of God.' [2] According
to the teaching of this Gospel, it is the function of the Spirit
to 'glorify' Christ, to take of that which is Christ's and to
'declare it.' [3] It is probable that the Gospel itself should be
regarded as being a concrete illustration of the process,
and it is difficult not to think that the Evangelist has allowed
himself a considerable amount of dramatic freedom in the
dialogue. There are sayings ascribed to our Lord in this
Gospel with regard to the Jews who had rejected the Messiah
which—to speak quite candidly—we should be reluctant to
regard as being literally His ; [4] there are sustained arguments
with the Jews which are most naturally explained as being
dramatized versions of subsequent controversies between
the Church and the Synagogue ; [5] and there are discourses
which it is difficult to regard as being anything more than the
setting forth of the Church doctrines of Holy Communion
and of Baptism. [6]

It has been noticed, moreover, as being in a conspicuous
degree a peculiarity of this Gospel, that our Lord is habitually
represented in its pages as proclaiming Himself in the first
person singular. ' I am '—He is represented as saying—
' I am the bread of life,[7] the light of the world,[8] the door of the
sheep,[9] the good shepherd,[10] the resurrection and the life,[11] the
true vine.' [12] ' I am the way, and the truth, and the life.' [13]

---

[1] Cf. Weinel, *Die Wirkungen des Geistes und der Geister*, p. 98 ; and
Streeter, *op. cit.* pp. 371 *sqq.*

[2] Rev. 2 [7] etc., 19 [9].

[4] Jn. 8 [23] *sq.*, [44] *sqq.*

[6] Jn. 6 [51] *sqq.*, 3 [3] *sqq.*

[8] Jn. 8 [12].

[10] Jn. 10 [11, 14].

[12] Jn. 15 [1, 5].

[3] Jn. 16 [14].

[5] Jn. 5 [17] *sqq.*, 8 [12] *sqq.*

[7] Jn. 6 [35, 48].

[9] Jn. 10 [7, 9].

[11] Jn. 11 [25].

[13] Jn. 14 [6].

'I am from above . . . I am not of this world.'[1] 'I am in the Father, and the Father in me.'[2] 'Before Abraham was, I am.'[3] Parallels have been sought for this type of religious self-proclamation in the usage of orientalized Hellenism. It is an usage which stands in sharp contrast with the manner and style of our Lord's teaching as set forth in the Synoptic tradition,[4] and it has been suggested—more particularly by scholars who are disposed to base inferences upon the description in Celsus, to which reference was made in an earlier lecture,[5] of the claims made for themselves by itinerant prophets and self-deified men—that such self-proclamation was regarded, in the orientalized Hellenistic world, as being appropriate and almost necessary on the part of One for whom it was claimed that He was the Divine Son of God. According to Wetter, the Evangelist simply makes our Lord speak in what was regarded in the Greek-speaking world as the inevitable style of a 'Son of God.'[6] According to Norden, the usage in question goes back behind Hellenism to the type of self-proclamation which in early Sumerian, Babylonian, Assyrian and Egyptian hymnology is ascribed to the gods, and which appears in a secularized form in the inscriptions of oriental Kings from the period of the first Babylonian dynasty onwards.[7]

The researches of Norden are of singular interest ; but it would seem that in the case of the Fourth Gospel so recondite an explanation is hardly required. That our Lord should be represented in this Gospel as proclaiming Himself was really inevitable—it was involved in the Evangelist's whole method. It matters but little whether

---

[1] Jn. 8 23.   [2] Jn. 14 11.   [3] Jn. 8 58.
[4] In the Synoptists the solemn ἐγώ εἰμι of Jesus appears only in the story of the walking on the water (Mk. 6 50, Mt. 14 27) and in the Marcan version of our Lord's admission of the Messiahship at His trial (Mk. 14 62).
[5] Lecture III. pp. 69 sq.
[6] G. P. Wetter, Der Sohn Gottes, p. 170.
[7] E. Norden, Agnostos Theos, pp. 177 sqq., 207 sqq.

we regard the book as being ' a doctrinal work in the form of a Gospel ' or (as Lagrange would prefer to express it) ' a doctrinal Gospel.' [1] The Evangelist has in either case, whether consciously or unconsciously, dramatized doctrine by representing it as being taught by our Lord ; with the result that the affirmations of Christianity with regard to Him become in this Gospel His own self-affirmations, introduced by the formula 'I am.' If any analogy is required, it is to be found in the Old Testament. The solemn self-affirmations of our Lord in this Gospel suggest powerfully, no doubt, and are meant to suggest, His Divinity and Saviourhood ; it appears probable that the saying, 'Before Abraham was, I am,' in particular, is meant definitely to recall the mysterious ' I AM ' of the Old Testament Jehovah,[2] and to suggest that our Lord shares, as the pre-temporal Word, the uncreated eternity of God.

' The Word,' writes the Evangelist, ' became flesh.' What is meant by the expression ' the Word ' ? The writer does not explain it ; he assumes that it is familiar already to his readers. It occurs, as we were reminded in the course of the last lecture,[3] in a passage of the Apocalypse. It is unlikely that it was derived either by the writer of the Gospel from the Apocalypse, or by the writer of the Apocalypse from the Gospel.[4] The inference suggests itself that the title ' Word ' was already in current use in the Christianity of Ephesus as a recognized designation of Jesus. It has been held to present affinities with the Logos doctrine of Philo,

---

[1] Lagrange, op. cit. p. lxix.

[2] Jn. 8 [58] ; cf. Ex. 3 [14]. The problematical meaning of the Hebrew of Ex. 3 [14] is for our purposes less important than the fact that the LXX renders ἐγώ εἰμι ὁ ὤν. [3] Lecture VII. p. 191.

[4] The Apocalypse was probably written about A.D. 96. In the last lecture it was implied that the Gospel was written later. This is the usual assumption, but it is probable that the two books were nearly contemporary, and it is by no means inconceivable that the Gospel might have been written a year or two earlier than the Apocalypse. The dependence of either upon the other is in any case improbable.

with the World-Reason of Stoicism, with the use of the term *Memra* or ' Word ' in the Jewish Targums as a paraphrastic expression to avoid the direct use of the Divine Name in referring to God, and with the use of the term ' Logos ' in connexion with Hermes in the type of theology represented by the *Corpus Hermeticum*. It has been argued by Krebs that in such a city as Ephesus all or most of these various notions were probably current, and that in a general way the term ' Logos ' would be understood, in the light of its contemporary associations in various quarters, as conveying the idea on the one hand of a Divine Word of Revelation, on the other hand of a cosmic and soteriological principle, a Divine Being intermediate between God and the world. The term, he suggests, may have been selected deliberately in opposition to the various Logos doctrines of heathenism, the true Logos being opposed to the false.[1] Like most Catholic expositors, Krebs desires to lay stress upon the creative and cosmic as well as upon the revelational and soteriological functions which in this Gospel are ascribed to the Word—a line of interpretation which leads on to the more definitely philosophical and speculative Logos Christology of the Apologists and of the early Greek Fathers.

The remarkable thing is that the Logos conception as such—though the term is introduced in the first sentence of the Prologue and recurs later in the statement that ' the Logos became flesh '—does not in any way dominate or pervade the theology of the Gospel as a whole. In a sense the Christological idea which is really characteristic of this Gospel is the idea of our Lord as the Son of God, with whom the Logos is identified. The doctrine of the Prologue, in

---

[1] Krebs, *Der Logos als Heiland im ersten Jahrhundert*, pp. 98 *sq.* The appendix to this book contains a valuable and extremely damaging criticism of Reitzenstein's *Poimandres*, in which the arguments by means of which Reitzenstein attempted to establish a date earlier than that of the *Shepherd* of Hermas for the *Poimandres* document are shown clearly to be devoid of foundation.

O

so far as it really governs the thought of the Gospel, must be held to do so, as the late Dr. Sanday pointed out (following Holtzmann and Grill), not directly through the Logos conception, but through the two closely-related doctrines of Life and Light which (in Sanday's phrase) 'together make up, and are embraced under, the doctrine of the Logos.'[1]   Now, there seems reason to think that the antecedents of both these conceptions in the mind of the Evangelist are not Greek but Semitic.   They appealed, no doubt, to the Greek mind ; but in themselves they are Biblical.   They have their roots in the characteristically Hebraic conception of God as the Living God, who at the creation breathed into man's nostrils the breath of life,[2] and who as the Creator said ' Let there be light.'[3]   *Dominus illuminatio mea*—' The Lord is my light '—so runs the motto of the University of Oxford,[4] derived from an Old Testament Psalm.   ' With thee is the fountain of life,' says a Psalmist, ' and in thy light shall we see light.'[5]   The difference ' that what in the Old Testament is ascribed directly to Jehovah, in the Gospel is ascribed to the Logos ' is part, as Sanday remarks, ' of the Evangelist's method, which we may assume to be at work all through.'[6]   That the Evangelist was in any way directly dependent either upon the speculations of Philo or upon any alternative form of Hellenistic religious philosophy appears highly improbable.   What he has done is to adopt from current usage at Ephesus the term Logos or ' Word,' in order to express by its means the same type of Christology—it is really a ' Wisdom ' Christology—which had been developed by S. Paul and by the writer of the Epistle to the Hebrews.   ' By the word of the Lord were the heavens made,' writes a Psalmist, ' and all the host of them

---

[1] Sanday, *The Criticism of the Fourth Gospel*, p. 194.
[2] Gen. 2 [7].   [3] Gen. 1 [3].
[4] Ps. 27 [1].   [5] Ps. 36 [9].
[6] Sanday, *op. cit.* p. 195.

by the breath of his mouth.'[1] From the point of view of
the Old Testament, the Word was as capable as was the
Wisdom of God of being personified as a Divine Principle
intermediate between God and the world. It presented,
moreover, the advantage that in Greek the term Λόγος is
masculine, whereas Σοφία or ' Wisdom ' is feminine.

The Evangelist reads the Old Testament in the light of
his Christianity. He identifies Jesus with the creative,
personified Word, the self-utterance of God. The Gospel
according to S. Mark had begun simply ' The beginning of
the Good News of Jesus Christ, the Son of God [5] (in accordance with Old Testament prophecy), was John who baptized
in the desert.'[2] The later Evangelist must begin further
back. His mind goes back to the first beginning of all
things—to the first day of creation, when God spake, and
said, ' Let there be light.'[3] A true follower of S. Paul, he
will connect the work of redemption with the work of
creation.[4] He believes the same Christ to have been the
Divine Agent and Instrument of both. The beginning of
all things was the utterance by God of His Word—nay, the
Word uttered by God was already in existence. Already,
in the very beginning, the Word was ' with God,' and the
Word ' was God '—the expression, as it were, of God's
Being ; ' the same was in the beginning with God,' and by
Him were all things made, and ' that which was made, was
life in Him.'[5] I need not follow out the majestic words of
the Prologue in detail. They strike the keynotes of Life
and of Light—the Light shining in darkness, and yet not
overwhelmed.[6] The opening verses of the Gospel according
to S. Mark are recalled once more by the reference to the

[1] Ps. 33 [6].   [2] Cf. Mk. 1 [1] sqq.
[3] Gen. 1 [3].   [4] Cf. Lecture VI. pp. 160 sq.
[5] So the most probable, because the most difficult, punctuation of Jn. 1 [3]
sq. The meaning presumably is that all created life pre-existed in the
life of the Word before issuing into distinct and created being.
[6] Jn. 1 [5] (R.V., marg.).

coming and witness of the Baptist [1]—it is tempting to suppose that the Evangelist had S. Mark lying open before him as he was writing. The tragedy of the world that knew not its Creator, and of the coming of the Messiah to His own people—the Jews who rejected Him—foreshadows a theme which will recur later in the Gospel. The Jews who rejected Jesus serve as a kind of foil to the Gentiles who were willing to receive Him—' as many as received him, to them gave he the right to become children of God.' [2] ' And the Word became flesh and dwelt in our midst '—that is the supreme theme of the Gospel : the Word dwelt amongst men, as the *Shekhinah* or visible manifestation of the Divine Presence was believed to have dwelt in the Temple [3]—' and we beheld his glory, glory as of the only-begotten from the Father, full of grace and truth.' [4]

The Fourth Gospel—from a doctrinal point of view the crown and culmination of the New Testament—retells the story of Jesus from the point of view of the developed theology of the Church. But the point is not to be over-looked—for it is part of the Evangelist's contact with history—that the book contains also quite primitive Christ-ology. ' Rabbi,' says Nathanael to Jesus, ' thou art the Son of God, thou art King of Israel.' [5] The title ' Son of God ' is, as I have already hinted, even more than the term Logos, the real key to the Christology of this Gospel, and its significance is developed by the Evangelist in a very definitely theological sense. Nevertheless, in the passage just quoted he betrays the fact that he is well aware that originally, and in a purely Jewish as distinct from a specifically Christian context of thought, the title ' Son of

---

[1] Jn. 1 [6].   [2] Jn. 1 [12].

[3] ' The Greek word *skēnē* (tabernacle) and its derivatives were, perhaps, chosen on account of their assonance with the Hebrew word to express the *Shekhinah* and its dwelling with men ' (Oesterley and Box, *The Religion and Worship of the Synagogue*, p. 220).

[4] Jn. 1 [14].   [5] Jn. 1 [49].

God ' was synonymous with that of Messiah, and denoted simply the theocratic King of the people of God. So again in this Gospel our Lord is repeatedly designated simply as the Messiah—' We have found the Messiah,' say the earliest disciples, and the Evangelist adds the explanation, 'which is, being interpreted, Christ.' [1] The Evangelist even remains faithful to the historical fact that our Lord during His ministry upon earth was addressed normally by the disciples by the pre-christological title of ' Rabbi,' [2] and shows acquaintance with the early form of Christological thought which identified our Lord with the ' prophet like unto Moses ' of Deuteronomy,[3] though he repeatedly sets our Lord in pointed antithesis to Moses, as being a Greater than he.[4] He is familiar with the early Christian use of the title ' Son of Man,' and in the Gospel employs it in a sense at once primitive and Pauline. It is as the Son of Man that our Lord is to execute judgment.[5] It is as the Son of Man that He is to be exalted—the Evangelist uses the expression ' to be lifted up,' with an allusion primarily to our Lord's Passion : [6] but that it was by the way of the Cross that the Son of Man must pass to the throne of His glory was the teaching also of the Synoptic tradition of our Lord's words.[7] It is as the exalted Son of Man that our Lord gives His flesh and His blood to be mystically eaten and drunk by the faithful in the Eucharist.[8] As the Son of Man also He is in the Pauline sense pre-existent—He came down from heaven, and to heaven He returns.[9] Even during His life upon earth

---

[1] Jn. 1 [41] : cf. 4 [25, 29] ; 7 [26] sqq., 7 [41] sqq. ; 9 [22] ; 10 [24] ; 11 [27]. Cf. also 6 [15], 12 [13, 34], 18 [33] sqq., 19 [19].

[2] Jn. 1 [38, 49], 4 [31], 9 [2], 11 [8] ; cf. 20 [16] (' Rabboni ').

[3] Deut. 18 [15] sqq. See Lecture II. p. 37, and cf. Jn. 1 [22, 25], 6 [14].

[4] Jn. 1 [17] ; cf. Jn. 5 [45], 9 [28] sqq.

[5] Jn. 5 [27].

[6] Jn. 3 [14], 8 [28], 12 [34] ; cf. 13 [31].

[7] Cf. Mk. 8 [31], 9 [12, 31], 10 [33, 45], 14 [21, 41].

[8] Jn. 6 [53] : cf. 6 [62].

[9] Jn. 3 [13], 6 [62].

heaven stands open, and the angels of God ascend and descend upon the Son of Man, as upon Jacob of old.[1]

The title ' Lord,' on the other hand, is, relatively speaking, not prominent in this Gospel. It has been argued by Bousset—who notes also that it is nowhere found in the Johannine Epistles—that the Johannine writings proceeded from a circle of Christians to whom this particular title was uncongenial.[2] ' Ye are my friends,' says our Lord in this Gospel, ' if ye do the things which I command you. No longer do I call you servants ; for the servant knoweth not what his Lord doeth : but I have called you friends ; for all things that I heard from my Father I have made known unto you.'[3] According to Bousset, the writer thinks of himself and of his circle as being not the 'servants' or ' slaves,' but the ' friends ' of our Lord : and he holds that it is no longer, therefore, natural to them to address Him as ' Lord.' I cannot think that Bousset has here made out his case. The title ' Lord,' though it is relatively infrequent, is by no means avoided in the Gospel. It occurs not merely as a form of address in the vocative (in which usage it can sometimes, but not by any means always, be interpreted as meaning simply ' Sir ')[4] but as a description of our Lord by the Evangelist in more than one passage,[5] as a title claimed by our Lord for Himself,[6] and—most strikingly of all—in the solemn confession of the risen Lord by S. Thomas in the words ' My Lord and my God.'[7] It appears evident that Bousset has drawn the inferences too

[1] Jn. 1 [51] : cf. Gen. 28 [12].
[2] Bousset, *Kyrios Christos*, 2nd ed., p. 155.
[3] Jn. 15 [14] *sq.*
[4] So (e.g.) Jn. 4 [11, 15, 19, 49], 5 [7], 6 [34]; cf. 12 [21], 20 [15]. But contrast Jn. 6 [68], 13 [6, 9, 25, 36] *sq.*, 14 [5, 8, 22].
[5] Jn. 6 [23], 11 [2].   [6] Jn. 13 [13].
[7] Jn. 20 [28]. The title further occurs no less than eight times in the twenty-first chapter, which, however, is sometimes held to be an appendix by a different hand from that of the writer of the rest of the Gospel (cf. Jn. 21 [7, 12, 15, 16, 17, 20, 21]).

confidently from what appeared to him to be the implications of a particular saying.

It has been argued further by Bousset that the type of
piety—the kind of religion—which is reflected in this Gospel
is essentially non-Jewish. The Gospel ought to be interpreted, as he believes, from the point of view of Hellenistic
religion, and more particularly in the light of certain conceptions which he believes to have been characteristic of the
theology of the Mysteries. He draws attention to such a
saying as that which occurs in the fortieth verse of the
sixth chapter of the Gospel : 'For this is the will of my
Father, that every one that beholdeth the Son, and believeth
on him, should have eternal life.' [1] He compares a verse
from the first Epistle of S. John, which, as he believes,
contains not a 'Christ-mysticism,' but a God-mysticism,'
viz. : 'Beloved, now are we children of God, and it is not
yet made manifest what we shall be. We know that, if
he shall be manifested, we shall be like him ; for we shall
see him even as he is ' [2] The latter of these two passages,
as he suggests, contains the clue to the proper understanding of the former, and the religious conception to which
the two passages, taken together, give expression is that
which is familiar to the student of Hellenistic religion as
the idea of *deification by means of the vision of God*. The
actual word 'deification' the Evangelist avoids, but he
has that for which, in the type of religion in question, it
essentially stands, namely, eternal life, immortality, incorruption. A number of other passages in the Gospel then
fall into line—such sayings, for example, as 'the Word

---

[1] Jn. 6 [40]. The concluding words of the verse, viz. 'and I will raise
him up at the last day,' are discarded by Bousset as the 'pointless
addition' of an ecclesiastical redactor (*Kyrios Christos*, 2nd ed., p 177 *n.*).

[2] 1 Jn. 3 [2]. I cannot believe that Bousset is right in the distinction
which he here draws between a 'Christ-mysticism' and a 'God-mysticism.'
The 'manifestation' to which the writer of 1 Jn. 3 [2] looks forward is the
parousia of Christ, not a theophany of God.

became flesh . . . and we beheld his glory ; ' [1] ' He that hath seen me, hath seen the Father ' ; [2] ' The world beholdeth me no more ; but ye behold me : because I live, ye shall live also ' ; [3] ' Father, that which thou hast given me, I will that, where I am, they also may be with me ; that they may behold my glory, which thou hast given me.' [4]

These and similar passages Bousset would illustrate by comparing the importance attached in the Eleusinian Mysteries to the ἐποπτεία or ' ceremony of beholding,' the significance of which he would interpret in the light of the description in Apuleius of the initiation of Lucius into the Mysteries of Isis—' I beheld the sun shining with a bright light at midnight ; I saw likewise the gods both celestial and infernal ; I was admitted into their presence, I worshipped them face to face.' [5] He quotes further from the Greek text of a document in the Corpus Hermeticum, as conjecturally emended by Reitzenstein—' We rejoice, that while we are yet in our bodies thou hast made us divine by the vision of thyself.' [6] The same type of general conception he believes to be illustrated also in a different way by the ' astral mysticism ' of the astronomers and astrologers of the period, in so far as they may be said to have sought mystical union

---

[1] Jn. 1 [14].   [2] Jn. 14 [9].   [3] Jn. 14 [19].   [4] Jn. 17 [24].

[5] ' Accessi confinium mortis et calcato Proserpinae limine per omnia vectus elementa remeavi ; nocte media vidi solem candido coruscantem lumine ; deos inferos et deos superos accessi coram et adoravi de proximo ' (Apuleius, Metamorph. xi. 23).

[6] χαίρομεν ὅτι ἐν σώμασιν ἡμᾶς ὄντας ἀπεθέωσας τῇ σεαυτοῦ θέᾳ. The Greek text of the passage, which forms part of the concluding prayer of the series of ' Asclepius ' documents in the Corpus Hermeticum, has been edited by Reitzenstein from a magical papyrus, written probably about the end of the 3rd century A.D., and now in the Louvre (the so-called Papyrus Mimaut). The ' Asclepius ' documents as a whole are known only in a Latin translation. Unfortunately, the Greek text of the fragment is corrupt, and the crucial words τῇ σεαυτοῦ θέᾳ are simply a conjectural restoration by Reitzenstein. Cf. Reitzenstein, Die hellenistischen Mysterien-religionen, 2nd ed., p. 136 sq.; and see also W. Scott, Hermetica, vol. i. pp. 376 sq., where the text is printed in both Latin and Greek, with critical apparatus.

with God and life eternal by means of the contemplation of the stars as the ' visible gods.' [1] A third series of parallel instances he finds in the prominence given to the closely-related conceptions of Life and Light, not in the Johannine literature only, but in the literature of Gnosticism, both Christian and non-Christian, and especially in the so-called *Poimandres* document of the *Corpus Hermeticum*.[2]

It is not suggested by Bousset that the Evangelist was directly dependent upon any of these sources ; and indeed the greater part of his evidence is derived from documents which, as documents, are demonstrably later in date than the Gospel. What he suggests rather is that the notion that deification—or eternal life as its practical equivalent—could be attained as a result of beholding or gazing upon God was already in the air, and that it is this general conception which provides the right clue to the historical understanding of the Gospel. He thinks that our Lord in this Gospel is conceived both as a Mystagogue, revealing to His own the true *gnosis*, the *gnosis* which deifies, the miraculous ' words of eternal life ' [3]—' Never man spake like this man ' [4]—and also at the same time as a Divine Being, in whom men may ' see God,' and, as a result of seeing Him, become like Him.[5] The terms ' faith,' ' vision ' and ' knowledge ' in this Gospel, he suggests, are all virtually equivalents of one another— they all denote the same process of adoring and mystical contemplation of Jesus. It is a question of ' seeing ' or of ' beholding ' Jesus, of ' believing on ' Jesus, in order to ' see ' or ' behold ' the Father in Him, and to ' know ' God as the result of ' knowing ' Him whom God sent, Jesus Christ.[6]

His general conception of the Gospel Bousset sums up in

---

[1] Cf. Lecture III. pp. 63 *sqq.*

[2] Cf. (e.g.), *Corp. Hermet.* i. 9, ὁ δὲ νοῦς ὁ πρῶτος . . . ζωὴ καὶ φῶς ὑπάρχων, and i. 32 (of the soul that has received enlightenment), εἰς ζωὴν καὶ φῶς χωρῶ. Cf. also *Corp. Hermet.* xiii. 18, ζωὴ καὶ φῶς, ἀφ᾽ ὑμῶν εἰς ὑμᾶς χωρεῖ ἡ εὐλογία.

[3] Jn. 6 [68].   [4] Jn. 7 [46] (A.V.).   [5] Jn. 14 [9], 1 Jn. 3 [2].

[6] Jn. 17 [3, 25].

a short paragraph which may be quoted as follows. ' The Johannine writings,' he says, ' with their conception of life as being attainable through vision, with their doctrine of the Saviour's words of miraculous power, with their ideas of faith, knowledge, truth, light and darkness, light and life, have their roots in the soil of contemporary Hellenistic mysticism. To say this is not to detract from the Evangelist's originality. On the contrary, it is only from this point of view that we can begin for the first time to appreciate the grandeur of the conception which he proclaims. " He that beholdeth the Son, hath eternal life." The new message of the writer to his contemporaries is just this :—It is not by means of the contemplation of the starry heavens and the *pleroma* or " fulness " thereof, the multitude of gloriously shining divine beings who there move in their courses ; nor again is it by means of the vision of God as experienced at the supreme moment of the sacred initiation by the devotee of the Mysteries—it is not by these means that eternal life—exaltation into the sphere of divinity—is attained. On the contrary, *here* is the " fulness " of grace, here is the true light and life, and here, too, is the perfected *gnosis* : " He that beholdeth the Son and believeth on him, hath eternal life." ' [1]

I have summarized Bousset's position, not because I think he is right from the point of view of the Gospel itself, or that he has rightly understood the Evangelist, but because his position really does illustrate the kind of sense in which the Gospel might be read by a certain type of Greek reader. It is, moreover, the real purpose of the Evangelist to show Jesus to the Greeks, that they may believe on the Son of God, and he had perhaps learnt by experience how best to present Him in such a way as to appeal powerfully to the Greek mind. The actual origin of the doctrines of life and

---

[1] Bousset, *Kyrios Christos*, 2nd ed., p. 176. For Bousset's discussion of the Gospel as a whole, see *Kyrios Christos*, 2nd ed., pp. 154 *sqq*.

of light we have found in the Old Testament ; the special
prominence which is given to them in the Gospel, and the
half-mystical atmosphere of the whole book, may be due
to the fact that the Evangelist was writing in an environment
which was sensitive to mysticism, and in particular, perhaps,
to the appeal of a ' life and light ' mysticism—an appeal to
which, doubtless, he was himself also by temperament and
cast of mind sympathetic.

The conception of life eternal in Christianity was originally
eschatological : to 'enter into life,' or to ' inherit eternal
life,' in the Synoptic tradition, means to enter into life in
the eschatological sense.[1] Nevertheless, as we have seen,
it was the conviction of Christianity that the ' powers of the
coming age ' were already at work ;[2] and already in the
Epistles of S. Paul we have found prominence given to the
doctrine of the new supernatural life as a present possession
which at the same time is the ' earnest ' and ' first-fruits '
of a fuller inheritance hereafter.[3] The doctrine of the
Fourth Gospel is essentially similar, save only that the
balance of emphasis has been altered.   The doctrines of the
Parousia,[4] of the final Resurrection,[5] of the Judgement,[6]
and of the Life of the World to Come [7] are not abandoned,
but they have ceased to occupy the foreground of thought.
To speak more accurately, there is a spiritual sense in which
all these things are regarded as being already actualized here
and now in the life of the Church.   They are future events,
but they are also—and it is upon this fact that the stress of
the Evangelist's emphasis falls—present processes, eternally
going on. The *parousia* or ' presence ' of the Christ is
already realized in a secondary or spiritual sense—which for
the Evangelist tends already to become the primary sense,

[1] Cf. Mk. 9 [43], [45], 10 [17], [30] ; Mt. 19 [16] *sq.*, [29] ; 25 [46] ; 18 [1] *sq.* ; etc.
[2] Cf. Lecture II. p. 33.   [3] Lecture VI. pp. 154 *sq.*
[4] Jn. 14 [3], 21 [22] ; cf. 1 Jn. 3 [2].   [5] Jn. 6 [39] *sq.*, 11 [24].
[6] Jn. 5 [27] *sq.* ; cf. 1 Jn. 4 [17].   [7] Jn. 5 [29].

since that which is spiritual is in the fullest sense vital and real—through the coming of the Spirit. In this sense the Christ is already 'manifested'—to the Church, though not to the world.[1] The Spirit is sent by the Father in Christ's name,[2] and the coming of the Spirit is at the same time also a 'coming' of the Father and the Son.[3] The Judgement is similarly a spiritual process. It is happening now. Men are being judged by their response, or by their failure to respond, to the light.[4] The word spoken by Christ shall be the final judge of men.[5] So likewise with regard to the Resurrection. S. Paul had taught that there was a sense in which the faithful already were risen with Christ,[6] and our Lord in this Gospel is similarly represented as saying, 'Verily, verily, I say unto you, he that heareth my word, and believeth on him that sent me, hath eternal life, and cometh not into judgement, but is passed out of death into life.'[7] 'We know that we have passed out of death into life,' writes the Evangelist in the first Epistle of S. John, 'because we love the brethren.'[8] In all this the Evangelist is no doubt both drawing out and developing the significance of Christianity from the point of view of the life of the spirit, and also doing much to commend it in such a way as to appeal to the Greeks. His doctrine, nevertheless, presupposes from first to last as its basis the original eschatological tradition ; and in so far as there has been a development, it is a development which in principle is already anticipated by S. Paul.

Throughout the Gospel the Evangelist presents Christ to his readers as being the eternal Son of God, only-begotten,[9] unique, one with the Father,[10] to whom the Father has given

---

[1] Jn. 14 [22]. [2] Jn. 14 [26].
[3] Jn. 14 [23]. [4] Jn. 3 [17] *sqq.*, 9 [39] *sqq.*
[5] Jn. 12 [48]. [6] Col. 3 [1]. [7] Jn. 5 [24]. [8] 1 Jn. 3 [14].
[9] Jn. 1 [14, 18], 3 [16, 18] ; 1 Jn. 4 [9]. The title μονογενής in the Johannine literature is a virtual equivalent of ἀγαπητός in the Synoptists ; see pp. 79, 121 *sq.* [10] Jn. 10 [30].

His own holy name,[1] who alone ' cometh from above ' and is ' above all,'[2] the Son whom the Father sanctified and sealed,[3] and to whom He has given the Spirit without measure, so that the words which He speaks are ' the words of God.'[4] He is a proper object of worship—men are to ' honour the Son even as they honour the Father,' and the Jews who refuse thus to ' honour ' the Son are refusing to ' honour the Father which sent him.'[5] The Jews accuse Jesus of blasphemy, because, ' being a man,' he makes Himself God.[6] The Father is in Christ, and He in the Father.[7] He came forth from God into the world, and again, He leaves the world to go unto the Father.[8] He was in the bosom of the Father from the beginning.[9] Christian faith is faith in the Name of the Son of God,[10] prayer is prayer in His Name,[11] the new commandment of love, the fulfilment of which is the hall-mark of Christian allegiance, is the commandment given by the Son.[12] To see the Son is to see the Father,[13] to know the Son is to know the Father also.[14]

Behind this Christology is the Christian attitude towards Jesus, the Christian worship of God the Son. It has been suggested by Wetter, who like Bousset would interpret the Gospel from the point of view primarily of Hellenism, though on lines other than Bousset's, that our Lord is here set forth as a typical Hellenistic ' Son of God ' in implicit polemic against rivals.[15] He believes that the claims made for our Lord in this Gospel are typical claims made in the Hellenistic world for ' divine men '—prophets, miracle-workers, revealers of *gnosis*, supernatural in knowledge

[1] Jn. 17 11.   [2] Jn. 3 31 ; cf. 8 13.
[3] Jn. 10 36, 6 27.   [4] Jn. 3 34.
[5] Jn. 5 23.   [6] Jn. 10 33 *sqq.*
[7] Jn. 10 38, 14 10.   [8] Jn. 16 28.
[9] Jn. 1 18.   [10] Jn. 1 12, 2 23, 3 18.
[11] Jn. 14 13 *sq.*, 15 16, 16 23 *sq.*
[12] Jn. 13 34 *sq.*, 15 12 ; cf. 1 Jn. 3 11, 23, 4 7 *sqq.*, 21.
[13] Jn. 14 9.   [14] Jn. 14 7.
[15] G. P. Wetter, *Der Sohn Gottes*, esp. pp. 163 *sqq.*

and power.[1] At the same time, he recognizes that there
is an essential *differentia*. The Gnostic teacher and thaumaturge, the Hellenistic and heathen 'son of God,' proclaims primarily himself, concentrates everything upon
himself and his own claims, believes that divine, semi-
magical power and divine 'knowledge' are his to dispose
of according to his own will. The Jesus of the Fourth
Gospel proclaims also Himself, but in essential subordina-
tion to God. He comes not in His own name, but in the
name of His Father.[2] He can do nothing of Himself; He
seeks not His own will, but the will of Him that sent Him.[3]
He glorifies not Himself, it is His Father who glorifies Him.[4]
He 'keeps the word' of His Father.[5] The 'truth,' which
He tells to the Jews, is the truth which He 'heard from
God.'[6] It is the Father who is alone and always the
Giver: the Son receives from the Father. 'The Father
loveth the Son, and hath given all things into His hand.'[7]
Nevertheless, the Father is greater than He.[8] The supreme
doctrine of the Gospel is the doctrine of the eternal mystery
of the Divine Love—the love of the Son for the Father,
the love of the Father for the Son. 'Therefore doth the
Father love me,' says our Lord in this Gospel, 'because
I lay down my life, that I may take it again.'[9] 'The good
shepherd layeth down his life for the sheep.'[10] Nevertheless, the Father loved the Son before the foundation of the
world.[11] The Christian life is conceived by this Evangelist
as being before all things a life of fellowship—fellowship
with the Father, and with His Son Jesus Christ.[12]

But such fellowship with the Father and the Son is at
the same time also fellowship in the Spirit, fellowship in
the Church. The doctrine of the Church is set forth in

[1] Cf. Lecture III. pp. 70 *sqq*.   [2] Jn. 5 [43].   [3] Jn. 5 [30].
[4] Jn. 8 [54].   [5] Jn. 8 [55].   [6] Jn. 8 [40].
[7] Jn. 3 [35].   [8] Jn. 14 [28].   [9] Jn. 10 [17].
[10] Jn. 10 [11].   [11] Jn. 17 [24].   [12] I Jn. 1 [3].

the last discourses of Jesus, and especially in the allegory of the Vine. Continuance in the Vine is continuance in the love of Jesus, who has loved the disciples, as the Father hath loved Him.[1] With the coming of the Spirit the Father and the Son come also to take up their abode with the disciples,[2] and the unity of the disciples with one another is of the same kind as the unity between Christ and the Father, because it is an unity of love—the love wherewith the Father loved Christ is in them, and Christ is in them thereby.[3] Christians are to be one, even as Christ and the Father are one, that the world may believe.[4] ' God is love '—so the matter is summed up in the first Epistle of S. John—' and he that abideth in love abideth in God, and God abideth in him.'[5] The Evangelist proclaims a high mystical doctrine, upon the basis not of pantheism, but of Jewish and Christian monotheistic faith.

For he remains to the end essentially Jewish, despite the fact that there is a sense in which he has travelled far from Judaism. The Jews *are* the people of God, and if they had failed tragically to recognize the Messiah, it was because they had misread their own Scriptures.[6] The Evangelist's ' very anger with his own race,' writes Lord Charnwood, ' is that of a Jew. . . . His anger is the inverted patriotism of the prophet rebuking his people. . . . Intense as is his forward gaze upon a future in which mere Judaism counts for nothing, it is not without a passionate backward glance at the past. Consider, for example, what is signified by his only very important quotation from the Old Testament. It stands, in chapter xii., at what may be called the crisis of his argument, at the conclusion of his long insistence upon the Jews' rejection of our Lord. It is just because the testimony of the prophets has now been fulfilled to the uttermost that this most deeply Jewish of all

[1] Jn. 15 [9].   [2] Jn. 14 [23].   [3] Jn. 17 [11, 26].
[4] Jn. 17 [21].   [5] 1 Jn. 4 [16].   [6] Jn. 5 [39].

the Jews who wrote in the New Testament has, more markedly than any of them, now turned his face away from Judaism.' [1]

He has turned his face away from Judaism, in order to proclaim Jesus to the Greeks. He would set forth to the Greek world, with its pantheon of deities and its half-religious, half-philosophical agnosticism about God, the great message that God is knowable and revealed in Jesus. But the claim that in Jesus the true God is revealed, and that eternal life has at last been made possible for men, is made in the context and on the basis of the historic claim of the Jewish race to be the repositories of the true revelation of God. We are not allowed to forget in the Gospel that it was as a Jewish Messiah that the Saviour was crucified, and that the inscription over His cross was set forth to all the world in Greek, Latin and Hebrew— ' Jesus of Nazareth, the King of the Jews.' [2] ' Ye worship ye know not what '—so runs the Evangelist's message to his non-Jewish readers (and the saying is ascribed in the Gospel to the Lord Jesus Himself)—' we worship that which we know : for salvation is from the Jews.' [3] ' This,' writes the Evangelist, in what are almost the final words of the first of his Epistles, ' this is the true God, and eternal life.' [4]

I allow myself some concluding reflections. The attempt has been made in these lectures to interpret historically, and to study as objectively as possible, the successive and various forms which, within the period of the New Testament itself, were assumed by the Christian doctrine of the Person of Christ. The survey has been in some respects incomplete. I have been able to say little in detail about the Christology of the Synoptists, nothing at all about the writings traditionally ascribed to S. Peter, S. James

---

[1] Charnwood, *According to S. John*, p. 52 ; cf. Jn. 12 [37] *sq.*
[2] Jn. 19 [19] *sqq.*   [3] Jn. 4 [22].   [4] 1 Jn. 5 [20].

and S. Jude. Nevertheless, I believe that the chief types of New Testament Christology have been reviewed. We have recognized frankly a development. Christianity begins with the confession of Jesus as the Messiah, a confession which is accepted by Jesus Himself. It is in the capacity of a Jewish claimant of Messiahship that He allows Himself to be crucified. He is regarded after the Resurrection as the exalted Messiah, who is expected in the near future to return as the Son of Man coming in the clouds. Meanwhile He is the present 'Lord' of the Church. S. Paul introduces the idea of His pre-existence—an idea derived, as I have suggested, from the conception of Christ as the 'heavenly Man,' but involving also the identification of Christ as the 'heavenly Man' with the 'image' of God. The idea of His Sonship is at the same time read back into the past. He pre-exists from all eternity with God as His 'Son.' He is identified with the Divine 'Wisdom,' and in that capacity He is regarded as having been the mediator not merely of redemption but of creation. The Epistle to the Hebrews introduces the conception of His eternal High Priesthood. The Fourth Gospel presents Him as the eternal Son of God who is also God's 'Word,' and proclaims the final doctrine—that the Word who was with God and was God from the beginning, became flesh for the salvation of the world in Jesus Christ.

The categories of New Testament thought are not ours, and there is a tendency at the present day to be impatient with them. There is an even more strongly marked tendency to be impatient with that which is Jewish in Christianity, and to seek to get rid of it. The Dean of S. Paul's, in his recently published Hulsean Lectures delivered at Cambridge, has argued that the most desirable form of Christianity would be neither the Catholicism nor the Protestantism of history, but a kind of Christianized Platonism, in which 'the Christian element' would be 'supplied mainly by the identification of the inner light with the Spirit of the living, glorified, and indwelling Christ.'[1] He describes it as 'an autonomous faith which rests upon experience and individual inspiration.' 'We may call it,' he says, 'the Platonic tradition. . . . We may venture to call it the true heir of the original Gospel, while admitting that no direct Hellenic influence can be traced in our Lord's teaching. We may confidently call it Pauline and Johannine Christianity, though the theology of S. Paul is woven of many strands. . . . The tradition has never been extinct.'[2] It will be obvious that the Dean's point of view is the precise antithesis of that which has been maintained in these lectures. I have argued (with the writer of the Fourth Gospel) that ' salvation is from the Jews '; and the reading of Pauline and Johannine Christianity which I have put before you has been directed to emphasize the point that the whole development of Christianity in the New Testament period was continuously faithful to its originally Jewish beginnings. I made the point in my first lecture that what is really at stake in the modern discussion of Christianity is the validity of the essentially Jewish religious faith in the Living God, active in history, concretely real and personal, the Creator of the ends of the earth. I have sought to show that Christianity—in any form of it that matters— presupposes that essentially Jewish faith, and presupposes also the validity of the Jewish religious hope in God's purpose of redemption, and the doctrine of its fulfilment in Jesus. The Christological doctrine of the New Testament developed very rapidly, and quickly assumed, as we have seen, a variety of differing forms, some more and some less adequate as an interpretation of the experienced significance of Jesus. There are three elements which remained constant through-out. There is in the first place the religious cult of the

[1] W. R. Inge, *The Platonic Tradition in English Religious Thought*, pp. 33 *sq.*   [2] *Op. cit.* pp. 27 *sq.*

Lord Jesus—He becomes from the very beginning an object of faith ; He has, in modern phrase, the value of God ; He is the Lord of the Church, who can be invoked in prayer, side by side with the Father. In the second place, there is the insistence on monotheism. The Church did not become polytheistic. There is a constant straining, throughout the whole development of New Testament thought, to find ways in which the cult of the Lord Jesus might be reconciled with the belief that there is only one God. The solution was not finally reached until it was affirmed at Nicaea that the Son of God, in His essential being, is one with the Father—a solution which can only be repudiated at the cost of regarding Christianity as having involved from the beginning the idolatrous deification of a Jew. In the third place, implicit in the earliest and most rudimentary affirmation of the Messiahship of Jesus, and involved equally in every form of Christology, is the affirmation that the Person of Jesus is of absolute and ultimate religious significance for mankind, for the reason that through Him is the redemption of God's people. And because *it is of importance to affirm that the God of Redemption is also the God of Nature*, there is a religious truth also implicit in the Wisdom-Logos Christology, which affirms that the Christ who redeems is also the beginning and end of the Creation of God, the First Principle and Goal of Creation.

I am dissatisfied personally with every form of purely speculative or philosophical Christology which is known to me. I am prepared to recognize that in the Creed of the Church there are mythological elements, and I am content that it should be so. I am content personally to affirm that the Son of God ' for us men and for our salvation came down from heaven and was made man,' and I am unable to state my faith in any less frankly mythological form.[1]

---

[1] Mythological, because expressed in terms of pictorial metaphor. ' Heaven ' is not a place, from which earth could be reached by means of

Meanwhile I am prepared also confidently to prophesy that the future lies, not with any reduced, watered down, or attenuated version of Christianity, but with the full religious faith of the New Testament. The method of these lectures has throughout been historical and critical. I make no apology for this. In the modern educated world the historico-critical method of study is inevitable—as applicable and as fruitful in relation to the New Testament as in relation to any other body of ancient literature. Nevertheless, the last word is not with the historico-critical method. The things of the Spirit are spiritually discerned.[1] It is the Spirit who takes of the things of Christ, and declares them unto the Church.[2] 'The Spirit searcheth all things, yea, the deep things of God.'[3] The Church, taught by the Spirit, is enabled ultimately to know all things. The individual, taught by the same Spirit, may be enabled to know some things, and even, it may be, in some measure to make known to his fellows whatsoever it has been given him to apprehend of the unsearchable riches of Christ.

a literal ' coming down.' The language in terms of which theology expresses the doctrine of the Incarnation is riddled with metaphor through and through. But I believe that we have no more adequate means of expressing what nevertheless needs to be expressed.

[1] I Cor. 2 14.   [2] Jn. 16 14.   [3] I Cor. 2 10.

APPENDED NOTES

APPENDED NOTE I

The title ' Lord ' in pre-Hellenic Christianity.

IT has been assumed in the text of these lectures (see above, pp. 37, 76 *sqq.*) that behind the absolute description of Jesus in Greek-speaking Christianity as ὁ κύριος (' the Lord ') there lay an earlier description of Him as ὁ κύριος ἡμῶν (' our Lord '), corresponding to the Aramaic *Maran* ; and that consequently the belief of the Christian community in the religious lordship of Jesus must be traced back behind Greek-speaking Christianity to the original Aramaic-speaking Church. This view has been challenged by Bousset in the interests of his theory that in the earliest Christianity there was no element of present devotion to Jesus as the exalted ' Lord ' of the Church—that there was merely the hope of His future advent from heaven as the ' Son of Man.' Bousset stated his position in *Kyrios Christos* and defended it in *Jesus der Herr*, to which in turn frequent reference is made in the second edition of *Kyrios Christos* (see especially *Kyrios Christos*, 2nd edition, pp. 77-84 ; *Jesus der Herr*, pp. 13 *sqq.*).

Bousset's arguments may be briefly summarized. He begins by drawing a sharp distinction between the use of the vocative κύριε as a form of address, and the full use of ὁ κύριος as a title. The former, he urges, is without significance, inasmuch as the word κύριε may be used as a form of address not only to Christ or to God, but (e.g.) to the ' elder ' of Rev. 7 [14], or again by a slave in addressing his master (Mt. 13 [27], 25 [11], [20], [22], [24] ; Lk. 13 [8], 14 [22], 19 [16] *sqq.*), by a son to his father (Mt. 21 [30]), or, more generally, in addressing any one who is superior in rank (Mt. 27 [63]), or to whom it is intended to show respect (Jn. 11 [21], 20 [15] ; Acts 16 [30]). He concerns himself, therefore, exclusively with the use of ὁ κύριος, and proceeds to point out that

231

in the Synoptic Gospels it is least frequent in Mk. (according to Bousset the only relevant instance is Mk. 11 ³, where it occurs in what Bousset regards as a ' secondary amplification' of the story of our Lord's entry into Jerusalem), that Mt. ' follows for the most part the usage of his sources,' except that ' in a number of passages the vocative κύριε makes its way into the text,' but that in Lk., apart from a still more frequent use of the vocative, the title ὁ κύριος is introduced in about a dozen additional passages. Lk. of course represents Hellenistic Christianity, and with his Gospel ' the period of later usage clearly begins.'

Against this evidence it is useless, says Bousset, to appeal to the early speeches in Acts (e.g. Acts 2 ³⁶, ἀσφαλῶς οὖν γινωσκέτω πᾶς οἶκος Ἰσραήλ, ὅτι καὶ κύριον αὐτὸν καὶ χριστὸν ὁ θεὸς ἐποίησε), since the speeches in Acts are either free compositions on the part of ' S. Luke,' or at least have been freely redacted by him. Nor, again, does Bousset see any force in the suggestion that the earlier evangelists avoided the introduction of ὁ κύριος into the narrative of our Lord's earthly life with a certain historical tact, as being an anachronism before the period of our Lord's exaltation. He believes that the description of our Lord as ' the Son of Man ' was avoided in the Gospels (except as a mysterious proleptic self-revelation on the part of Jesus Himself) on the ground that this title had reference to the future—a future which was *still* future when the Gospels were written. For the avoidance of the title ὁ κύριος, which denoted Jesus as the *present* Lord of the Church, no such reason existed ; and the virtual non-appearance of this title in the earliest strata of the Gospel tradition is clear evidence to Bousset's mind that it was not known as a title of Jesus in the earliest period of the life of the Church.

Bousset proceeds further to argue the question upon linguistic grounds also. If the title ' Lord,' as applied to Jesus, goes back to a period when the Church spoke Aramaic, what are we to take to have been its equivalent in that language ? The Aramaic word *Mar* (= ' Lord ') is, strictly speaking, incapable of being used absolutely as the equivalent of ὁ κύριος. It can only be used as a title in com-

bination with a pronominal suffix, as in the forms *Mari*
(='my Lord') or *Maran* (='our Lord'). There is evidence
in the Gospels that our Lord was called 'Rabbi,' and there
is evidence in the Talmuds that a Rabbi was sometimes
greeted respectfully as 'my lord.' It is uncertain whether
the latter usage goes back to the first century, but it may
possibly have done so. Were the disciples, then, accustomed
to speak of their Master as 'our Lord,' in the sense of 'our
Teacher'? Very possibly, remarks Bousset; but the
problem is not thereby solved, since it is a far cry from the
use of *Maran* in this sense to such a religious use of the
title ὁ κύριος as appears in S. Paul.

On the other hand (he continues), it is still more impossible
to understand the term κύριος, on the assumption that it
represents some form of the Aramaic word *Mar*, as involving
in a religious sense the application to Jesus of a title of God.
The word in question was not in use as a title of God. It is
true that in the public reading of the Scriptures the word
Adonai (which in Hebrew means 'Lord') was habitually
substituted (probably already in the time of Christ) for the
personal name 'Jahve,' wherever the latter occurred; but
the practice did not pass over into the usage of ordinary
speech, and in *quoting* from Scripture (as distinct from reading it aloud in the synagogues) it was customary to substi-
tute not '*Adonai*,' but a word meaning simply 'the Name.'[1]
'The significant transition,' writes Dalman, 'from the divine
name "Jahve" to the divine name "Lord" did not take
place in the region of Hebraic Judaism. It is rather a
peculiarity of Jewish Hellenism, and from that source found
its way into the language of the Church, even of the Semitic-
speaking part of it.'[2] The word *Mar* (as distinct from
Adonai) is applied to God twice in the Book of Daniel; but
it is not there used absolutely. It occurs only in phrases
which affirm respectively that the God of the Jews is 'the
Lord of kings' (Dan. 2 [47]) and 'the Lord of heaven' (Dan.
5 [23]). Apart from these instances, there is no evidence of
the use of the word by the Jews as a title of God; nor, of

[1] Dalman, *The Words of Jesus*, E.T., p. 182.
[2] Dalman, *op. cit.* pp. 179 *sq.*

course, is it upon other grounds probable that a title understood as being distinctively divine would have been applied
without qualification to Jesus in a Jewish environment.

Bousset therefore regards himself as being justified in
maintaining that in Christianity also (and not merely in
Judaism), the 'significant transition' to the divine title
'the Lord' first took place (under the influence of the
Septuagint) upon Greek soil, and that the application to
Jesus of the title ὁ κύριος in a sense properly religious is
inconceivable at any stage earlier than that of definitely
Hellenistic Christianity.

I have attempted to state Bousset's position with fair-
ness. It must be pointed out in criticism that it depends,
for very much of its plausibility, upon the drawing of too
rigid a distinction between the sacred and the profane uses
of the term ' lord.' Wherever the title is used, in whatever
language, in application either to gods or to men, it denotes
always that the ' lord ' in question, whether human or
divine, has a just claim to the devotion, loyalty and reverence
of his slaves, subjects or worshippers. Thus if a Rabbi or
' teacher ' is addressed as ' lord,' the title thus given him,
even though in effect a mere piece of conventional politeness,
is nevertheless not a mere synonym of ' teacher.' It implies,
strictly speaking, that he is *more* than a ' teacher '—that he
is in fact a ' lord,' who has the rights of a ' lord ' over his
disciples. That the disciples of Jesus ever spoke or thought
of their Master as ' lord ' in this merely conventional sense
may be doubted. It was not as Rabbi, but as Messiah, and
(to judge by the evidence) more particularly as the *exalted*
Messiah, that they spoke of Him as their ' Lord.' It may be
conceded to Bousset—on grounds mainly linguistic—that
the ' absolute ' use of the title ' the Lord,' corresponding to
ὁ κύριος in Greek, would have been impossible in Aramaic,
and further, that the title carried with it a more absolute
meaning in Greek, and played a much more determinative
part in the Christology of the Greek-speaking Church—
more especially in view of its use as a designation of God in
the Septuagint—than it could ever have done, as a mere
title, in pre-Hellenic Christianity. But that the title was

used in pre-Hellenic Christianity, and that the Aramaic-speaking Church spoke of Jesus, in view of His exaltation to the right hand of God, as *Maran* (i.e. ' our Lord '), in a sense implying religious devotion, is surely clear from the Aramaic prayer-formula *Marana tha*, which S. Paul quotes in warning against his Judaistic opponents (1 Cor. 16 [22]). ' Teacher, come ! ' is an impossible rendering in such a context : the phrase means, and can only mean, ' Come, *Lord* ! '

The phrase *Marana tha* is in fact the Achilles' heel of the theory of Bousset. He attempts in various ways to get rid of it. In the first edition of *Kyrios Christos* he suggests that the phrase arose in bilingual Antioch : our Lord was first called κύριος, he thinks, by the Greek-speaking Christians in that city, but there were also Aramaic-speaking Christians in Antioch, and in imitation of their Greek-speaking brethren they adopted the title and rendered ὁ κύριος into Aramaic as *Maran*. In *Jesus der Herr* he resorts to a different explanation. For the moment forgetting that he had previously laid stress upon the point that *Maran* was not in use in Jewish circles as a title of God, he suggests that the formula, as used by S. Paul, was a Jewish curse (like ἀνάθεμα),[1] and meant ' Our Lord (i.e. *God*) will come and judge you ! ' (*Jesus der Herr*, pp. 22 *sq*.). In the second edition of *Kyrios Christos*, this new explanation in its turn is revoked, and the former suggestion that the title *Maran* arose in bilingual circles at Antioch is reasserted as ' a possibility which cannot be ignored,' and which ' must be taken seriously.' It would be a pity to allow one piece of evidence to upset Bousset's whole theory ! (*Kyrios Christos*, 2nd edition, p. 84.)

A further difficulty for Bousset's theory is the Christian use of Psalm cx. (for which cf. Mk. 12 [35-37] and parallels). That the Gospel section in question must be assigned to Palestinian Christianity is admitted by Bousset, though he regards it as containing ' Church-theology,' rather than as

---

[1] ἀνάθεμα=*Corban*, for which, as a Jewish oath-formula, cf. Josephus, *c. Apion*, i. 22, and Mt. 23 [18]. An oath-formula not infrequently in usage serves also as a curse-formula.

enshrining any actual words of our Lord. Nevertheless, the full force of the passage, as suggesting the application to Jesus of the term ' lord ' in a sense distinctively religious, is dependent, he pleads, on the Greek text of the Septuagint. In the Greek version the same word κύριος is used of the Messiah as of God (εἶπεν ὁ κύριος τῷ κυρίῳ μου . . . αὐτὸς Δαυεὶδ λέγει αὐτὸν κύριον). In the Hebrew (Ne'um Jahve l' Adoni) this point disappears, and in any Aramaic version of the words ascribed to our Lord the comment ' David himself calleth him Lord ' must have run ' David himself calleth him his lord.' According to Bousset, the term Adoni, supposed in the Psalm to be applied by David to the Messiah, can only be taken as meaning ' lord ' in the ' profane ' and not in the ' religious ' sense of the word. A strange argument, which betrays the whole weakness of Bousset's rigid distinction of the ' religious ' from the ' profane ' uses of the term ! For to a Hebrew the king, as the ' Anointed ' of Jahve, was already a religious personage, invested with the prerogatives of sacrosanct majesty ; and the expected ' Messiah ' was no ordinary king—he was the mediator of Israel's redemption, the supreme Agent, according to not a few forms of Messianic expectation, of the ' Restoration ' of all things. The argument of Mk. 12 [35] sqq. is that the Messiah had been called ' lord ' by King David himself : He is a fortiori the ' Lord,' divinely appointed, of the whole redeemed people of God. We have here, surely, an obvious basis for the description of the exalted Messiah as Maran (i.e. ' our Lord ') by all those who accepted His sovereignty, and it is probable, in effect, that it was precisely this Scriptural argument which gave rise to the title, the more usual Aramaic Maran being employed as a natural equivalent for the Hebrew Psalmist's Adoni.

Behind Bousset's denial to the Palestinian Church of the use of Maran as a title of Jesus there lies, of course, the more important denial to Christianity in its original form of any element of cultus (i.e. of properly religious devotion) on the part of Christians towards Christ. It is a leading contention of the present work that the cult of the Lord Jesus was inherent in Christianity from the beginning, and

that the eventual formulation of an explicit doctrine of our
Lord's deity as the incarnate Son of God was necessitated
by the fact that it provided the only ultimate intellectual
justification of such a *cultus* which was compatible with
monotheism. I am glad to be able at this point to refer to
a note by Johannes Weiss, who, after conceding to Bousset
that the title κύριος arose in a Greek-speaking *milieu*, and
that it implies as its correlative a *cultus*, proceeds to ask
how then, on Bousset's showing, is it to be supposed that
the alleged Gentile converts who first gave Jesus the title of
' Lord ' were led so to describe Him ? On what grounds did
they come to regard as a proper object of *cultus* a Person of
whom—simply as a human being—they can have known
relatively little ? The adoption of κύριος as a title presupposes a *cultus*—that is undoubtedly true. But the possibility of such a *cultus* presupposes in its turn the existence
already of an attitude of essentially religious devotion
towards Jesus (*eine im eigentlichen Sinne religiöse Verehrung*)
which must be credited, in the first instance, to the missionaries and not merely to their converts, and which must be
held to go back to the original Christianity of Palestine (see
J. Weiss, *Das Urchristentum*, p. 576, *n.* 2 ; and cf. also E.
Meyer, *Ursprung und Anfänge des Christentums*, iii. p. 218 *n.*,
and Deissmann, *Paulus*, 2nd edition, pp. 90, 98 *sqq.*).

APPENDED NOTE II

The designation ' Servant ' as applied to our Lord.

As according to Bousset the title ' Lord ' cannot go back to
the earliest Christianity, so also it has been argued by Professor F. C. Burkitt in *Christian Beginnings* that the application to Jesus of the passages referring to the Lord's Servant
in the second half of the Book of Isaiah arose first at the
stage of Greek-speaking Christianity, and depends upon the
use of the Septuagint (Burkitt, op. cit. pp. 35 sqq.).

Burkitt refers first, in justification of his position, to the
evidence of quotations in the New Testament—on the one
hand to the relative infrequency of references to, or echoes of,
the ' Servant ' passages in the Gospels, and to the virtual
absence of such quotations from the Apocalypse and from the
writings of S. Paul ; on the other hand to the exploitation of
the Servant passages in Acts (cf. especially Acts 8 ^{32} sq.),
and to the use made of them by ' S. Matthew ' (8 ^{17}), by
1 Peter (2 ^{22} sqq.), and by the author of the Epistle to the
Hebrews (9 ^{28}). ' The distribution of the two classes here,'
he writes, ' is quite significant. On the one side are Luke,
Hebrews, " 1 Peter," the editor of the First Gospel ; on the
other are Paul, " John," and the Apocalyptist, together with
the silence of Mark and of anything that could be grouped
under " Q." That is to say, the writers who use the Greek
Bible exclusively are on one side, while those who, like
S. Paul, have access to Semitic forms and interpretations
of the Old Testament are on the other.

' This is significant enough. It is enough to create a
strong presumption that the application of Isaiah 53 as a
prediction of the Passion of Jesus was the work of Gentile
Christians, familiar only with the Bible in Greek. But it
does not stand alone. . . .

' The matter can be stated in a single sentence. The

" Servant of the Lord," " My servant," etc., is in Hebrew
" the Lord's *slave*," " My *slave*." In the Greek translation
of Isaiah, this notion, not very attractive to Greek ears, was
not unsuitably softened by rendering '*ebed*, i.e. " slave,"
by πais, a word which, like " boy " in English, means both
son and *servant*. But this is peculiar to the Greek Bible.
Now, the earliest believers may very well have started with
a " low " Christology, but I do not think that any of them,
whether Greek or Jew, ever thought of Jesus, their Master,
as God's slave. . . . With the Greek-speaking Christians
it was different. There was nothing in the Greek Bible
to show that the Servant (or Son) of the Lord spoken of by
Isaiah was a bondservant, a slave, and so they applied the
phrases used of the Servant to Jesus. This stage is represented in Acts : it is a very early stage of Greek-speaking
Christianity, but it is not quite primitive or apostolic.' [1]

A writer who can claim no knowledge of Semitic languages
must necessarily differ with some hesitation from a scholar
like Burkitt with regard to a point of this kind. Nevertheless, I remain wholly unconvinced by his argument. I
have attempted to argue on the other side in a note appended
to my edition of *The Gospel according to S. Mark* in the
' Westminster ' series of commentaries (*op. cit.* pp. 251-256).
To what I have there said I would add only that Professor
Burkitt's insistence upon the idea that to describe our Lord
as ' God's slave ' would have appeared derogatory to any
early Christian who understood the true meaning of the
Hebrew word '*ebed* appears to me to betray a Greek, rather
than a Hebrew, valuation of slavery, and particularly to
suggest the wrong *nuance* of meaning, when what is in
question is the description of a person as the ' slave ' of a
god. I would refer once more in this connexion to the
passage in Robertson Smith's *Religion of the Semites*, from
which a quotation has already been made in the third
lecture (Lecture III. *supra*, pp. 77 *sq.*). ' In all parts of
the Semitic field,' writes Robertson Smith, ' the worshipper
calls himself the servant or slave ('*abd*, '*ebed*) of his god, just
as a subject does in addressing his king. The designation

[1] Burkitt, *op. cit.* pp. 38-41.

" servant " is much affected by worshippers, and forms the basis of a large number of theophorous proper names— 'Abd-Eshmun, " servant of Eshmun," 'Abd-Baal, 'Abd-Osir, etc. At first sight this designation seems to point to a more rigid conception of divine kingship than I have presented, for it is only under a strict despotism that the subject is the slave of the monarch ; it has been taken as a fundamental distinction between Semitic religion and that of the Greeks, that in the one case the relation of man to his god is servile, while in the other it is not so. But this conclusion rests on the neglect of a nicety of language, a refinement of Semitic politeness. When a man addresses any superior he calls him " my lord," and speaks of himself and others as " thy servants," and this form of politeness is naturally *de rigueur* in presence of the king ; but where the king is not addressed, his "servants" mean his courtiers that are in personal attendance on him, or such of his subjects as are actually engaged in his service—for example, his soldiers. . . . And so the servants of Jehovah are sometimes the prophets, who hold a special commission from Him ; at other times, as often in the Psalms, His worshipping people assembled at the temple ; and at other times, as in Deutero-Isaiah, His true servants as distinguished from the natural Israel, who are His subjects only in name. . . . Thus, when a man is named the servant of a god, the implication appears to be, not merely that he belongs to the community of which the god is king, but that he is specially devoted to his service and worship. Like other theophorous names, compounds with *'abd* seem to have been originally most common in royal and priestly families. . . . That the use of such names was not connected with the idea of slavery to a divine despot is pretty clear. . . . ' [1]

To these considerations should be added the fact that in Jewish exegesis, at least as represented by the Targum on the prophets, the ' Servant of the Lord ' of Deutero-Isaiah is explicitly identified with the Messiah in those passages which refer to his exaltation and glory, though the passages which refer to his humiliation and suffering are expounded

[1] Robertson Smith, *The Religion of the Semites,* pp. 68-70.

as referring not to the Messiah, but to the nation.[1] To identify the 'Slave of Jehovah' *in the capacity of a sufferer* with the Messiah was a Christian novelty, which for my own part I believe to have gone back (despite the relative infrequency of allusions to the 'Servant' passages in the Gospels) to the historical mind of the Lord Jesus Himself. Meanwhile, that to Jewish minds there was nothing either impossible or derogatory in the identification of the Messiah with the 'Slave of Jehovah' as such is abundantly clear from the exegesis of Isaiah in the Talmud.

The most remarkable thing about the New Testament evidence—accurately summarized by Burkitt—is the virtual absence of any references to the 'Servant' passages in the Epistles of S. Paul. If this is not accidental, I should be disposed to explain it by means of the hypothesis that S. Paul was affected not by Hebrew but by *Greek* social ideas about slavery. The occurrence of the 'Servant' Christology in the early chapters of Acts in the form, not merely of the explicit quotation in Acts 8 [32] *sq.*, but of the ambiguous Greek use of the word παῖς (Acts 3 [13], [26], 4 [27], [30]), suggests to my own mind the probability that the title 'Servant' as applied to our Lord is pre-Pauline, and that behind the ambiguous passages in the Acts there lurks an original Aramaic tradition (whether written or oral), in which the Messiah was described unambiguously as the 'Servant' of the Lord.

[1] Oesterley and Box, *The Religion and Worship of the Synagogue*, p. 51.

APPENDED NOTE III

*On the meaning and use of the title 'Son of Man'
in the Gospels.*

IT has been assumed in the course of this book that the
Aramaic phrase *barnāshā* ('Son of Man') was in current
use as a title of Jesus in the Palestinian or Aramaic-speaking
Church, that it was familiar to S. Paul, and that it implied,
in the minds of the earliest Christians who used it, an identification of Jesus, at least in respect of His *rôle* in the future,
with the mysterious Figure 'like unto a son of man' who in
the vision of Daniel is represented as coming in the clouds
(Dan. 7 [13]).[1] That the passage in question was interpreted
in later Judaism, at least in some circles, as having reference
no longer merely to the nation of Israel, but to the Messiah,
conceived as a heavenly, pre-existent individual, a supernatural Man who was destined to be revealed in the 'last
times,' appears clear from the *Book of Enoch* (*Eth. En.* 46 [1]
sqq., 48 [2] *sqq.*, 62 [5] *sqq.*, 69 [26] *sqq.*, 71 [14] *sqq.*; cf. also 2 Esdras
13). A possible Scriptural basis for such an identification
with the Messiah may perhaps have been supplied by
Ps. 80 [17], where it is not improbable that by the phrase 'the
son of man whom thou madest strong for thyself' the
Messiah was intended. It has been objected by some
scholars that the passages in *Enoch* and Esdras do not prove
that the phrase 'the Son of Man' was in any sense a recognized technical term—it may still, in the contexts in
which it occurs, be no more than a description. Thus in
Eth. En. 46 [1], where the so-called 'Son of Man' is introduced
for the first time, we read simply that 'with Him [i.e. with
God] was another being whose countenance had the appearance of a man'; and in subsequent references to the Figure

---

[1] *Vide supra*, Lecture II. p. 34, Lecture III. p. 75, and Lecture V.
pp. 122 *sqq.*

so introduced we have invariably (except in *Eth. En.* 62 [7])
the phrase ' that Son of Man ' (and similarly in 2 Esdras 13 [12]
'*ille homo*'), which it is natural to interpret as meaning simply
'the human Figure already mentioned.' Nevertheless, it
appears evident that, whether the title ' Son of Man ' was
already technical or not, the ' Son of Man ' Figure, based
upon Daniel, had become already a familiar conception,
and that the actual phrase ' Son of Man ' was at least on
the way to becoming technical. It is believed, moreover,
by Dr. Charles that the demonstratives ' that ' and ' this '
in the Ethiopic text of *Enoch* are simply mistranslations of
the Greek article, that the phrase in the original Greek must
have been, as in the Gospels, ὁ υἱὸς τοῦ ἀνθρώπου, and
that the title is in the *Book of Enoch* ' the distinct designation of the personal Messiah ' (R. H. Charles, *Apocrypha
and Pseudepigrapha of the Old Testament*, ii. p. 214).

Except in Rev. 1 [13], 14 [14] (which depend closely on Dan.
7 [13]) and in Acts 7 [56] (with which cf. and contrast Lk. 22 [69]),
the phrase ὁ υἱὸς τοῦ ἀνθρώπου appears in the New Testament only in the Gospels, in which it occurs frequently,
never, however, in the narrative, but always in words of our
Lord, as an indirect self-designation in the third person
on the part of Jesus Himself. To the earliest Greek readers
it must inevitably have appeared enigmatic and puzzling.
The Greek phrase, taken literally, could mean only ' the
son of the man '—a very unnatural and not very intelligible
expression, which according to Dalman could only have
suggested the idea of ' an intentional veiling of the Messianic
character ' under a title which affirmed the ' humanity '
of Christ.[1] It became certainly in later times the accepted
opinion that the title ' Son of Man ' was the antithesis of
' Son of God,' and that our Lord bore appropriately both
titles, as being at once human and divine. This, of course,
was to lose sight of the historical meaning of both phrases
as originally used in a context of Judaism, nor did it in any
way explain the peculiarity of ὁ υἱὸς τοῦ ἀνθρώπου as a
form of expression in Greek. The sub-apostolic author of
the *Epistle of Barnabas* was apparently alive to the possibility

[1] Dalman, *The Words of Jesus*, p. 255.

that it might be taken to imply that our Lord was 'the son of a man': he remarks that our Lord was οὐχὶ υἱὸς ἀνθρώπου, ἀλλὰ υἱὸς τοῦ Θεοῦ (*Ep. Barn.* xii. 10). The Fathers occasionally suggest that the term ἄνθρωπος in the phrase ὁ υἱὸς τοῦ ἀνθρώπου might be taken in a feminine sense to denote or include our Lord's birth from the Virgin (so, e.g., Greg. Naz., *Or.* 30: υἱὸς δὲ ἀνθρώπου καὶ διὰ τὸν Ἀδὰμ καὶ διὰ τὴν πάρθενον). It is possible that the compiler of the Gospel according to S. Matthew was attempting to explain the strange phrase for the benefit of his Greek readers when he introduced it into our Lord's question at Caesarea Philippi. The question in Matthew, according to the most probable reading, runs, 'Who do men say that the Son of Man is?'[1] The sequel suggests that the Christian answer is that the Son of Man is 'the Christ, the Son of the Living God.'[2]

It is likely that to not a few readers the most probable inference suggested by the peculiar phenomena of the Gospels, as contrasted in this respect with the rest of the New Testament, will be the one drawn by the late Dr. Sanday, viz. that the phrase 'can only go back to our Lord Himself,' and that it 'bears speaking testimony to the fidelity with which His words have been preserved.'[3] Upon this view, the phrase appears in the Gospels for the reason that it was actually used by our Lord as His 'favourite self-designation.' It is a literal translation of the Aramaic *barnāshā*, and it was employed, in translating words of our Lord, from motives of reverence and fidelity to the original, even in a language in which it conveyed, strictly speaking, no intelligible meaning. It was misleading in Greek, but less misleading than the more idiomatic translation of *barnāshā* as ὁ ἄνθρωπος. It at least served to convey the suggestion of a characteristic, if enigmatic, *title*—a title which for some reason had been used by our Lord of Himself.

Nevertheless, this conclusion has been doubted. It was

---

[1] Τίνα λέγουσιν οἱ ἄνθρωποι εἶναι τὸν υἱὸν τοῦ ἀνθρώπου; (so ℵ B as against D and Old Latin, which insert με).

[2] Mt. 16 13-16.

[3] Sanday, *The Life of Christ in Recent Research*, p. 125.

argued by Lietzmann, in a work called *Der Menschensohn*,
published in 1896, that the title in question could not have
been used by our Lord, for the simple reason that in Aramaic
such a title did not exist, and on linguistic grounds could not
exist. In the language used by our Lord, *barnāshā* was a
mere periphrasis for ' man,' and therefore, in Lietzmann's
view, could not have been used as a title. ' Son of Man,' as
a title, could only have arisen in Christian Greek-speaking
circles, on the basis of Dan. 7 [13] as read in the Septuagint.
Lietzmann's view was supported by Wellhausen—there was
no possibility of distinguishing, in the Aramaic spoken in
Palestine, between ' the son of man ' and ' the man,' and
the proper translation was simply ' the man.' In the article
Israel, contributed by Wellhausen to the *Encyclopaedia
Britannica*, which in an expanded form was reprinted as an
appendix to the English edition of Wellhausen's *Prolegomena*,
the view was adopted that, although ' son of man ' must
mean ' man,' nevertheless our Lord did so speak of Himself,
using always and emphatically this general name of the
race to designate His own person.' [1] In the later writings
of Wellhausen this ' half-way position ' was abandoned.
It was denied, with Lietzmann, that Jesus could have spoken
of Himself as ' the Son of Man.' The title must have arisen
amongst Christians, who identified Jesus with the 'heavenly
Messiah' of the Book of Daniel. It became a technical
term for the Christian (as opposed to the Jewish) Messiah.
It was introduced into the predictions of the Passion
(Mk. 8 [31], 9 [12], [31], 10 [33]), because distinctive of the Christian
conception was the doctrine of the Messiah as a sufferer.
The contrast is pointed in Mk. 8 [27] *sqq*. In two passages
Wellhausen thinks that it represents in the Greek text a
mistranslation of the Aramaic *barnāshā* in the sense of ' man '
generally (Mk. 2 [10], 2 [28]). As a result of the misunderstanding of these sayings it came to be supposed that our Lord
was accustomed to use ' the Son of Man ' as a periphrasis
for ' I,' and the title thus came to be introduced here and
there into other sayings of His also. All this development Wellhausen believed to have taken place very early.

[1] Wellhausen, *Prolegomena to the History of Israel*, E.T., p. 511.

'Already,' he writes, 'the Christians of Jerusalem will have distinguished the specific *barnāshā* from the ordinary *barnāshā*.' But how then can Wellhausen maintain that it was impossible in Aramaic for such a distinction to be made ? [1]

The views of Lietzmann and Wellhausen on the issue of Aramaic usage were challenged by Dalman, according to whom in the Aramaic of Palestine in the time of our Lord it *was* possible to say *nāshā* (as distinct from *barnāshā*) for ' man,' and indeed *nāshā* was the ordinary term.[2] The theory that our Lord could not have called Himself in Aramaic ' the Son of Man ' is ' a grievous error, which careful observation of the biblical Aramaic alone would have rendered impossible.' [3] The term *barnāshā*, employed by our Lord, ' did *not* properly belong to the common language of Palestinian Jews as a term for " man " ; it was charac-teristic rather of the elevated diction of poetry and prophecy. To the Jews it will have been known purely as a biblical word.' [4] Wellhausen's rejoinder appeared in his *Skizzen und Vorarbeiten*, and is partly reprinted in his *Einleitung in die drei ersten Evangelien*,[5] and the English reader is warned by Professor Burkitt, in a note contributed to the English translation of Schweitzer's *Quest of the Historical Jesus*,[6] against supposing that Dalman has finally settled the question. Nevertheless, it appears now to be fairly generally held that the merely linguistic objections to our Lord's use of *barnāshā* as a self-designation are not in-superable. Bousset in *Kyrios Christos* discusses the point, and, after drawing attention to the conflict of authorities, concludes by remarking that, even if Dalman is mistaken, and if *barnāshā* was (as Lietzmann and Wellhausen suppose) in common use in Palestinian Aramaic as the ordinary word for ' the man,' there is still no reason why, given

---

[1] For the above discussion see Wellhausen, *Einleitung in die drei ersten Evangelien*, 2nd ed., pp. 123 *sqq*.

[2] Dalman, *The Words of Jesus*, E.T., pp. 234 *sqq*.

[3] *Op. cit.* p. 239.

[4] *Op. cit.* p. 256.

[5] *Op. cit.* pp. 124 *sq*

[6] *Op. cit.* p. 279.

certain presuppositions, a quite general expression of this
kind should not have come to be used in a specific sense
to denote the Messiah. ' Jewish Apocalyptic loves to coin
such mysterious, enigmatic expressions.'[1] On the question
whether the term was ever actually used by our Lord, Bousset
expresses himself doubtfully. He believes that the majority,
if not all, of the instances in which ὁ υἱὸς τοῦ ἀνθρώπου
occurs in the Gospels are to be explained as being due to
the intrusion of ' Gemeindetheologie.'[2] But that the phrase
could have been used as a title Bousset has no doubt at all,
and despite Bousset's own sceptical hesitation it is believed
now by most scholars that our Lord did use the expression,
i.e. that He was accustomed to describe Himself, in some
specific sense, as ' the Man.'[3]

Assuming, then, as an historical fact our Lord's use of
the title, in what sense did He use it ? To the earliest
disciples, among whom it was current, it appears to have
carried with it the identification of Jesus with the Son of
Man of apocalyptic expectation. Did it imply this to Jesus
Himself ? It has been noticed that the passages in which
the description occurs in the Gospels fall into three distinct
groups. There is a group in which the title is used, in con-
formity with its use in late Judaism, with explicit reference
to the future Parousia of the Son of Man at the End of the
Age ;[4] there is a second group, in which the reference is
to our Lord's anticipated sufferings and death ;[5] and
there is further a third group, in which it would be possible
to understand the expression as being simply a periphrasis
for ' I,' though the sayings in question become much more

[1] Bousset, Kyrios Christos, 2nd ed., p. 12.
[2] Bousset, op. cit. pp. 5 sqq.
[3] Cf., e.g., Meyer, Ursprung und Anfänge, ii. p. 337; Reitzenstein, Das iranische Erlösungsmysterium, pp. 117 sqq.; Foakes Jackson and Lake, The Beginnings of Christianity, i. p. 374.
[4] Mk. 8 38 and parallels, 13 26 and parallels, 14 62 and parallels; Mt. 19 28, with which cf. Lk. 22 30; Mt. 24 27=Lk. 17 24; Mt. 24 37=Lk. 17 26; Mt. 24 44 =Lk. 12 40; Mt. 10 23, 13 41. 25 31; Lk. 17 30, 18 8, 21 36.
[5] Mk. 8 31=Lk. 9 22; Mk. 9 9=Mt. 17 9; Mk. 9 12=Mt. 17 12; Mk. 9 31 and parallels, 10 33 and parallels; Mk. 10 45=Mt. 20 28; Mk. 14 21 and parallels; Mk. 14 41=Mt. 26 45; Mt. 26 2; Lk. 24 7.

pointed if the phrase be interpreted as a periphrasis for ' the Messiah.' [1]

The phrase, in other words, in the Gospels denotes simply the Christian Messiah, who on earth had not where to lay His head (Mt. 8 [20]; Lk. 9 [57]), who is destined to suffering and death, and came not to be ministered unto, but to minister, and to give His life a ransom for many (Mk. 10 [45]), but who nevertheless, even upon earth, has authority to forgive sins (Mk. 2 [10]) and is Lord of the Sabbath (Mk. 2 [28]), and who is destined hereafter to ' come with the clouds ' as the Representative of God and the Ultimate Judge. The three groups of passages in which the expression is used are all explicable if we suppose that the Christian synthesis of the *rôle* of the Son of Man with the *rôle* of the Lord's Servant had already been effected in the mind of our Lord. He could use the phrase ' Son of Man ' in a sense which to His hearers (until they became seized of the right clue) must have appeared enigmatic (for if Jesus were the ' Son of Man ' of apocalyptic expectation, what could be the meaning of His present *rôle* as a mere man upon earth ?), because in His own mind the solution already was found. He was the Anointed of the Spirit (Is. 61 [1]), the Lord's ideal ' Servant ' or ' Slave,' the King-designate who was the ' servant of all ' (Mk. 10 [44]) ; and He was at the same time the ' Son of Man.' He could combine both convictions, because He had understood the Scriptures. The vision of Daniel should yet be fulfilled ; but the predestined road by which the Son of Man must pass to His glory was the road of the Cross.

The attempts of scholars to explain our Lord's use of the expression ' Son of Man ' have been many and various. It has been held (1) that the phrase, in our Lord's use of

---

[1] Mt. 8 [20]=Lk. 9 [58]; Mt. 11 [19]=Lk. 7 [34]; Mt. 12 [32]=Lk. 12 [10]; Mt. 12 [40]=Lk. 11 [30]; Mt. 13 [37]; Mt. 18 [11] (omitted by א B) ; Lk. 9 [56] (omitted by א B *al.*) ; Lk. 17 [22], 19 [10], 22 [48]. To these should be added two passages (Mk. 2 [10], 2 [28] and parallels) in which it has been proposed by Wellhausen and others (probably wrongly—see the notes *ad locc.* in my *Commentary on S. Mark*, pp. 25, 34) to understand the expression as having arisen as the result of the mistranslation of an original *barnāshā* in the sense merely of ' man.'

it, had no Messianic significance, but was a mere periphrasis for 'I,' intended, perhaps, at the most to call pointed attention to the fact of His manhood. According to Colani and others, it meant no more than ' I, who am no more than a mere man.' According to another view, it meant ' I, who am the *ideal* man,' or the 'absolute' man, the 'universal' or ' representative ' man. According to the late Dr. Abbott, the meaning of the expression might be summed up in such phrases as ' divine Humanity,' or ' Man according to the intention of God.'[1] Such interpretations, it is now generally agreed, are too modern. ' Jesus,' in Wellhausen's words, 'was no Greek philosopher and no modern humanist, nor did He speak to philosophers and humanists.'[2]

(2) It has been argued (no doubt rightly) by Dalman that ' in view of the obvious reference by Jesus to Dan. 7 [13] in His apocalyptic discourse, Mt. 24 [30] (Mk. 13 [26]; Lk. 21 [27]), and in His testimony before the Sanhedrin, Mt. 26 [64] (Mk. 14 [62]),[3] it can scarcely be doubted that Dan. 7 [13] was the source from which He took the self-designation. This origin is further confirmed by the fact that it was also from Daniel that Jesus adapted the idea of the sovereignty of God.'[4] Dalman inclines to the view that our Lord did not use the expression ' Son of Man ' until after S. Peter's confession of faith at Caesarea Philippi, and that it meant (in dependence on Dan. 7 [13], but perhaps with some thought also of its use in Ps. 8 [4] *sq.*) *that member of the human race* (*Menschenkind*), *in his own nature impotent, whom God will make Lord of the world.*[5] It is admitted, however, by Dalman that the view that the title was not used until after Caesarea Philippi is a pure *a priori* conjecture, and

[1] E. A. Abbott, *The Message of the Son of Man*, p. 73.

[2] Wellhausen, *Einleitung in die drei ersten Evangelien*, 2nd ed., p. 126.

[3] It should be noted, however, that the first of these instances to which Dalman refers is derived from the supposed ' Little Apocalypse,' which may not historically go back to our Lord, and that the exact wording of the saying at the trial, in which our Lord acknowledges His Messiahship, may represent rather the terms in which the earliest believers confessed their faith than the *ipsissima verba* of Christ.

[4] Dalman, *The Words of Jesus*, E.T., pp. 257 *sq.*

[5] *Op. cit.* pp. 264 *sq.*

that ' as for the evangelists themselves, they take the view that Jesus called Himself " the Son of Man " at all times and before any company.'[1]

(3) According to Völter, the passages in which the title is used in the eschatological sense are not genuine words of our Lord but are in all cases products of the early (and mistaken) beliefs of the Church. Our Lord's own use of the title he thinks goes back to the use of the corresponding Hebrew phrase *ben adam* by Ezekiel, and means that our Lord thought of Himself as the Messiah in the sense of a Prophet who (like Ezekiel) was charged with a mission to the ' rebellious ' and ' stiff-hearted ' children of Israel,[2] a mission which would involve sufferings and ultimate death.[3]

(4) Conversely, it is held by many scholars that the ' eschatological ' passages in which the title occurs are alone genuine, or at least primary, and that the title came to be introduced wrongly into other sayings, or alleged sayings, of Jesus at an early stage in the development of the Christian tradition.

(5) F. Tillmann, who appears to have written the least unsatisfactory monograph on the subject, sums up his conclusions as follows : ' The name " Son of Man " is a title of the Messiah, just as much so as the names " Son of David," " the Anointed," etc. Jesus decided in favour of this name because it best expressed what He was and what He meant, and because it gave least support to the political and national hopes which His people attached to the person of the Messiah. If we ask further as to the specific content of this name as applied to the Messiah, the reference, implied in it, to the prophecy in Daniel gives the key : the Son of Man is the divine-human Bringer of Messianic salvation of the prophet's vision, He with whose coming begins the Kingdom of God upon earth.'[4]

[1] *Op. cit.* p. 259.　　　　　[2] Ezek. 2 [3] *sqq.*, 3 [4] *sqq.*

[3] D. Völter, *Die Menschensohn-Frage neu untersucht* (Leiden, 1916).

[4] F. Tillmann, *Der Menschensohn. Jesu Selbstzeugnis für seine messianische Würde* (Freiburg im Breisgau, 1907). The book appears with the *imprimatur* of the Archbishop of Freiburg. Despite the conservative presuppositions of Roman Catholic biblical scholarship, it is a scientific and competent piece of work.

APPENDED NOTE IV

The ' Filial Consciousness ' of Jesus.

THE phrase ' Son of God,' which in a context of Greek pagan thought appears to have denoted a θεῖος ἄνθρωπος, a ' supernatural person,' or ' manifest god ' (θεὸς ἐπιφανής),[1] and of which a Christian theological interpretation is developed in the writings of S. Paul and of ' S. John,' denoted in a context of purely Jewish thought either Israel,[2] or a righteous Israelite,[3] or the Messiah.[4] As applied by others to Jesus in a context of Jewish Christianity, the phrase can only have meant ' the Messiah,' and it is with this meaning, presumably, that it occurs in the story of our Lord's Temptation.[5]

Nevertheless, we have seen reason to think[6] that our Lord was accustomed not only to speak characteristically of God as His ' Father,' but also to think, and from time to time to speak, of Himself as ' the Son ' : and it appears likely that this phrase, upon His lips, was not *simply* a Messianic title, but that it was rather the expression of some profound and specific awareness of inner personal relationship to God, the characteristic form under which the ultimate mystery of His Person was interpreted to His own human mind. I have given tentative expression in Lecture II. to my agreement with those scholars who have regarded the ' filial consciousness ' of Jesus as constituting the indispensable psychological presupposition of the possibility of His acceptance of the Messianic vocation.

---

[1] *Vide supra,* Lecture III. pp. 70 *sqq.*
[2] Ex. 4 [22], Hos. 11 [1].
[3] *Ecclus.* 4 [10] ; *Wisd.* 2 [16, 18], 5 [5] ; *Pss. Sol.* 13 [8], 18 [4].
[4] 2 Sam. 7 [14]; Ps. 2 [7]; 2 Esdras 13 [32].
[5] Mt. 4 [3, 6]=Lk. 4 [3, 9].
[6] Pp. 50 *sq., supra.*

The broad case for this view I would rest primarily upon our Lord's characteristic use of the expression ' the Father ' in speaking of God (a use which appears to have gone beyond what was usual in Judaism),[1] and also—more generally— upon His whole doctrine of the Divine Fatherhood, which I believe to be adequately interpretable only in relation to His own human life as God's ' Son.' I believe further that the distinction between the ' son ' and the ' servants ' in the Parable of the Wicked Husbandmen (Mk. 12 [6] and parallels) goes back to our Lord, and that the same is true of the saying in Mk. 13 [32]. The argument for our Lord's ' filial consciousness ' is therefore essentially independent of the question of the authenticity, as literal utterances of Jesus, of the sayings of Mt. 11 [25-27] (with which cf. Lk. 10 [21] sq.).

The sayings in question, however, which have given rise to a great deal of discussion, may be shortly discussed here; and the discussion of them may usefully begin with a consideration of the views of Harnack with regard to the text.

The passage in Mt., as printed in Souter's Oxford text of the Greek New Testament, but arranged (as it should be) in stanzas,[2] runs as follows :—

Ἐν ἐκείνῳ τῷ καιρῷ ἀποκριθεὶς ὁ Ἰησοῦς εἶπεν,
Ἐξομολογοῦμαί σοι, πάτερ, Κύριε τοῦ οὐρανοῦ καὶ τῆς γῆς,
ὅτι ἀπέκρυψας ταῦτα ἀπὸ σοφῶν καὶ συνετῶν
καὶ ἀπεκάλυψας αὐτὰ νηπίοις·
ναί, ὁ πατήρ, ὅτι οὕτως ἐγένετο εὐδοκία ἔμπροσθέν σου·

πάντα μοι παρεδόθη ὑπὸ τοῦ πατρός μου·
καὶ οὐδεὶς ἐπιγινώσκει τὸν υἱόν, εἰ μὴ ὁ πατήρ·
οὐδὲ τὸν πατέρα τις ἐπιγινώσκει, εἰ μὴ ὁ υἱός,
καὶ ᾧ ἐὰν βούληται ὁ υἱὸς ἀποκαλύψαι.

[1] See the note on p. 50 *supra*. The usage in question is not distinctively Matthaean ; cf. (e.g.) Mk. 14 [36], Lk. 12 [32].

[2] That the passage constitutes a short poem has been recognized by many scholars : see esp. C. F. Burney (*The Poetry of our Lord*, pp. 133, 171), who attempts a retranslation of the stanzas common to Mt. and Lk. into Aramaic verse.

δεῦτε πρός με, πάντες οἱ κοπιῶντες καὶ πεφορτισμένοι,
κἀγὼ ἀναπαύσω ὑμᾶς·
ἄρατε τὸν ζυγόν μου ἐφ᾽ ὑμᾶς, καὶ μάθετε ἀπ᾽ ἐμοῦ, ὅτι
πρᾷός εἰμι καὶ ταπεινὸς τῇ καρδίᾳ,
καὶ εὑρήσετε ἀνάπαυσιν ταῖς ψυχαῖς ὑμῶν·
ὁ γὰρ ζυγός μου χρηστός, καὶ τὸ φορτίον μου ἐλαφρόν ἐστιν.

The first two stanzas appear also in Lk. 10 21 sq., as
follows :—

Ἐν αὐτῇ τᾷ ὥρᾳ ἠγαλλιάσατο τῷ Πνεύματι τῷ Ἁγίῳ,
καὶ εἶπεν,
Ἐξομολογοῦμαί σοι, πάτερ, Κύριε τοῦ οὐρανοῦ καὶ τῆς γῆς,
ὅτι ἀπέκρυψας ταῦτα ἀπὸ σοφῶν καὶ συνετῶν
καὶ ἀπεκάλυψας αὐτὰ νηπίοις·
ναί, ὁ πατήρ, ὅτι οὕτως ἐγένετο εὐδοκία ἔμπροσθέν σου·

πάντα παρεδόθη μοι ὑπὸ τοῦ πατρός μου·
καὶ οὐδεὶς γινώσκει τίς ἐστιν ὁ υἱός, εἰ μὴ ὁ πατήρ,
καὶ τίς ἐστιν ὁ πατήρ, εἰ μὴ ὁ υἱός,
καὶ ᾧ ἐὰν βούληται ὁ υἱὸς ἀποκαλύψαι.

The verbal agreement of the two versions, so far as they
are parallel, is very close. It is clear that the first two
stanzas, if not also the third, stood in ' Q ' (i.e. the Greek
source containing sayings of Jesus, believed by Streeter to
have been of Antiochene *provenance*, which was used in
common by Mt. and Lk.), and it appears probable that the
variations in Lk. from the wording as given in Mt. are merely
stylistic, and that Mt. represents the more accurately of
the two the original wording of ' Q.'

The text of the passage as given in the Greek MSS. does
not present any particular problems, and the MS. evidence
as a whole is almost unanimous, except that there is one
cursive MS. of the Old Latin version of the Gospels (*Codex
Vercellensis*) which stands quite by itself in omitting from
the text of Lk. 10 22 the clause which refers to the Father's
knowledge of the Son, so that the verse reads in this MS. :
' *Omnia mihi tradita sunt a patre, et nemo novit quis est pater
nisi filius et cuicumque voluerit filius, revelavit.*'

The text, however, as read (or, at least, as quoted) by early Church Fathers and by their heretical opponents presents numerous and interesting variants, and the evidence of patristic quotations (with partial support from the versions) is held by Harnack to point back to the original existence of a form of the text, at least of Lk. and of ' Q,' which differed in two important particulars from the text as it now stands in the Greek MSS. The two chief variants which appear in the patristic quotations of the passage are :

(1) The substitution for γινώσκει of ἔγνω, a reading asserted by Irenaeus to be an heretical forgery on the part of certain persons who desire to be ' *peritiores apostolis* '—Harnack thinks that Irenaeus was quite right in feeling that the sense of *cognovit* (ἔγνω) was different from that of *cognoscit* (γινώσκει), but wrong in regarding ἔγνω as being an heretical corruption—and

(2) The placing of the Son's knowledge of the Father before the Father's knowledge of the Son. This might be held to suggest that originally the text contained only one of these clauses, and that the other is a gloss. We have noted already that *Codex Vercellensis* omits the words which refer to the Father's knowledge of the Son from the Lukan version of the saying. Harnack believes that it was right in so doing.

His conclusion, therefore, is that the text as it originally stood in ' Q ' and in Lk. was as follows :—

Ἐξομολογοῦμαί σοι, πάτερ, κύριε τοῦ οὐρανοῦ καὶ τῆς γῆς,
ὅτι ἔκρυψας ταῦτα ἀπὸ σοφῶν καὶ συνετῶν
καὶ ἀπεκάλυψας αὐτὰ νηπίοις·
ναί, ὁ πατήρ, ὅτι οὕτως ἐγένετο εὐδοκία ἔμπροσθέν σου·

πάντα μοι παρεδόθη ὑπὸ τοῦ πατρός,
καὶ οὐδεὶς ἔγνω τὸν πατέρα [*vel.* τίς ἐστιν ὁ πατήρ] εἰ μὴ ὁ υἱὸς
καὶ ᾧ ἂν ὁ υἱὸς ἀποκαλύψῃ.

In favour of this text Harnack argues :—

(1) That we do not expect to find the clause concerning ' knowing the Son ' in this connexion, since the passage

—an ascription of praise—is concerned both at the beginning and at the close with the *knowledge of God.*

(2) ' The historic aorist ἔγνω suits excellently the Son's knowledge of the Father, *but it does not suit so well the Father's knowledge of the Son* ; this has been noticed by thoughtful copyists, who have tried to overcome the difficulty in various ways.'

(3) ' *The clause* καὶ ᾧ ἂν ὁ υἱὸς ἀποκαλύψῃ *only suits the clause* οὐδεὶς ἔγνω τίς ἐστιν ὁ πατὴρ εἰ μὴ ὁ υἱός, *but not the other clause with which it is connected above in St. Luke (the Son is God's interpreter and not His own). This also has been correctly seen by the copyists, who accordingly overcome the difficulty by transposition (or even by changing* υἱός *into* αὐτός, *which then refers to the Father).*'

(4) ' *In Cod. Vercell. of St. Luke we even now read* (vide supra) *the saying without the clause concerning " knowledge of the Son."* '

Harnack believes the saying, in the short form of text which he defends, to be genuine. He thinks it was uttered just after some conspicuous success in our Lord's ministry —some acceptance of His message on the part of simple folk (νήπιοι), who *through Him and through His teaching* have for the first time attained the full knowledge of God's Fatherhood. The word πάντα means here not ' all things ' but ' the whole doctrine . . ., the complete revelation of the knowledge of God.' The doctrine came to Jesus Himself as a παράδοσις ; it was ' delivered ' to Him by the Father, and now He has succeeded in passing on the παράδοσις to others. Only from Him can they learn it. (For the whole discussion, which I have summarized, see Harnack, *The Sayings of Jesus,* E.T., pp. 272 *sqq.*)

Harnack's views on the text have not won general acceptance. They were sharply challenged by Dom Chapman, who in an elaborate article contributed to the *J. Th. S.* pointed out that the passage, just because in the ancient Church it was continually being quoted and discussed, was commonly quoted from memory. The variations in the order of the clauses were to be explained in this way, and the reading ἔγνω (which would not really differ in meaning from γινώσκει, any more than the Latin *novit* really differs in meaning from *cognoscit*), if it ever stood in any Greek codices, was probably only an eccentric reading of some copies, not of Lk. (as Harnack supposed), but of *Mt.* The text of the Gk. MSS., according to Chapman, is right, and the saying means that ' the Father has revealed the Son to the disciples (as he did to St. Peter and to St. Paul) : it was His good pleasure, for without such a revelation none could know the Son, whom the Father alone knows ; similarly, the Father is only known by the Son, and by those to whom it is His good pleasure to reveal Him ' (see J. Chapman, O.S.B., *Dr. Harnack on Luke x. 22: No Man Knoweth the Son*, in the *J. Th. S.*, July 1909, pp. 552 *sqq.*).

A solution differing from Harnack's, though influenced by his textual discussion, is suggested by B. S. Easton, the most recent editor of S. Luke. Dr. Easton shares acutely the difficulty which has been felt by many recent writers with regard to the possibility of the clause about *the know-ledge of the Father* on the lips of our Lord. ' This verse,' he writes, ' certainly enunciates the basic principle of the mystery religions ' [he should have said rather ' the Gnostic sects '—for the distinction see the note *supra*, pp. 67 *sq.*], ' that true knowledge of God is hidden, and is conveyed only to a chosen few by a Divine mediator, and this principle is most difficult to reconcile with the other teaching of Christ.' Dr. Easton would therefore *reverse* Harnack's solution, i.e. of the two clauses of which the order is varied in patristic quotations, he would omit the saying about the knowledge of the Father. He agrees that πάντα means not ' all power ' but ' all knowledge,' and holds that the ' knowledge ' in question means the knowledge of the full secret of the Messiahship. ' Only the Father knew the real meaning of Messiahship, but now the Son knows, and He has communi-cated His knowledge to His chosen disciples.'. The verse as a whole means, he thinks, ' the Father has (at last) granted me full knowledge of the Messianic mystery ; no one knew the nature of the Son's work but the Father, and now only those know it to whom the Son reveals it ' (B. S. Easton, *The Gospel according to S. Luke*, pp. 166 *sq.*).

A consideration which tells strongly against all such
arguments as those of Harnack and Easton in favour of a
shortened form of the text is the rhythmic structure of the
whole passage. If the whole is cast in the form of a poem
the clauses about the Son's knowledge of the Father and the
Father's knowledge of the Son are *both* necessary, on grounds
of form, for the sake of the parallelism. The most thorough
discussion of the whole group of sayings from this point of
view is that of Norden, who in *Agnostos Theos*, pp. 277 *sqq.*,
draws attention to the similarity of structure between
Mt. 11 [25-30] and *Ecclus.* 51. In each case we have (1)
a thanksgiving to God—Mt. 11 [25] *sq.*, cf. *Ecclus.* 51 [1-12],
followed by (2) the revelation of a mystery—Mt. 11 [27], cf.
Ecclus. 51 [13-22], and (3) an appeal to men to draw near—
Mt. 11 [28-30], cf. *Ecclus.* 51 [23] *sqq.* With both passages he
compares (*inter alia*) the conclusion of the *Poimandres* document in the *Corpus Hermeticum*, where, after the revelation
has been received from the mysterious ' Poimandres,' the
initiate concludes :—

' Therefore with all my soul and with all my strength
did I give praise to God the Father, saying :
' " Holy is God the Father of all, who is before the first
beginning. . . .
' " Accept pure offerings of speech from a soul and heart
uplifted to thee, thou of whom no words can tell, no tongue
can speak, whom silence only can declare. . . ."
' And when I had given thanks and praise to the Father
of all, I was sent forth by him, having had power given
me. . . . And I began to preach to men the beauty of
piety and of the knowledge of God, saying : " Hearken, ye
folk, men born of earth, who have given yourselves up to
drunkenness and sleep in your ignorance of God ; awake
to soberness, cease to be sodden with strong drink and
lulled in sleep devoid of reason." '—(*Corpus Hermeticum*,
i. 30 *sqq.*, translated by W. Scott.)

Norden believed all these passages to have been independent of one another, but concluded that behind all of them
there was a common traditional scheme, derived from the

' mystical-theosophical literature of the East,' of which the
Hermetic passage has preserved the true logical order,
which was as follows :—

      (1) Revelation of a μυστήριον.
      (2) Thanksgiving for the γνῶσις of God.
      (3) Appeal to men to learn the true γνῶσις.

In both *Ecclus.* and Mt. the order is distorted by the placing
of the thanksgiving first, with the result that in Mt. the ταῦτα
of verse 25 is left hanging in the air, with nothing to which
it can refer : it should really refer to the revelation of truth
in verse 27, which now follows it. He thinks that the compiler of ' Q ' was acquainted with some mystical-theosophical
writing which afforded an example of such a scheme, and that
he adapted it, making use of the *motifs* which it contained
in order to set forth our Lord as the sole Revealer of the
true *gnosis*, though in the authentic spirit of the Gospel he
directs the Christian appeal not to the adepts of Gnosticism,
who are ' wise,' but to the ' weary and heavy-laden,' who
from the point of view of Gnosticism are νήπιοι.

Against Norden it has been argued that *Ecclus.* 51 does
not really fall into three sections, but into two : verses 1-12
are a thanksgiving for deliverance from danger, quite
separate structurally from the rest of the chapter, and
verses 13-30 go together and form a distinct alphabetical
poem (so, e.g., McNeile, *The Gospel according to S. Matthew*,
p. 165, and E. Meyer, *Ursprung und Anfänge*, i. p. 281).
It may further be pointed out that the early date of the
Poimandres document, assumed by Norden to have been
established by Reitzenstein, is now widely rejected (see
Krebs, *Der Logos als Heiland*, pp. 133 *sqq.*, Meyer, *op. cit.* ii.
p. 372 *n.*, W. Scott, *Hermetica*, ii. p. 11). It is argued by
Bousset that the absence from Lk. of the saying contained
in Mt. 11 [28-30] makes it doubtful whether more than the
first two stanzas stood in ' Q,' and that if the third stanza
was missing Norden's whole case falls to the ground. Even,
however, if a literary scheme does underlie the composition
in Mt., it may still be the case that the passage has preserved
genuine words of our Lord, though arranged and perhaps
editorially adapted by the Evangelist. Of the three sayings

the only one which is really difficult is the second (Mt. 11 [27] ; Lk. 10 [22]), the tone of which—as occurring in the *Synoptic* tradition of our Lord's words—is certainly ' singular ' (Bousset, *Kyrios Christos*, 2nd edition, pp. 45 *sqq.*).

In *Die Schriften des N.T.* (earlier editions) the attempt is made by J. Weiss to interpret the saying as having been uttered by our Lord in a moment of sudden revelation, in which He rejoiced in the illuminating knowledge of the Father, and at the same time felt clearly how little He was Himself understood ; no one knew what He, the Son, really was, except the Father. It was the secret of His own personality, His Messiahship, which came as a solution of the question which had troubled His soul. He had thought that His call to the Messiahship involved the huge burden of winning the whole nation ; and yet the mass of them, especially the scribes, remained so dull and unimpression-able ! Was He the Chosen of God after all ? The doubts melted away at this supreme moment. He realized that the secret of His Person was meant only for a few, to whom it was specially revealed ; and, freed from the greater burden, He now understood that His work was to bring this revela-tion to the few. (So J. Weiss, summarized by McNeile.) McNeile justly remarks that this explanation (which neces-sitates the placing of the clause ' knoweth the Son ' after ' knoweth the Father ') is ' largely subjective,' and that it presupposes too detailed a knowledge of our Lord's inner life. In the third edition of *Die Schriften des N.T.* (revised by Bousset) it is withdrawn. In *Das Urchristentum*, Weiss attempts only to understand the passage from the point of view of the Evangelists. It enshrines ' the utmost that the earliest Church was able to assert of the earthly Jesus. There can be no question but that He here stands solitary amongst the children of men, as " the Son " over against " the Father." Between Him and the Father there subsists a relationship of mutual knowledge which is wholly unique.' [1]

Among other interpretations of the passage may be mentioned those of B. W. Bacon, A. H. McNeile, and P. W. Schmidt.

---

[1] J. Weiss, *Das Urchristentum*, p. 87.

Bacon thinks that the saying is authentic, but that it had originally no specifically Christological reference. He believes that the whole group of sayings gives expression simply to our Lord's championship of the 'lost sheep of the house of Israel,' the despised *am ha-aretz* or 'people of the land,' who are supposed to have been 'dispossessed of their spiritual inheritance' by the Pharisees and scribes. Bacon would print the word 'son' with a small letter, not with a capital. He believes that the meaning is 'Only a father can know his son, only a son can know his father. I have learnt to know God as my Father, because God has acknowledged me as His son. But the knowledge is not for me only, but for all those who are sons and daughters of God. And because I have learnt it myself, I can give the knowledge to others. It is the son who is competent to give revelation of the Father ; but this knowledge is not that of the wise and understanding, it is such as is given to those who are simple-hearted as babes.' (See Bacon, *Jesus the Son of God*, pp. 1-33.)

McNeile follows Bacon, but with a difference. He accepts the theory of Bacon about the reference of the saying to our Lord's championship of spiritual outcasts, but he recognizes that the title 'the Son' on our Lord's lips is distinctive. He builds upon the idea that the Messiah, as ' Son of God,' is the Representative of the sonship of Israel. Our Lord, he writes, ' knows Himself to be the Champion and Representative of the true Israel, the pious, humble and oppressed. He thanks His Father for revealing truths to them, the " babes," not to the privileged, learned class, the "wise and prudent." Even so, Father, for so it was Thy good pleasure. To Me, their Representative, " the Son," the whole truth has been entrusted. None except Thee can know My Sonship, i.e. that I hold this representative office ; none has the immediate, experimental knowledge of Thy Fatherhood, which is the prerogative of My Sonship, except Myself, the Son, and those to whom I reveal it.' (McNeile, *New Testament Teaching in the Light of S. Paul*, pp. 28 *sq.*)

The view of P. W. Schmidt is more interesting. He believes that Norden has rightly recognized the affinities of the passage with *Ecclus.* 51 (to which attention had been drawn also by Loisy [1] and at an earlier epoch by Strauss), and further that Norden's argument is conclusive (as against Harnack) that the clause about the Father's knowledge of the Son is, on grounds of literary form, indispensable. On the other hand, since both *Ecclus.* and Mt. have the three elements in the scheme (thanksgiving, revelation, invitation) in the same order, there is no need to appeal with Norden to any further traditional scheme, supposed to have been disseminated in the Hellenistic East, which had the order (1) revelation, (2) thanksgiving, (3) invitation. Schmidt believes that our Lord really uttered the sayings, and that He had the concluding chapter of *Ecclus.* (with which He may have been familiar in the Hebrew original) in mind. The relation between Mt. 11 [28] *sqq.* and *Ecclus.* 51 [23] *sqq.* is particularly close, as may be seen by placing the parallel passages side by side, thus :—

Jesus ben-Sirach, 51 [23] *sqq.*	' *St. Matthew,*' 11 [28] *sqq.*
(23) Draw near unto me, ye unlearned.	(28) Come unto me, all ye that labour and are heavy laden.
(26) Put your neck under the yoke, and let your soul bear her burden [so the Hebrew text of Sirach].	(29) Take my yoke upon you, and learn of me. . . .
(27) Behold with your eyes, How that I laboured but a little, And found for myself much rest.	(30) For my yoke is easy, and my burden is light.
	(29) For I am meek and lowly in heart : and ye shall find rest unto your souls.

The parallelism in the last words (' for myself ' . . . ' for your souls ') is especially striking in view of the fact that the Hebrew word for ' soul ' or ' life ' (*néphesh*) can mean also ' self.' [2]

Schmidt draws attention to the fact that the passage

[1] Loisy, *Les Évangiles Synoptiques,* i. p. 913.

[2] It is possible, however, that Mt. 11 [29] is based on the Hebrew text of Jer. 6 [16] (' and ye shall find rest for your souls '). The LXX of the passage has a different reading (ἁγνισμόν, where we expect ἀνάπαυσιν).

in Mt. (and so also, apparently, in ' Q ') follows (separated from it only by the Woes on the Cities of Galilee) the Rebuke to the Generation which had responded neither to the appeal of the Baptist nor to the appeal of the Son of Man, and that the latter passage concludes with the comment ' *Wisdom* is justified by her works ' (so Mt. 11 [19]) or ' of all her children ' (so Lk. 7 [35]). He believes that our Lord was deliberately identifying Himself with the Divine Wisdom. Like Ben-Sirach, He begins with a thanksgiving (' I thank thee, O Father, Lord of heaven and earth '—cf. *Ecclus.* 51 [1], ' I will give thanks unto thee, O Lord, O King ') : the saying about the mutual knowledge of the Father and the Son follows, and takes the place of the account in *Ecclus.* 51 [13] *sqq.* of Ben-Sirach's search after ' Wisdom ' ; the invitation at the end of our Lord's group of sayings corresponds with the invitation at the end of Ben-Sirach—but with the significant difference that, whereas Ben-Sirach invites the ' unlearned ' to put their necks under the yoke of the Divine Wisdom and (encouraged by the fact that he himself has found rest by so doing) to ' receive instruction ' from her, our Lord deliberately puts *Himself* in the place of the Divine Wisdom, and invites all them that labour to take *His* yoke upon them, and to learn of *Him*, who is ' meek and lowly in heart.' (See P. W. Schmidt, *Menschheitswege zum Gotterkennen*, München, 1923, pp. 195 *sqq.*)

Did our Lord in His human life thus actually, as a matter of historical fact, identify Himself with the Divine Wisdom of the Old Testament and of Jesus ben-Sirach ? It is easier to ask than to answer the question. On the other hand, that the group of sayings under discussion, in the full form in which they appear in Mt., stands in some kind of literary relation to the Hebrew original of Ben-Sirach appears not to be doubtful. That the passage as it now stands in the Gospels—and especially the saying of Mt. 11 [27], Lk. 10 [22] —is ' Johannine ' in character appears also to be really unquestionable. It would be possible, in effect, to regard the saying in question as having been the germ from which was ultimately developed the whole Johannine theology of our Lord as ' the Son.'

Was the saying actually uttered by Jesus? It is hard to give a confident answer. There are those to whom the fact of its occurrence in ' Q ' will be sufficient evidence that (in the words of Bishop Gore) it is ' authentic beyond all reasonable dispute.' [1] But it is strange that—in so far as the evidence enables us to judge—it does not appear to have influenced the very earliest Christology of the Church, and the saying stands wholly isolated in ' Q.' As an expression of Christian belief about Jesus, which eventually came to be attributed to Jesus Himself, it is wholly intelligible. As a saying uttered by Jesus it is less easy, though perhaps not impossible, to explain. For myself, I am not ashamed to confess that I am not able to make up my mind. It appears to me to be not impossible for a saying which was not literally authentic to have come to be included in ' Q.'

On the other hand, it certainly cannot truthfully be maintained that the fundamental idea of the passage—the idea of ' knowing and being known ' in relation to God—is essentially Hellenistic. The idea is not only found in S. Paul ; [2] it is conspicuous in the theology of the Old Testament. It is the duty of Israel to ' know Yahweh,' and in the day of the New Covenant every true Israelite shall know Him. [3] ' The Lord hath a controversy ' with Israel, because ' there is no truth, nor mercy, nor *knowledge of God* in the land.' [4] The Lord desires ' the knowledge of God ' more than burnt-offerings. [5] But the reason why Israel may be expected thus to ' know Yahweh ' is that Yahweh Himself first has known Israel. ' You only have I known of all the families of the earth.' It is this fact which makes Israel peculiarly responsible. [6] So also the greatness of Moses as a prophet is explained by the consideration that he was one ' whom the Lord knew face to face.' [7]

I would conclude this note by drawing attention to a passage in a book by an American writer, Dr. Paul Elmer More. [8] ' Mrs. Humphry Ward in her *Recollections*,' he

[1] Gore, *Belief in Christ*, p. 56.
[2] Gal. 4 [9]; I Cor. 13 [12].   [3] Jer. 31 [34].   [4] Hos. 4 [1].
[5] Hos. 6 [6].   [6] Amos 3 [2].   [7] Deut. 34 [10].
[8] P. E. More, *The Christ of the New Testament*, pp. 239 *sqq.*

writes, ' tells how once in Oxford she was expatiating to Pater on the certain downfall of the orthodox views of Christ under the blows of historical criticism, expecting his assent, and how she was surprised by his answer :

' " I don't think so," he said. Then with hesitation : " And we don't altogether agree. You think it 's all plain. But I can't. There are such mysterious things. Take that saying, ' Come unto me, all ye that are weary and heavy laden.' How can you explain that ? There is a mystery in it—a something supernatural." '

Dr. More adds a comment of his own : ' There it is, the mystery, the something supernatural, the words that never man spake, the veiled utterance of a pretension that opens the door to strange speculations. Other leaders of religious movements have assumed the authority of divine inspiration, but I do not know where in the books of the world you will find anything quite equivalent to that " Come unto me " spoken by an historical man who professed in the same breath to be, and in life showed himself to be, " meek and lowly in heart." If the saying is genuine, as we have reason to hold it, then we must acknowledge that Jesus arrogated to himself something more than belongs to humanity.'

APPENDED NOTE V

On the alleged 'Adoptionism' of Primitive Christianity.

THE term 'Adoptionism' is familiar to students of the history of Christian doctrine as the name of a heresy which appears to have been current at Rome in the last quarter of the second Christian century. According to the teaching of the Adoptionists, our Lord was originally a man who, by a special decree of God, was miraculously born of a Virgin, and who subsequently (after the piety of His life had been thoroughly tested) was equipped by the Holy Spirit with supernatural powers at His Baptism. Eventually, as the reward of His achievement, He was raised from the dead and adopted into the sphere of the Godhead. He was a man who had become God.

It was a crude theory—in essentials the familiar Greek pagan conception of apotheosis. But it was a theory which it was easy for pagan minds—or for the minds of raw converts to Christianity from paganism—to entertain. It appeared to afford at once an intelligible account of our Lord's human career and a justification of the Church's attitude towards Him. The Fourth Gospel was apparently either not as yet known to the Roman Church, or not as yet fully accepted as canonical. To simple-minded readers it is obvious that the Adoptionist theory might easily appear to be the natural meaning of the Synoptic accounts of our Lord's life, and the *prima facie* implication of the early Christology of Acts.

The Roman Adoptionists claimed that their theory was the original teaching of Christianity, and that down to the time of Pope Victor (A.D. 190-198)—by whom the Adoptionist leader Theodotus of Byzantium was excommunicated—it had been the accepted teaching of Christianity at Rome.[1]

---

[1] Euseb., *H.E.* v. 28.

There are modern scholars by whom this assertion is regarded as containing a substratum of truth. It is believed by Harnack that in early Gentile Christianity there were two distinguishable types of Christology—a ' pneumatic ' or incarnationist type, and an ' adoptionist ' type—which were both widely prevalent side by side, and which competed for the mastery. According to the one view, our Lord was regarded as ' a heavenly spiritual being (the highest after God) who took flesh, and again returned to heaven after the completion of his work on earth.' According to the other view, He was regarded as ' the man whom God hath chosen, in whom the Deity or the Spirit of God dwelt, and who, after being tested, was adopted by God and invested with dominion.' Harnack adds in a footnote the remark that ' both were clearly in existence in the Apostolic Age.'[1] The work known as the *Shepherd* of Hermas[2]—a true example of the type of popular uninstructed Christianity (*vulgär Christentum*) of which the heart was in the right place though the head was confused—has been thought to exhibit a blend of both theories, though by some scholars it is held that the Christology of Hermas is Adoptionist *sans phrase*.

The theory of an original Roman Adoptionism has been carried furthest by Lake, who in *Landmarks of Early Christianity* argues desperately that it would be possible to interpret in an Adoptionist sense *all* the documents of the earliest Christianity at Rome—the Epistle to the Romans, the Epistle to the Hebrews, 1 Peter, 1 Clement, Hermas, and the Gospel according to S. Mark![3] The religion of the Roman Church as revealed in 1 Clement he would sum up as ' hellenized Judaism, without the ceremonial law, but with a belief in Jesus and the Church'; and Jesus, he thinks, was regarded simply as ' the divine messenger of God, who in turn had appointed the Apostles as the foundation of the Church.'[4]

---

[1] Harnack, *History of Dogma*, E.T., i. pp. 190 *sqq.*

[2] The *Shepherd* of Hermas was written at Rome—according to some scholars as late as A.D. 140, according to others considerably earlier.

[3] K. Lake, *op. cit.* pp. 102 *sqq.*   [4] *Op. cit.* p. 110.

Other scholars, without attempting so definitely as Lake to establish the existence of a continuously Adoptionist tradition in a particular Church (e.g Rome), have nevertheless held that the New Testament evidence suggests that the original doctrine of Christianity was Adoptionist, and in particular that Adoptionism represents the theory originally held with regard to the Divine Sonship of Jesus. 'According to the most ancient opinion,' writes Pfleiderer, 'the man Jesus Christ was raised to be the Son of God by a divine act of adoption, which was at first connected with the Resurrection from the dead and the Ascension to Heaven, and afterwards with the Voice from Heaven at the Baptism, when by the descent of the Spirit He was endowed with miraculous Messianic power.'[1] Not infrequently a neat theory of development is constructed, according to which the Divine Sonship, originally dated from the Resurrection,[2] is supposed to have been first transferred to our Lord's Baptism,[3] then to His Birth,[4] and at last carried back, as in the theology of S. Paul and of S. John, to a pre-mundane eternity, in which the Divine Son, as the pre-existent Word, was already 'with God' from the beginning.[5]

I cannot help thinking that the plausibility of this theory depends largely upon the failure of those critics who hold it to recognize clearly the distinction between the Jewish-Christian and the Gentile-Christian conceptions of what was meant by Divine Sonship. To a Jewish mind, as we have

[1] O. Pfleiderer, *The Early Christian Conception of Christ* (Crown Theological Library), pp. 16 *sq.*

[2] Rom. 1[4]; Acts 13[33]. The Transfiguration (cf. Mk. 9[7] and parallels) is capable of being fitted into the scheme also at this point if the theory of Wellhausen and Loisy be adopted, that the narrative represents in reality the story of a post-Resurrection appearance of Jesus, which in the Gospel tradition has been thrust back into His life upon earth.

[3] Mk. 1[11] and parallels. J. Weiss (*Die Schriften des N.T., ad loc.*) and Harnack (*Sayings of Jesus,* E.T., pp. 310 *sqq.*) both maintain, in the interests of this theory, that the eccentric reading of Dabeff[2] in Lk. 3[22] (υἱός μου εἶ σύ · σήμερον γεγέννηκά σε) represents the original text. But the reading in question can perfectly well be explained as the result of a slip on the part of a scribe, who mechanically completed the familiar quotation from Ps. 2[7] without noticing that the original which he was copying had a different conclusion.

[4] Lk. 1[35].   [5] Jn. 1[1].

seen,[1] the title 'Son of God,' as applied to our Lord, was equivalent to 'Messiah.' It denoted our Lord as the Messianic King of the People of God. It expressed, as such, no theory of His ultimate nature as Divine : it was a title of office, and Jewish Christians, in so far as they were content to think simply in terms of the categories of Messianism, were not constructing a theology of the *Person* of Christ ; what they were doing was to recognize His *function* as the Chosen of God, who was the Mediator of Redemption to Israel. When they affirmed, on the basis of their belief in His Resurrection and Ascension, that God had made Him 'both Lord and Christ,' [2] they were not giving expression to anything remotely resembling a theory of apotheosis, which to a Jew would have been impossible. What they meant was that the Messiah had been enthroned. When they affirmed that He had been 'anointed' at His Baptism,[3] this did not imply of necessity any development of doctrine. He had been predestined to the Messiahship all along, from the time of His Birth,[4] and no doubt also from all eternity in the counsels of God. But Messiahship was a *career*, to which Jesus had been called, and it was possible in the course of such a career to pick out and distinguish the critical points—the Messianic Anointing at the Baptism, followed in due course by the Messianic Enthronement, which was connected in their minds with the Ascension.

The Gentile-Christian conception of the matter was quite different. No doubt Gentile Christians also accepted (in so far as they understood it) the doctrine of Messiahship. But the term 'Son of God' to a Gentile meant a supernatural Being. It suggested that our Lord was Divine. And no doubt many Gentiles were content simply to recognize Jesus as Divine without speculating further.[5] On the other hand,

---

[1] *Supra*, pp. 212 *sq.*, 251.   [2] Acts 2 [34] ; cf. Acts 13 [33].
[3] Acts 10 [33].   [4] Lk. 1 [35].
[5] The popular 'untheological' conception of our Lord's Divine Sonship, as it existed, no doubt, in the minds of many Gentile believers, is represented in the New Testament by the Gospel according to S. Mark, the author of which, though a Jew, was sufficiently in touch with the Gentile-Christian mind in this matter to reflect it in his presentation of Jesus. S. Mark is not an 'Adoptionist,' and, on the other hand, he appears

it was inevitable that in the Gentile Church speculation should arise, and no doubt at first speculations were many and various. The ideas of many a simple-hearted representative of *vulgär Christentum* (i.e. of the Christianity of the plain man) in the Gentile-Christian Church were no doubt as vague and confused as are the ideas of many plain men in the Christian Church of to-day. It is possible that, *left to themselves*, Gentile Christians (more particularly when the Synoptic Gospels and the Acts began to circulate) might very easily have come to explain the Divinity of Jesus in an 'adoptionist' sense—that is to say, as the result of an apotheosis. But the Gentile Christians were not left to themselves. On the contrary, the theology of the Divine Sonship of Jesus in the Gentile-Christian sense was thought out, as we have seen, by Jewish-Christian apostles and teachers (S. Paul, 'S. John,' and the writer of the Epistle to the Hebrews), with the help of the Wisdom-Logos conception and upon a basis of monotheism ; with the result that the 'incarnationist' type of theology (which alone was capable, in the long run, of providing an adequate interpretation of the meaning of Christianity) prevailed, and 'Adoptionism,' when it definitely made its appearance, was condemned as a heresy.

to have no explicit theology of the Incarnation. He simply takes it for granted that Jesus, as the ' Son of God,' is a supernatural Being; and the supernatural voices from Heaven at the Baptism and Transfiguration are for him Divine testimonies to this effect (so rightly J. Weiss, *Das Urchristentum*, p. 545).

APPENDED NOTE VI

Christianity and the ' Mystery Religions;'

IT will be obvious that, unless the whole argument of the present work is mistaken, the idea that the development of Christianity in Apostolic times was in any appreciable respect influenced either by the ' theology ' or by the ceremonial rites of any contemporary pagan ' mystery cult ' must be regarded as erroneous. I deliberately write ' mystery cult ' in the singular, because although there was already a good deal of syncretism and cross-identification of the divinities of different races and peoples, the days of what Professor Phillimore has described as the ' grand East-and-West-Amalgamation Religion ' [1] were not yet, and much confusion has been caused by the procedure of scholars who have made use of evidence derived from second and third century writers, or even from those of the fourth century or later, and have proceeded virtually to argue as though such evidence were immediately applicable to the conditions of the first century A.D. It is sometimes forgotten that what was true of the paganism of the period of Julian the Apostate was not necessarily true of the paganism of the period of the Apostles. Dr. Armitage Robinson, writing in the *Journal of Theological Studies* for January 1913, took occasion to remark, with reference to some paragraphs on this subject in *Foundations*,[2] that ' the curious amalgam

[1] The phrase occurs in Professor Phillimore's introduction to his translation of Philostratus' work on Apollonius of Tyana (p. lxviii).

[2] In the paragraphs in question Dr. Parsons and I had followed Lake in supposing, not indeed that S. Paul himself was directly influenced by notions derived from the Mysteries, but that his converts had previously in some cases been initiates of ' mysteries ' involving the idea of the death and ' resurrection ' of a ' redeemer-god ' (see *Foundations*, pp. 181 *sqq.*). I should now agree with Dr. Robinson that Lake's suggestion had been ' taken over much too hastily,' and in particular that the

which goes by the name of the " theology of the mysteries "
falls to pieces when it is confronted by the original texts.'[1]
In this judgement I should now be disposed to concur.
There were ' mysteries ' or secret rites in many parts of
the Greek world, of which those connected with Eleusis
were of more than local importance, and the others, for the
most part, were not.[2]   There were also mythologies, by no
means secret, connected with the worship of such non-Greek
divinities as the Phrygian Attis, the Egyptian Osiris, the
Syrian Adonis, the Phoenician Esmun, and the Babylonian
Thammuz.[3]   In all these cases there were festivals, annually
held, as a rule in the spring, which commemorated the
death of the god in some form, and his subsequent restoration to some kind of life.   Thus, for example, the slain
Attis was supposed to have been changed into a pine tree;
or, again, in the Egyptian myth the *disjecta membra* of the
murdered Osiris were collected by Isis, and the defunct
deity became lord of the dead.   In all these cases the
fundamental idea underlying both the myth and the ritual
was that of the decay and revival of vegetable life.   The
myth could be interpreted in a more refined sense as a
parable of life out of death, and in the case of the Osiris
and Attis cults—perhaps also eventually in that of the
others—it was in civilized times so interpreted.   But there
was no definite orthodoxy upon the subject.   Plutarch, for
example, in his treatise *De Iside et Osiride*, after noticing
some half a dozen rival and variant interpretations of the

protest of Schweitzer against the use of the phrase ' redeemer-god ' in
such a connexion is justified by the facts (*vide supra*, p. 152, and cf.
Schweitzer, *Paul and his Interpreters*, E.T., p. 193).

[1] J. A. Robinson in the *J. Th. S.*, vol. xiv. p. 198.

[2] An exception should perhaps be made also in favour of the Samo-
thracian mysteries of the Kabeiroi, a pair of divine brothers of whom the
one was alleged to have murdered the other.   In the Hellenistic period
their cult appears to have had a considerable vogue, more particularly
amongst sailors.   As divinities of a storm-swept island they were regarded
as the protectors of mariners.   For the little that is known of their worship,
see Pauly-Wissowa, *Real-Encyclopädie der classischen Wissenschaft*, s.vv.
Kabeiros und Kabeiroi.

[3] The cults of Adonis, Esmun, and Thammuz have been elaborately
studied by W. W. von Baudissin (*Adonis und Esmun*, Leipzig, 1911).

Osiris-Isis mythology, sums up by remarking that ' to put the matter shortly, it is not right to identify Osiris or Isis with water or sun or land or sky, or again Typhon with fire, drought, or sea ; but in general, if we assign to Typhon whatever in these departments of Nature is disproportionate or unruly by way of excess or defect, and pay reverence and honour to whatever is well ordered and useful and good as being the work of Isis, and the image, representation, and utterance (λόγου) of Osiris, we shall not be falling into error.' [1]

The cult of Osiris and Isis, or rather a hellenized form of it, which identified Osiris with Serapis, became widely known to the Greek world as the result of the syncretistic religious policy of Ptolemy I. (B.C. 305-285), who for reasons of state introduced into Alexandria, as a deity who might be worshipped in common by Greeks and Egyptians, the god Serapis, believed by some scholars to have been simply a combination of Osiris and Apis, by others to have been an originally foreign deity brought in from abroad, but in any case promptly identified with the Egyptian Osiris. The mythological basis of the cult of Serapis was Egyptian, the language was Greek. Associated with the public worship of the god there were also ' mysteries ' in the strict sense (i.e. secret rites, in which only the initiated might take part). According to a tradition in Plutarch, the first Ptolemy, in instituting the cult, was assisted by the advice of the Eumolpid Timotheus : [2] it is not impossible, therefore, that the development of the worship of Osiris into a ' mystery cult ' may have been directly fostered by Greek influence from Eleusis.[3] But it would seem that Osiris was already in the purely Egyptian system the Lord of life and death, and in the Hellenistic mysteries of Serapis he continued to exercise this rôle. Of the votary of Osiris it was written in ancient Egyptian texts : ' As truly as Osiris lives shall he live ; as truly as Osiris is not dead, shall he not die ;

---

[1] Plutarch, op. cit. 64.   [2] Op. cit. 28.

[3] The converse theory that the Eleusinian Mysteries themselves were derived originally from Egypt, maintained by Foucart in his book, Les Mystères d'Éleusis, is untenable.

as truly as Osiris is not annihilated, shall he not be annihilated.'[1] It is thought by many scholars that in the later Serapis-Isis cult the initiate came actually to be identified with Osiris himself and deified, thus definitely becoming immortal. In the second-century romance of Apuleius, the hero Lucius, as the climax of his initiation into the mysteries of Isis, comes forth in the array of the sun-god, and stands upon a pulpit of wood before the image of the goddess, while the people stream past and behold.[2] So too in the Hermetic literature we read that 'this is the blessed end for those who have attained knowledge, namely, deification.'[3] It would seem probable that Egypt is the true home of the idea of deification, whether attained, as in the mysteries of Isis, by means of a series of ceremonial initiations, or (as in the Hermetic religion) by means of a *gnosis* imparted by the communication of a λόγος τέλειος, or 'initiatory *discourse*.'[4] It is perhaps a permissible conjecture that the idea in question may have arisen as a result of the extension by analogy to ordinary mortals of a divinity originally ascribed to the Pharaohs. The dead Pharaoh appears from quite early times to have been identified with Osiris, as the living Pharaoh had been Osiris' image upon earth. The extension of this later to the initiates of Osiris in general would be a not unnatural development.

As a result of the policy of the Ptolemies the religion of Serapis and Isis became disseminated in various parts of the Mediterranean world in the course of the first two centuries before Christ, the area of its extension being, as we should anticipate, in rough correspondence with the sphere of influence of the Ptolemaic dynasty. We hear of associations of 'Ἰσιασταί at Rhodes and elsewhere, as well as of *collegia* of Isis-worshippers at Rome, just as we hear

---

[1] Cited by Cumont, *Les Religions Orientales dans le Paganisme Romain*, 2nd ed., p. 149.

[2] Apuleius, *Metamorphoses*, xi. 24.

[3] Τοῦτο ἐστι τὸ ἀγαθὸν τέλος τοῖς γνῶσιν ἐσχηκόσι, θεωθῆναι (*Corp. Hermet.* i. 26). W. Scott somewhat arbitrarily removes the word θεωθῆναι from his edition of the text as a gloss.

[4] On the importance of this distinction see the note *supra*, pp. 67 *sq.*

frequently of θίασοι and of associations of the μύσται of Dionysus.[1] It would be a mistake to infer hastily that wherever evidence can be found of the existence of an association of the worshippers of Isis there existed also a temple, at which it was possible for initiations to take place. It is known, however, that a temple of Serapis existed at Athens from the time of Ptolemy I. (Soter) onwards;[2] a temple of Isis has been found among the ruins of Pompeii; and an inscription of the year B.C. 105 refers to a Serapeum at Puteoli.[3] The first temple of Isis at Rome appears to have been built by Caligula in the year A.D. 38.[4] In the time of Apuleius it was possible to be initiated into the Isiac mysteries both at Rome and at Corinth,[5] and very likely at other places also.

The history of Attis-worship was different. Its home-land was in Phrygia, where the worship of the Great Mother goddess, known to the Greek world as Cybele, appears to have been associated with that of Attis from time immemorial. According to some forms of the legend, Attis, a beautiful youth, the beloved of the goddess, was killed by a boar sent by Zeus.[6] According to another version, the goddess killed him herself out of jealousy. According to yet another, Attis castrated himself, and so perished. At the spring festival of the goddess there was wild mourning for the dead Attis, which, however, ended in outcries of joy. In the ritual as practised in historical times at Rome the 24th of March was known as the *dies sanguinis*. A pine-tree, representing the dead Attis, was solemnly buried, and the self-emasculated priests of the goddess flogged them-

---

[1] Cf. H. A. A. Kennedy, *St. Paul and the Mystery Religions*, pp. 72 *sqq.*, where reference is made to the works of Poland and Kaerst.

[2] Cumont, *op. cit.* p. 119.   [3] Cumont, *op. cit.* p. 121.

[4] Cumont, *op. cit.* p. 126.

[5] In Apuleius' romance the first initiation of Lucius, described subsequently (*Metamorph.* xi. 27) as having been an initiation primarily into the Mysteries of Isis, takes place at Corinth, or perhaps rather at Cenchreae (*Metamorph.* x. 35). His subsequent initiation into the Mysteries of Osiris takes place at the temple of Isis Campensis at Rome (*Metamorph.* xi. 26).

[6] It is thought that this version of the story is the result of contamination of the Attis legend with the Syrian myth of Adonis.

selves, tore their own flesh, and cut themselves with knives.
It is believed also that it was on this day that new recruits
for the priesthood made the sacrifice of their virility. Two
days later ensued the joyous festival of the *Hilaria*, when
the pine-tree was disinterred, and the worshippers, according
to the conjectures of modern scholars, were assured by the
priests that the god had been ' saved.' [1]

This barbarous and horrible worship was brought to
Rome in the year 204 B.C. in obedience to an oracle obtained
by consulting the Sibylline Books. The Romans were
shocked by it when it arrived, and down to the time of
the Emperor Claudius Roman citizens were forbidden to
take part in it. The worship was carried on, but it was
carried on in a quasi-private manner in the temple of
Cybele on the Palatine hill by a *personnel* consisting exclusively of Phrygians. According to the statement of a
late Byzantine writer, John the Lydian, accepted by Hepding
and Cumont as being historical, Claudius allowed its rites
to be celebrated in public and gave recognition to its festival
in the calendar.[2] Henceforward the *archigalli*, or chief
priests of the goddess, bear Roman names, and presumably,
therefore, are citizens. It is probable that it was at this
time also that the ' mysteries ' or secret rites (as distinct
from the public festivals) were thrown open to such as
desired to be initiated. Both the character and the development of the Attis Mysteries are exceedingly obscure, and
Hepding's chapter on the subject contains a paragraph in
which he remarks that he is ' well aware that this account
of the Phrygian Mysteries is in its details for the most
part hypothetical.' [3] A formula cited in slightly divergent
versions both by Clement of Alexandria and by Firmicus
Maternus runs (according to a version obtained by combining the data of these two authors), ' I have eaten from

---

[1] This is based upon the famous fragment, believed to have been derived
from the Attis cult, which is quoted by Firmicus Maternus (*De err. prof.
relig.* 23 ; *vide supra*, p. 152, *n.* 3).

[2] Cumont suggests as the motive of Claudius' action the desire to
provide a counterpoise to the growing influence of Isis-worship, which
he thinks Claudius viewed with dislike (Cumont, *op. cit.* p. 84).

[3] Hepding, *Attis, seine Mythen und sein Kult*, p. 199.

the *tympanum*, I have drunk from the *cymbalum*, I have carried the *kernos*, I have crept into the bridal chamber, I have become an initiate of Attis.'[1] The similarity of this to the Eleusinian formula, ' I have fasted, I have drunk the *kykeon*, I have taken from the *cista* ; having wrought,[2] I have put back in the *calathus* and from the *calathus* into the *cista*,'[3] suggests the hypothesis that the Attis Mysteries, in the form in which they became ultimately known to the Greek world, had been influenced, like those of Serapis and Isis, by the Mysteries of Eleusis.[4] Except possibly at Rome, it does not appear that they were of any great importance until a period considerably later than that of the New Testament, and the same may be said also with certainty in respect of the Mysteries of Mithras, which became prominent in the Latin-speaking world in the second and third centuries A.D.[5]

The Mysteries of Eleusis were adopted by Athens at a very early period as a state cult, into the secrets of which all adult citizens of Athens were initiated. At a somewhat later date they were thrown open to the citizens also of other Greek states,[6] and eventually to all who could speak the Greek language. What is known about them has been elaborately studied by Foucart in *Les Mystères d'Éleusis*

---

[1] Firmicus Maternus, *De err. prof. relig.* 19; cf. Clem. Alex. *Protrept.* ii. 15.

[2] The alternative rendering ' having tasted ' or ' having partaken ' depends upon a conjecture of Lobeck's (ἐγγευσάμενος for ἐργασάμενος), which, though widely accepted, is probably wrong (so Loisy).

[3] Clem. Alex. *Protrept.* ii. 21.

[4] So Foucart, *Les Mystères d'Éleusis*, p. 384 *n.*

[5] A community of Mithraic worshippers appears to have existed in Rome itself from Pompey's time (B.C. 67), and there are Mithraic sanctuaries at Rome and Ostia which may go back to the first century. Justin Martyr, who taught at Rome and was martyred there in A.D. 165, betrays an at least external acquaintance with the cult (Justin, *Apol.* i. 66). The real diffusion of Mithraism, however, only begins about the end of the first Christian century. It was spread mainly by soldiers, and its monuments are found chiefly on the sites of the great military camps along the frontiers of the Empire. Cumont notes that it passed direct from Asia Minor to the *Latin* world—' *les Grecs n'accueillèrent jamais le dieu de leurs ennemis héréditaires* ' (Cumont, *op. cit.* p. 220).

[6] The ' sacred truce ' for the celebration of the Eleusinian Mysteries is mentioned in an inscription of the time of Pericles.

(Paris, 1914). There was, of course, no mystery about the public parts of the ceremonial, which have often been described. The actual secrets of the mysteries themselves have been well kept. It is known that certain preliminary rites, described as the ' Lesser Mysteries,' were first celebrated at Agrae on the left bank of the Ilissus in the spring The ' Great Mysteries ' took place at Eleusis some six months later. They were preceded by the arrival at Athens of the ' sacred objects ' (τὰ ἱερά)[1] from Eleusis, which were ceremonially received and deposited in the Eleusinium. Five days later the ' sacred objects ' were solemnly escorted back to Eleusis by all the initiates and candidates for initiation in procession. The procession arrived at Eleusis after nightfall, and the actual initiatory ceremonies began the next day. There were two grades of initiation, the simple μύησις, with which many were content, and the ἐποπτεία, or ' ceremony of beholding,' to which those who had been initiated already as μύσται were admissible after an interval of not less than a year. It is believed by Foucart that at the first initiation the secrets were revealed of the Under World, and that in connection with this there was enacted a sacred drama of Demeter and Kore. The second initiation, at which according to Hippolytus the initiates were shown ' an ear of corn reaped in silence,'[2] was connected more particularly, he thinks, with the cult of Dionysus. It seems probable that there was celebrated also, by the hierophant and the priestess of Demeter, a marriage-ritual, commemorative of the marriage of Zeus and Demeter, in connection with which the announcement was made to the initiates : ' The divine Brimo hath brought forth a sacred child, Brimos.'[3]

As early as the date at which the Homeric *Hymn to Demeter* was composed[4] it was believed that initiation at

---

[1] It is not known what these were.

[2] 'Αθηναῖοι μυοῦντες Ἐλευσίνια καὶ ἐπιδεικνύντες τοῖς ἐποπτεύουσι τὸ μέγα καὶ θαυμαστὸν καὶ τελειότατον ἐποπτικὸν ἐκεῖ μυστήριον ἐν σιωπῇ τεθερισμένον στάχυν (Hippol. *Refut. omn. haeres.* v. 8. 39).

[3] ἱερὸν ἔτεκε πότνια κοῦρον Βριμὼ Βριμόν (Hippol. *op. cit.* v. 8. 40).

[4] The *Hymn to Demeter* may be as early as the seventh century B.C., and is probably not later than the sixth.

Eleusis secured to the initiates a prospect of happiness after death,[1] and the belief in question persisted throughout the whole period of classical antiquity until the downfall of paganism. From all parts of the Greek-speaking world men came to Eleusis to be initiated, and Cicero can write of '*Eleusina sanctam illam et augustam,*

Ubi initiantur gentes orarum ultimae. [2]

Nevertheless, it does not appear that any particular doctrine or 'theology' was taught at Eleusis. The point of the initiation was simply that the initiates might behold certain sacred objects and take part in the secret rites. The instructions which they received from the ' mystagogues ' beforehand are believed to have been directed wholly towards the proper performance of the ritual and of the preliminary ceremonies, and the words spoken by the hierophant to have been confined to the repetition, at the proper moments, of the traditional formulae of the rite. According to a remark attributed by Synesius to Aristotle, the purpose of the initiation was not that the initiates should learn anything, but that they should receive an impression and that (if suitably disposed) they should be put in a certain frame of mind.[3] Other references in ancient writers tend to confirm this conclusion. They speak of what the initiates have experienced or *seen*, not of what they have learnt.[4] It may be added that there is good reason to believe that certain parts of the Eleusinian ritual

---

[1]   "Ολβιος, ὃς τάδ' ὄπωπεν ἐπιχθονίων ἀνθρώπων·
      ὃς δ'ἀτελὴς ἱερῶν, ὅς τ' ἄμμορος, οὔποθ' ὁμοίως
      αἶσαν ἔχει φθίμενός περ ὑπὸ ζόφῳ εὐρώεντι.
                              Hymn to Demeter, lines 480 *sqq.*
   Cf. Sophocles, *Frag.* 719 (ed. Dindorf) :
                              'Ως τρισόλβιοι
      κεῖνοι βροτῶν, οἱ ταῦτα δερχθέντες τέλη
      μόλωσ' ἐς "Αιδου· τοῖσδε γὰρ μόνοις ἐκεῖ
      ζῆν ἐστι, τοῖς δ' ἄλλοισι πάντ' ἐκεῖ κακά.

[2] Cicero, *De natura deorum,* I. 119.

[3] 'Αριστοτέλης ἀξιοῖ τοὺς τετελεσμένους οὐ μαθεῖν τι δεῖν, ἀλλὰ παθεῖν καὶ διατεθῆναι, γενομένους δηλόνοτι ἐπιτηδείους (Synesius, *Dion,* p. 48 [ed. Petavius]).

[4] Cf. (e.g.) the passage from what is believed to have been a lost writing of Plutarch, quoted by Halliday, *The Pagan Background of Early Christianity,* p. 272.

were open to the reproach of being grossly indecent. The insinuations of Christian writers to this effect [1] would have been singularly ineffective as polemics if every initiated pagan had been in a position to be aware that they were groundless. The pagan conscience was habituated to tolerate such things, and the pagan mind, in some cases, to discover in them an edifying meaning.[2] As T. R. Glover expresses it, ' Greek polytheism had always been weak in moral content. . . . Neither Demeter nor Isis was very squeamish.' [3]

There is really no likelihood at all that Christianity in any of the forms in which it is presented to us in the New Testament has been influenced in any degree whatever by any of the ' mystery cults ' which have been described. The current impression to the contrary is due to the habit of thinking in terms not of the concrete facts of history, but of a kind of idealized composite photograph of the ' mystery religions ' in general—a sort of typical or universal ' mystery religion ' which (as Schweitzer remarks) ' never actually existed, least of all in Paul's day.' [4] The illusion is further enhanced by the procedure, adopted by certain writers (among whom Frazer and Loisy are conspicuous), of freely ascribing Christian ideas to the ' mysteries,' and of describing their rites, usages, and supposed doctrines in Christian terminology. The reader is then expected to be proportionately impressed by the resulting resemblances to Christianity.[5]

[1] Cf. (e.g.) Greg. Naz. *Orat.* 39. 6 ; Arnobius, *Adv. Gent.* v. 26. Loisy thinks in this connexion of a phallic symbolism (Loisy, *Les Mystères païens et le Mystère chrétien*, p. 68).

[2] Cf. Plutarch, *De Iside et Osiride*, 36.

[3] T. R. Glover, *Paul of Tarsus*, p. 133.

[4] Schweitzer, *Paul and his Interpreters*, E.T., pp. 192 *sq.* I am afraid it must be said with regret that the latest book in English upon the mystery cults—*The Mystery Religions and Christianity*, by Dr. S. Angus of Sydney—is rendered for scientific purposes almost useless, despite the enormous erudition of the author, by the complete absence of any real attempt either to use evidence critically or to discriminate the various ' mystery religions ' from one another.

[5] See the examples quoted by Gore (*The Holy Spirit and the Church*, pp. 80 *sq.*), who protests with justice against this illegitimate begging of the questions at issue.

The suggestion which is most frequently put forward in England with regard to the supposed influence of the 'mystery cults' upon the beginnings of Christianity is to the effect that it was to this source that the Church was indebted for the idea of sacramentalism. It has been recently pointed out by Mr. N. P. Williams [1] that in the world of scholarship outside Great Britain the 'Mystery-Religion' theory of the origin of sacramentalism does not stand by itself, but is part and parcel of the whole *religionsgeschichtliche* explanation of Christianity, the untenability of which it has been part of the purpose of these lectures to demonstrate. As a matter of fact, quite apart from the enormous *a priori* improbability of any influence of the supposed 'sacramentalism' of the 'mystery cults' upon the mind of S. Paul (with regard to which Mr. Williams' discussion, in the essay to which I have referred, is in my judgment conclusive),[2] the actual evidence for the existence, in the period of the New Testament, of a sacramentalism akin to that of Christianity in connexion with any of the 'mystery cults' is exceedingly scanty. It is only necessary to read critically the relevant portions of Dieterich's book, *Eine Mithrasliturgie*, with close attention both to the dates of the documents quoted and to the (frequently forced) interpretation which is placed upon them by Dieterich, in order to be aware that this is so. Neither in the case of the Eucharist nor in the case of the initiatory sacrament of Baptism are the alleged parallels at all close, nor do they necessarily, or even probably, bear, in the majority of instances, the interpretation which has been placed upon them by Dieterich and others. It is not certain that the

---

[1] N. P. Williams, 'The Origins of the Sacraments,' in *Essays Catholic and Critical*, p. 391.

[2] *Essays Catholic and Critical*, pp. 397-399. On the other hand, I should not wish to be regarded as being committed in detail to the whole of Mr. Williams' somewhat speculative handling, on pp. 399 *sqq.* of the same essay, of the New Testament evidence in favour of the explicit institution of the sacraments by our Lord. I think the sacraments of Christianity arose out of what our Lord said and did, and are in accordance with 'the mind of Christ' in the Church. I should be indisposed personally to speculate further.

sacred meals of the mysteries were regarded in any specific
sense as being media of communion with the deity. It is
in any case extremely improbable that they were of the
nature of 'theophagic' meals. The argument derived from
the supposed originally totemistic character of the Dionysiac
omophagia, upon which stress has been laid by Frazer and
Loisy, has no bearing upon the significance which is likely
to have been attributed to the rite in historical times;[1]
and apart from this, it is extremely doubtful whether in
the period of the New Testament such abominable orgies
persisted at all, though it is just conceivable that they were
still practised by the peasantry in remote and uncivilized
districts.[2] 'Baptisms' (in the sense of ceremonial lustra-
tions with water)[3] are of course frequent in all forms of
ceremonial religion, and formed part of the preparatory
ceremonial purification of the initiates in most of the
mysteries.[4] In no case, however, does there appear to be
any suggestion that 'baptism' constituted, in itself, the
actual rite of initiation—it was essentially a preparatory
rite, which preceded initiation, as it might precede in the
ancient world participation in *any* particularly sacred religious ceremonial. The ideas of 'regeneration' and of a 'voluntary death' are brought into connexion with the process
of initiation into the mysteries by more writers than one,[5]
but the pagan writers who speak of 'regeneration' in this
sense do not connect the idea specifically with 'baptism,'
and their phraseology suggests rather the conscious use
of a metaphor than the echo of a recognized technical

[1] See Gore, *The Holy Spirit and the Church*, pp. 105 *sq.*, and the letter
from Dr. Edwyn Bevan there quoted.

[2] If a statement in Firmicus Maternus is to be trusted, they survived
in Crete down to the fourth century A.D. (cf. Firmicus Maternus, *De err.
prof. relig.* 6).

[3] Cf. the reference in S. Mark's Gospel to Jewish Pharisaic 'baptism'
of 'cups and pots and brazen vessels' (Mk. 7[4]).

[4] On the Eleusinian ceremonial bath of the initiates and of their sacrificial pigs in the sea (ἅλαδε μύσται), see Foucart, *Les Mystères d'Éleusis*,
pp. 314 *sqq.*; and for Isiac 'baptisms,' cf. Apuleius, *Metamorph.* xi. 23.

[5] For the idea of 'voluntary death,' cf. Apuleius, *Metamorph.* xi. 21 ;
and for 'regeneration,' see the passages quoted *supra*, p. 153, *n.* 8.

term.[1] It is the Christian writer Tertullian who connects with pagan 'baptisms' the ideas of regeneration and of the forgiveness of sins. It is by no means certain that he was right in so doing. ' It is Tertullian,' writes Mr. A. D. Nock, ' who supplies the motive, and Tertullian adopts Justin Martyr's thesis, that the Devil ingeniously counterfeited in advance Christian ritual : it was to the interest of this theory to see more similarity than existed, not less.'[2] It is certainly difficult to believe that ' baptism ' had the significance which Tertullian assigns to it in either of the two instances to which he actually refers.[3] It is known, of course, that the idea of regeneration became eventually attached to the repulsive ceremony known in different forms as the *taurobolium* or *criobolium*—a kind of blood-baptism in the gore of a slaughtered animal, a bull or a ram, which appears to have been connected in later times with the Mysteries of Attis ; [4] but the evidence is exceedingly late. The inscriptions imply in some cases that the efficacy of the rite lasted for twenty years ; in other cases we find the phrase *taurobolio renatus in aeternum*. It appears not improbable, in view of the lateness of the evidence, that the latter formula may represent pagan competition with Christianity. According to Hepding, the *taurobolium* was originally a sacrifice offered on behalf of the community— it might be offered, for example, for the welfare of the emperor, or for the safety of the state. It was only at a late period that (very likely as a consequence of some kind of contamination of cults and beliefs) it began to be offered also as a sacrifice for the ' regeneration ' of individuals. The earliest historical individual who is known to have

---

[1] Apuleius speaks of being ' *in a sense* born again ' (*quodam modo renatos*). Sallustius (writing in the fourth century) speaks of ' feeding upon milk, *as though* we were being born again ' (ὥσπερ ἀναγεννωμένων).

[2] I owe this quotation to an essay by Mr. Nock which is shortly to be published, and to which I have been allowed to have access.

[3] The reference in Tertullian (*De bapt.* v.—see the quotation *supra*, p. 153, *n.* 8) is to the Eleusinian Mysteries and to the *ludi Apollinares* at Rome.

[4] The connexion of the *taurobolium* ceremony with Mithraism is doubtful, except as a result of syncretism with the mysteries of the Great Mother and Attis—see Cumont, *Les Mystères de Mithra*, pp. 152 *sqq*.

undergone the *taurobolium* ceremony is the Emperor
Elagabalus, and the earliest known epigraphical evidence
for the *taurobolium* as offered for the 'regeneration' of an
individual is an inscription of the year A.D. 305.[1]

'Christianity,' writes Professor Kirsopp Lake, 'has not
borrowed from the Mystery Religions, because it was always,
at least in Europe, a Mystery Religion itself.'[2] The epigram
contains a modicum of truth. As having passed outside the
country of its origin and become missionary, Christianity
resembled the 'mystery cults' (and differed from the established and traditional religions of paganism) in offering to
individuals the privilege of membership, irrespective of sex,
race or class, in a spiritual brotherhood of which the sole
bond was community of religion. It may further be said
to have resembled the 'mystery cults' in possessing in the
sacrament of Baptism an initiatory rite and in the Eucharist
a divine drama, commemorative of its Lord, at which only
initiates might assist. Yet a third point of resemblance
lay in the fact that it held out to its initiates the prospect
of life after death. But the differences were fundamental
and far-reaching. The whole character of Christianity as
an historical religion was in the strongest contrast with that
of the pagan 'mystery cults.' The 'good news' of
Christianity was rooted in history. Its Christ was an
historical Person. Its strength lay in its Jewish past, and
not in any affinities or parallels with pagan mysteries.
Its theology was monotheistic, jealous on behalf of the
Divine majesty, intolerant of paganism, uncompromisingly
hostile in its attitude to all forms of idolatry and syncretism.
It proclaimed 'good news from God,' and not least the
good news of the forgiveness of sins. Christians and pagans
alike were acutely conscious, both in the New Testament
period and later, of a radical difference between paganism
and Christianity. The '*religionsgeschichtliche* explanation'
of Christianity, in so far as it fails to account for the differences, breaks down.

It may be added, in conclusion, that the actual use in the

---

[1] Hepding, *Attis : seine Mythen und sein Kult*, pp. 199 *sq.*
[2] Lake, *The Earlier Epistles of S. Paul*, p. 215.

New Testament writings of the Greek word μυστήριον is not in accordance with its use in connexion with the 'mystery cults.' It denotes in the New Testament not an esoteric religious ceremonial which the initiated are pledged to preserve inviolably secret, but (in Dr. Armitage Robinson's words) 'the great truths of the Christian religion, which could not have become known to men except by Divine disclosure or revelation. A mystery in this sense is not a thing which *must* be kept secret. On the contrary, it is a secret which God wills to make known and has charged His Apostles to declare to those who have ears to hear it.'[1] S. Paul, when he writes to the Corinthians, ' Let a man so account of us, as of the ministers of Christ, and stewards of the mysteries of God,'[2] is not thinking of himself and of his fellow-Apostles as hierophants, charged with the custody of secret rites and the function of admitting men thereto under the pledges of secrecy. He is thinking of himself as an evangelist, entrusted with the proclamation of the Gospel, which was God's revealed message for mankind. The eventual usage by which in the Greek Church the word μυστήρια became a technical term for the sacraments is much later than the period of the New Testament.

[1] J. A. Robinson, *St. Paul's Epistle to the Ephesians*, p. 240.
[2] 1 Cor. 4 [1].

INDICES

I

INDEX OF AUTHORS

II

INDEX OF SUBJECTS

Printed in Great Britain
by T. and A. CONSTABLE LTD., Hopetoun Street,
Printers to the University of Edinburgh